AT THE DOG IN DULWICH

At the Dog in Dulwich

Recollections of a Poet

PATRICIA DOUBELL

Edited by
CLIVE MURPHY

SECKER & WARBURG
LONDON

First published in England 1986 by
Martin Secker & Warburg Limited
54 Poland Street, London W1V 3DF

Copyright © 1986 by Patricia Doubell and Clive Murphy

British Library Cataloguing in Publication Data

Doubell, Patricia
　At the Dog in Dulwich: recollections of a poet.
　1. Doubell, Patricia – Biography　2. Poets,
　English – 20th century – Biography
　I. Title　II. Murphy, Clive
　821′.914　　　PR6054.07/

ISBN 0–436–29671–3

Set in 11/12 pt Monotype Lasercomp Photina
by Richard Clay (The Chaucer Press) Ltd, Bungay, Suffolk
Printed in Great Britain by
Redwood Burn Ltd, Trowbridge, Wiltshire

I first heard Patricia Doubell recite a poem on Thursday, 17 October 1968. Occasion – the journal *Adam's* concert at the Institut Français to celebrate its temporary affiliation to the University of Rochester, New York. Poem – 'The Runaway Heart'. Voice (her poems often dictate a special voice) – American Western Movie. Miss Doubell was already a member of the Dulwich Group of poets which met at the Crown and Greyhound public house, the 'Dog', in the centre of Dulwich village I have heard her using many voices there, and elsewhere, since. During June and July 1983 I recorded this book in the living-room of her Council flat in Tulse Hill, London, to learn the background to so versatile a gift.

Clive Murphy

1

You must have got a whiff as you came in. The men from the Gas Board say it's a blow-back from the chimney. I'd be worried if it was the old gas which would kill you, but North Sea Gas is safe. I've been a Samaritan for several years, and we've had people trying to commit suicide with this new gas by putting their head in the oven, but it can't be done. You know my husband committed suicide? . . . My brother's wife committed suicide, too. You see, we three children – myself, my brother Tim, and my sister Felicity who emigrated to Australia – we all married what I would consider to be very *insecure* people. My father and mother were rock-solid, they loved each other very much and, because we had a very secure childhood, I think the people who attracted us were rather unstable. Have a sandwich! It's crab that side and Lymeswold cheese that side – I'm a great Lymeswold fan. Take two or three! These are home-made Florentine biscuits.

Well, I suppose I'd better begin with being born. I *was* born! – on the 6th of May 1923, at The Glebe Farm, a mile from Charlton Marshall, which is two miles south of Blandford Forum in Dorset, very beautiful country, Hardy country which has changed little. It was a Sunday morning at eight o'clock which must have been rather a beautiful time – I can still remember the sound of Sunday morning bells ringing from Charlton church. The farm once belonged to the church. Now it belonged to my Great Uncle Gilbert, and was managed by my father, his adopted son, the third child of his sister Marjorie, who had been left a widow with four young children. Uncle Gilbert was tall and straight with a waistcoat and

1

a watch chain, and very kind, dark brown eyes and a drooping moustache. He used to stand behind my chair and say very politely, 'Allow me to assist you,' and proceed to cut things up and put them into my mouth. He was a great churchgoer, and wanted me to be called Faith, so he always called me that and never Pat as everyone else did. He died of a brain haemorrhage caused by a rodent ulcer when I was two.

The Glebe Farm was about six hundred acres of dairy pasture and woodland. The large, rambling, draughty old farmhouse must have been a nightmare for my mother, though at first we had money and those were the days when servants did a lot of the work. My father's name was Bob Burgess. I was born Patricia Nora Burgess – the French 'Doubell', which I took for my pen name, was my maternal grandmother's maiden name; her father was a London wine merchant who originated from Bordeaux. My mother, Margaret, was the daughter of Edwin Westcott, a jeweller in The Market Place, Blandford. My father came originally from a family reputed to be gypsies. My great grandfather, on his mother's side, was a cattle dealer. He could be heard late at night coming home from the cattle fairs, driving a pony and trap, and singing at the top of his voice in a foreign language, but which language nobody knew. I like to think it was Romany, but I hae ma doots.

It's amazing really that any servant girl was willing to stay in such an isolated place as The Glebe with its huge kitchen and long stone passages that all had to be scrubbed. But there was one girl who *did* stay, and this was the girl who took charge of me from the first, a Scottish girl by the name of Jean. She came from Galashiels. Her father was a miner and she used to tell me about her family's poverty and how, as children, there were never any Christmas presents except that their stockings would be filled with coal, the best present they could have to keep the fire going on Christmas night, which I thought was very dreadful. She had married a soldier when she was very young. His name was Frank and he was stationed in India. She used to write to him. She had a beautiful singing voice and, like many people with beautiful voices, she wasn't really conscious of it. Sometimes she sang Calvinist hymns, and sometimes Scottish ballads which I liked much better. Later, she turned up in my poem 'The Weir', a long poem which was an attempt to understand the state of mind of my husband who had committed suicide. The poem was about a man drowning and

2

going back over his life, and some of the images that come back from his childhood belong to my own experience:

> There was a fat girl once – and a litter of puppies –
> Ran through the daisies – Oh! my legs were short –
> They scratched and bit – six monsters – how I screamed!
> Till the fat girl took my hand,
> Cuddled the wolf-pack into sleepy fatness,
> Sang The Four Marys in the voice of a pearl,
> With creeping sadness, eerily serene.

Jean did rescue me from a litter of black retriever puppies, and she took my hand while she cuddled the pack into sleepy fatness, singing 'The Four Marys':

> I wrapped ma babe in a blanket,
> I tossed him in the sea,
> Cried, 'Sink or swim, my bonnie bairn!
> I want nae mair o' thee!'

'The Four Marys' is a very sad song and it made me feel sad but, as with such a lot of beautiful things, there was the enjoyment of being sad; it is a tragic beauty. I think that was really my first experience of poetry. Later, when I was two and a half, I uttered a poem of my own. My brother, Tim, had just been born and it was a windy day and all the napkins were out on the line and I came running in and said, 'The napkins and dishcloths are all in a flutter and houses are built without walls!' I don't remember that, and it was probably based unconsciously on a nursery rhyme. My mother wrote it down. What I do remember – and it's the very first thing I can remember, although I know I rode before I could walk and I've got photographs of myself being led on a pony – is being buttoned up into those diabolical gaiters that children used to wear to go out walking. They had to be done up with a button-hook and they always pinched your legs. In cold weather I always had to have these put on, and I remember going out in them with Jean when it was frosty to cut cabbage, and Jean was cursing though I think she rather liked hard, physical work.

Because I spent such a lot of time with Jean, I was completely unaware at two and a half that my brother was on the way. But I remember being *furious* and kicking and screaming because I couldn't see my mother at breakfast. I suppose in the last stages of pregnancy she was sick in the mornings and used to stay in bed. I'd never experienced *that* before and I used to run up the back stairs and hide in places so that I could go and see her; I was very angry that anyone should keep me *away* from her. Then she disappeared and I didn't know *why* she'd gone. Jean didn't explain anything but she did her best to make it not so dreadful. Next, a very white, starchy nurse appeared who finally took pity on me. She realised that I hadn't the faintest idea of what was happening and she said that I was going to have a little brother. I suppose she was getting ready for my mother coming home from the hospital. She had in her hand a baby's brush, a little blue brush, so I thought a brother was a little blue brush, and ever since then I've connected the word 'brother' with this little blue brush – it's quite ridiculous.

I was born at The Glebe Farm, but Tim was born at the Blandford Cottage Hospital. I remember going there in October with a little bunch of pink, very sweetly scented flowers. I was very, very glad to see my mother who had been snatched away from me, and I was picked up and made to look into this little bassinet with blue curtains, and I saw my brother and I thought, 'Yes, that's it. That's the little blue brush.' His hair stood on end like a brush, and he was asleep, so I don't think I really thought he was alive: I just thought that he was a little brush in the bassinet! When he eventually came home, the impression of the brush gradually faded and I realised it was something alive.

When my Auntie Nora saw him, she was really concerned. Auntie Nora was my godmother, my mother's elder sister. They were not at all alike. Mother was small and dark, and quick in her movements. Auntie Nora was tall, and there was an endearing vagueness about her; her hair was grey, but hairdresser smart. She and Mother were great friends. They both thought that Tim was very ugly. I'm told that Auntie Nora said to my mother, 'You'll have to put up with that all your life!' She was crying. I think she thought there was something *wrong* with the child.

Jean continued to look after me, but once the nurse was gone a nursemaid came to look after Tim. She was called Beatrice and she was very, very beautiful and very tall, and she was from an orphanage in London. Nobody approved of Beatrice very much – she was rather a high-flier; she was inclined to be what grown-ups called 'fast'. But we couldn't get rid of her because we couldn't get anybody to replace her. Her boyfriends used to come on motorbikes and fetch her to go to village dances and social evenings. I know that very often the dresses she wore were my mother's dresses which she filched from the wardrobe; my mother never, never knew that they had been worn.

I fell in love with one of Beatrice's boyfriends at the age of three. He was one of the men who cleaned the stables. She used to invite him into the kitchen when my mother was out and I used to sit by the fire and Bert Fiander used to come in and I would do anything to sit on Bert's knee. I was very much in love; I knew all about it; there was that feeling. Beatrice read poetry – Kipling, very blood and thunder poems. 'The Road to Mandalay' was her favourite. Another one was 'Gunga Din' – de de de-de de-de *dah*, de de de-de de-de *dah*, a-serving of Her Majesty the Queen. There was also a very scary serial story called 'The Wild Cat of the Woods' which she read aloud from a magazine. She and Jean and Bert and perhaps one or two others were sitting there in front of the fire, and they would make up a little sort of entertainment with poetry and stories. Anyway, Bert was my first love, and I didn't feel love again until I was about eight, and then it was for another grown-up person.

The awful thing was that, when Beatrice had been with us a little while, Jean began to change. Jean, up to now, had been completely devoted to me and to my mother, and to the work of the house and farm, but now she began to worry about her appearance and began to dress in different clothes. She became more and more friendly with Beatrice, and very much under her influence. Frank, who she had hardly seen since she married, finally wrote that he was coming home. And when he did come home and she was expecting him, he was killed on his motorbike *en route* to The Glebe Farm to see her. This knocked her for six. Soon after, about 1926, when I was getting on for four, Beatrice and Jean both left: they decided to go to London together, and I never saw Jean again. I hope things went well for her.

I used to stay for a few days, every now and then, with my grandparents in Blandford, especially after Tim arrived, because I think my mother wasn't too well. Of course my grandmother was always trying to get me there because I was her first grandchild. I used to go in a pony and trap with my nightie packed in a little crocodile-skin suitcase. It was an old, hopelessly inconvenient and uncomfortable house with three storeys over the shop, very dark and troubled. There was no running water except in the kitchen which was in the basement; hot water had to be carried up to the bathroom in the attic in copper water-jugs. Servants wouldn't do such work, and my grandmother couldn't cope.

She used to read to me from a book of poems illustrated with black Victorian woodcuts – *The Prisoner of Chillon*, *Eugene Aram*, who was a murderer, 'The Ancient Mariner' . . . Well, my grandparents' house and the woodcuts and these poems and the blood and thunder poems and stories that Beatrice read at her parties round the kitchen fire at The Glebe induced night fears. The Glebe Farm itself was a spooky place and I was in a bedroom by myself there and, when my mother shut the door, I knew there was all that expanse – a long landing, a long staircase and then a passage – between me and anybody else; I knew that if I called she wouldn't hear me. So I used to *scream* at the top of my voice and, when she got used to the fact that I did this, she left the door open. Those fears have been very useful to me since, particularly as a Samaritan when I've had to deal with cases which are called now 'psycho-somatic'. Although I could see these pictures and I could see animals jumping at me or I knew there was something horrible in the room, it only happened when I heard people coming to the hall door or when I heard laughter and I knew there was a party going on, something that I didn't want to be left out of downstairs. The fears were real enough, but at the same time there was an element of naughtiness, and this has always helped me to under-stand the mixture of neurosis and manipulation in people who really have something wrong with them but enjoy manipulating you too.

We left The Glebe in 1927, and went to live in an old, tumbledown, derelict manor house with no farm attached to it although it was called Langton Farm. It was in the village of Langton Long, four miles by road from Charlton, and a much lighter place; I don't remember being afraid there at all. In the words of my mother, many years later over a bottle of wine, the reason for the move was that 'after Uncle Gilbert died, we had to take a long hard look at things and we had to admit that we were living far beyond anything that we could afford. Something drastic had to be done or we should lose everything.' The 'something drastic' was to sell first the horses, then half the farm. At Langton, Mother had to do much of the housework as there was only one maid. Daddy wore old clothes and went to the farm every day on his motorbike.

Alcohol disappeared completely after a mysterious stay of his in a nursing home at Paignton. Perhaps he was on the way to becoming an alcoholic because I once heard my mother crying at The Glebe, and she said to my father, 'I know you've been to The Blue Boar!' From Langton onwards, while my father was alive, she just wouldn't have drink in the house. I never asked her directly why. And I never asked *him* why – I never really knew him well enough.

I get the impression that his stay at Paignton was the beginning of a less flippant life-style for my parents. My father had gone straight into the army from boarding school, went right through the whole four years of the 1914 War, and, when he came out, he was pitifully ignorant of the ways and means of farming, let alone book-keeping. At The Glebe he didn't *look* like a farmer. He dressed very smartly, and he and Mother seemed much more interested in the local Hunt (the South Dorset) and point-to-point racing than the farm, which could be run by jobless ex-service men who he would always help by hook or by crook. Then there were trips to the theatre in Bournemouth, parties to go to, and parties at home when everyone usually chose to drink something called 'Gin and It' and gramophone records were played – 'Where Does Daddy Go When He Goes Out?', 'Ain't She Sweet', 'Bye-Bye Blackbird' and everything that Dennis O'Neill ever sang. I was named Patricia after one of his songs, 'Patricia Malone'. And Mother had insisted on having 'Peggy O'Neill', another of his songs, played at her wedding. That was Daddy's favourite, probably because he called Mother 'Peggy' . . .

I deviate, I'm sorry. I was saying that at Langton there were no more horses. And no more alcohol – I presume at the insistence of my mother. My father was completely, as you would say, under her thumb. She didn't have anything to do with the running of Birch Close (what remained of The Glebe Farm) – that was his – but for everything else she was the boss and he wouldn't allow her to be displeased in any way.

Langton Farm was a lovely place for a child growing up. It was so rambling and enormous – I don't suppose I would think it was so big now – I could always find something new. I could find new stairways and new passages and, if I went up to the attics, I could always find a new attic that I hadn't seen before. And there was this beautiful great big old drawing-room where we burned logs and had children's parties. There were games, and somebody

7

played the piano and you danced 'Sir Roger de Coverley' and sang 'Auld Lang Syne' at the end. Outside was a big garden, and you never seemed to get to the end of it; it included, a lovely walled garden with peach trees and an asparagus bed and a strawberry bed, never very well kept. It was in this garden that I began to see fairies. I wasn't actually having hallucinations but, being a lonely person, because my brother was still a baby, I invented people to go with the flowers and, well, they were fairies and they made the place even prettier than it was. I talked to them and they talked back and the garden became sort of enchanted. Much later, when the astronauts were making their first trip to the moon, it was this garden that came back to me. I didn't have a television, and I was sitting on a bench, watching the moon and thinking, 'The radio says that the astronauts are up there. They *are* up there, but you can't see them, you can't really tell.' So I wrote a poem called 'Windflowers', which was partly about Langton and me as a child looking at some little flowers in the garden which reminded me of stars.

Perhaps the poem was connected with my grandmother's garden, too. I've told you how I used to stay over Grannie and Grandpapa's shop in The Market Place, Blandford. Well, in 1928, when I was five, they moved to a small house in Whitecliffe Mill Street which was much more manageable. The new house had a walled garden. It wasn't very big, but it was something wonderful to me because it had a little rockery where I used to go and sit if my grandmother was busy. The whole house used to smell of the garden because of the pot pourri that she made, but it was nice to be able to sit in the rockery by myself because she used to talk to me for hours on end, just as she would to a grown-up. It was a sort of Samaritan experience. My grandfather was a very quiet man; she never talked to him. But she used to talk to me for literally hours. I think it's because of her that I've rather got a way of shutting off when somebody talks too much.

'. . . Oh, I had a letter from Susie today,' she might say – Susie was her sister. 'I was wondering when I was going to get a letter. She usually writes every week, but I didn't get one last week. Well, she's been busy. Do you know, she's seen Kate?' I hadn't the faintest idea who Kate was. 'I shall never forgive Kate. Never. Never until my dying day. She ruined my brother. He was called to the Bar. He was a brilliant lawyer. He would have been a famous judge. But Kate ruined him. She was only a housemaid and he had to educate her before they married. He just saw her one day

8

on the stairs and that was enough, he was finished. He sent her away to France to be educated and then he married her. And what happened? She went through his money like a dose of salts!' I didn't understand any of this, but the family scandal all poured out. 'They had a house on the Riviera. They couldn't possibly afford it: of *course* they couldn't. But Kate *would* stay there and she married him and the last I saw of my brother, my poor brother, he was living in one room, he'd gone bankrupt. Kate was living in a boarding house, living on the fat of the land, but there was my poor brother, and, the next thing I heard, he'd shot himself. I shall never forgive Kate. Oh, she's knocking around London still, with a dog, a poodle . . .'

In winter, I used to sit playing Snap with Grannie in a big armchair in front of the fire. Sometimes she read to me. What I liked best were still the old gruesome poems – 'The Ancient Mariner' for instance, could stop me and tell me his story whenever he liked. She did try to get me interested in *Alice in Wonderland* but, at that time, I wouldn't have anything to do with Alice. She was more successful with Edward Lear. So Grannie and I would hibernate through the winter afternoons until my grandfather came home from the shop, which he ran in partnership with his son Leonard. The evening meal was often followed by band practice. An orchestra would gather – I say orchestra for want of a better word. There was old Mr Butt on the trumpet – he was the only one to have beer with his supper and he used to drink it with great relish and then wipe his moustache. There was somebody on cello, somebody on double bass. My grandmother, who had been a professional pianist, played the piano, and my grandfather played the violin. They all belonged to the orchestra of the Operatic Society, which gave performances in The Corn Exchange. Mother sang in the Operatic Society because she was a trained singer; she was also a trained actress and directed plays for the Blandford Dramatic Society and the Shakespeare Festivals held at Dorchester.

When Grannie went out to bring in the supper, Grandpapa would play a little solo on his violin. At first this made me cry. Their dog Badger, a little fox terrier, used to join me, and we both set up a *howl*. I used to cry and cry and cry and shout for Grannie, and eventually Grannie had to be fetched from the kitchen and I used to go out and help her make the supper instead of listening. My grandfather played first violin for the Operatic Society, and conducted the orchestra. I can remember him sitting there with

9

music manuscripts on his knee writing out sheets and sheets of band parts, mostly Gilbert and Sullivan. Grannie played the piano and I danced. He would sometimes look up from his eternal copying and interrupt with an old Music Hall song:

> My Maria's a fairy queen.
> Such a fairy ne'er was seen.
> Round she goes on her darling toes.
> She's all the world to me.

I must have been three when I began to dance. I used to dance when I heard music. I couldn't help this: it was a natural thing. My mother deduced that I was likely to be a dancer, so she would put a record on the gramophone and watch me dance and say, 'Oh, that's not very good. Up on your toes!' and so I went up on my toes, and then she would say, 'Yes, but you're not listening to the music!' and so I listened to the music. I used to take off my shoes and dance for her in my socks on the carpet in the drawing-room. From the age of ... it may have been three, it may have been four, she drove me on Saturday mornings to the Baby Class at the Norman and Saxon School in Bournemouth. It was quite a long way from The Glebe – I think it was about twenty miles – and she drove me in our small yellow Standard.

This Standard was something of a curiosity in the neighbour-hood as there were not many cars on the roads in those days. It was a two-seater with a hood that could be put up in wet weather, and there were celluloid windows in this hood that became rather cracked. At the back was the 'dickie', which looked like the boot of some modern cars, but when you lifted the lid it turned into the back of a seat for two more people. You put a rug over your knees if the weather was cold and, if it rained, there was a waterproof sheet that buttoned over you right up to the neck. I was about three when I began to travel in this way, and I enjoyed it tremendously. Tim was still a baby and I have an old photograph with my mother at the wheel and Jean in the dickie holding Tim with one arm and clutching me with the other, and looking rather grim. Sometimes Beatrice would come as well, so then there would be a lap for each child, and this would be better than ever because you were high up and could see all round you. The car never refused to go anywhere. It went through fields and over sand dunes and down muddy tracks. When we moved to Langton Farm, a

10

new car arrived, perhaps because I was starting at St Christopher's School, Blandford, and I had to be got there every day. This was an enormous saloon car, an ancient Daimler. It was dark red and it had little blinds with hanging tassels at the windows. There were also quilted leather straps to hang on to when you were going round corners. Tim and I thought it was very grand. When Mother and Daddy went out in the evenings in evening dress, they were usually going to a dance, so when we were in the car we always pretended we were 'going to a dance'. I can't remember any of the cars we had later. They were ordinary things for getting from one place to another. But there was magic about the first two.

The Norman and Saxon School of Dancing was started by Phyllis Saxon and Somebody Norman. There were large pictures of them in ballroom dancing poses – they were World Champions – in the changing rooms, she in short waistless evening dresses with a feather fan, he in white tie and tails. But, though it was still called the Norman and Saxon, it was now run by Miss Woodward, Alice Woodward. She was beautiful in her own way, very graceful, rather tall. She was an *extremely* good teacher. She had always wanted to dance but her mother wouldn't allow her to. When she was nineteen her mother died, and she then took the Royal Academy training up to Advanced Standard.

The dancing studio had a special smell of its own – a mixture of cosmetics and sweat and the resin that you put on your feet because the floor was slippery. It's very odd: as a baby I didn't notice the mirrors at all. It was only later, when I was in a practice dress and with my hair screwed up, that I began to notice the blinking mirrors. They're an awful eye-opener. I was very worried when I looked wrong in front of the mirror. Some babies that I've been teaching recently, I had to dress them as fairies. I tarted them all up in chiffon and flowers. They were *thrilled* with their dresses; they were dying to get into them. But although they were thrilled with them, not *one* of them asked to look in the mirror. It was enough that the dress was pretty; they knew *they* were pretty. I was the same when I was a small child in a party dress. The dress was pretty, so *I* was pretty. I think that's why it's so important to give handicapped children pretty dresses; they don't notice what they themselves look like; they don't bother with the mirrors. In the baby class we wore our party dresses, but I always had ballet shoes. It's much easier for children now. They just have these little slip-on things with a piece of elastic over the instep. But in those days we always had ribbons which crossed over the ankle, and you tied them at the back. It was ages before you could learn how to tie them properly.

My mother always watched the classes and then I would have to do an hour's practice at home every evening, rehearsing what had been done – the conventional ballet training of *pliés*, *grands battements*, *échappé* ... everything that's been going on for the last three hundred years. She adored making my party dresses: my school things were a mess because she never cared what I went to school in, but she adored making party dresses. I had shantung smocks. And a favourite material in those days was organdie, so I had two organdie dresses – one in pink and one in yellow – with tight bodices and full skirts. Because they were pretty I endured them, but they were very scratchy. I preferred to dance in a white chiffon dress with blue flowers and ribbons. I was very fair, and at the baby stage we all wore our hair loose. But later, of course, as soon as you passed the absolute baby stage, you had to do your hair up in a pony tail which you twisted up on top of your head and tied with a chiffon handkerchief so that it was well out of the way. By then I was having two classes a week.

Reading began at Langton Farm. I read very early because my mother taught me. I don't remember having many children's books. We had Grimm's Fairy Tales and Hans Andersen, Alice and Edward Lear, but as soon as I was fluent, which was probably after I went to St Christopher's, I wanted my mother's books. She had a copy of *The Knights of the Round Table*, done in story form from Malory's poem 'Morte d'Arthur'. That was the first book I can remember reading really fluently and really enjoying. Next, I read Shakespeare. My mother had a large illustrated Shakespeare. I thought it was marvellous. Between the ages of seven and ten I read it from cover to cover. For my tenth birthday my grandmother gave me a Shakespeare of my own because I loved it so much, but I wasn't nearly so interested in that because it didn't have the same pictures as the other. The other had those black Victorian engravings which I found very thrilling. The pictures of Macbeth and the witches and of the fairies in *A Midsummer Night's Dream*, these attracted me. And also the court scenes in *Romeo and Juliet*. You could see it all happening. There was a very horrible one of

12

Lady Macbeth in the sleepwalking scene. The Victorians really went to town on horror.

My love of Shakespeare, of course, was tied in with sex. I think I learned how to *feel* through Shakespeare. I read and re-read *Othello*. *Othello* is a very strange play – that and *A Midsummer Night's Dream*. Very strange. I read *Othello* in the same way as little boys would now watch rude videos. It was about something I was interested in, and it really told me. I don't know whether you've ever come across the play, but it has this sort of atmosphere of sex; it breathes sex even when it's not talking about it. Although it doesn't give the facts of life according to Dr Freud and the sex books, it tells you an awful lot. When I actually heard the facts as they are, it was some time before I actually believed them. I mean, the girls at school used to talk about little bits and pieces that they'd heard, and I knew about it all before my mother told me at thirteen just before I had my first period. But I wouldn't sort of believe it. I thought, 'It's not like that at all!' But I believed Shakespeare right away. I recognized it as the way you *do* feel . . .

2

We moved to The Long Cottage in Charlton Marshall when I was
seven. My mother couldn't cope with Langton, it was so huge.
Servants didn't like it: they wouldn't stay: they came and went.
After a lot of niggling and arguing with my father, who always
wanted to please her, my mother decided on this cottage. Six rooms
instead of ten. No more oil lamps to be cleaned and filled. No great
falls of soot from Jacobean chimneys. A constant flow of water. A
girl from the village coming in every day. Daddy only had to travel
about half a mile to Birch Close on his motorbike, and Mother
made the cottage very pretty and was much happier.

Charlton Church was a little way down the road, on the opposite
side, by the river, the River Stour. My Great Uncle John Hooper
lived on a farm at the top of the hill above the village. I had met
him when I was younger, usually on Market Days, but, now that
we lived in Charlton itself, I was more aware of his presence – his
regular pilgrimage to church every Sunday, and his life with the
tiny wraith-like Scotswoman who was his housekeeper. Many
years later, I wrote a poem about him called 'A God-Fearing Man'.
Part of it goes like this:

> There lived a woman in my uncle's house.
> A shy, grey creature, silent as himself,
> Her only grace was in the Highland Step,
> Taut as a bird, with all the heather spring.
> No breath of scandal ever touched her name –
> My uncle's fear of God was too well known.
> She shared the Sabbath pilgrimage to church,

14

Walking a step behind. They seldom spoke,
And yet I've watched them working side by side
In the damp garden where the blackbird sang.
There was a thread between them. Have you seen
A robin hopping by the gardener's spade?
Half proud, half prudent, but in partnership,
He loved that grey hen-robin thirty years . . .

Yes, I know all my poems by heart; I know them by heart before I write them down. But I always do take the sheaf for a special Reading in case I forget. By the way, there's a poetry reading tonight [18 June] out at Wallington, just the other side of Croydon. Peter Meares is fetching me and bringing me back. Peter has had some poems in magazines, and, a few years ago, he published a novel called *Fat Boy*. The group often asks me, but I never go unless I can get a lift. They meet in each other's houses once a month, and you all sit around and read your poetry. They appear to be wealthy people, up-market, arty housewives and so on, a kind of network. I take my sheaf of poems and somebody reads something and then, in a convenient lull, I say, 'Oh yes, well, I've got something here.'

As a child, I was taken to Charlton Church every Sunday. The rector, Mr Drury, was a wonderful man. He was an Irishman, an Oxford man, a bachelor who lived with an elderly sister, a very *grand* old lady. Her name was Alison and everybody called her 'Miss Alison'. Everything was so dignified, but he always had a twinkle in his eye. One afternoon, when I was about eight, he took my brother and me rowing on the river – the River Stour was just on the other side of the road from The Long Cottage. We came across this cow with its head sticking out of the water. Mr Drury at once said, 'Oh, poor cow! *Poor* cow! It's drowning! We must get it out!' There was a rope in the boat, so Mr Drury said, 'I'll put this rope round its horns and then we can lead it to the bank.' We pulled and we pushed and this cow wouldn't come out. He said, 'It must be stuck in the mud. I really don't know what to do. What do cows like to eat?' I said, 'Hay.' He said, 'Well, do you think if we held a little hay in front of its mouth?' I said, 'We haven't *got* any hay.' He said, 'Suppose we were to get on the bank and call it? What do you call cows when it's time to come to milking?' I said, 'Daddy usually calls

15

their names.' He said, 'That's no good because we don't know its name.'

So anyway, we went on pulling and pushing, and it was *so* hot. Finally the boat upset and Mr Drury got his trousers very wet. We stood on the bank and Mr Drury really pulled the rope and Tim and I pulled behind him like in a tug-o-war, and this cow did eventually splash out of the water. What had happened was that the poor thing had been bothered by the flies on this very hot afternoon and it had found a way of getting rid of them. As soon as we took the rope off its horns, it splashed back into the river again. But this was Mr Drury. I don't believe he really thought the cow was drowning.

He took to giving sherry parties in the rectory for the villagers. It was a standing joke – 'Oh yes. Remember when Mr Drury swore that he saw two moons!' In the 1930s when Hitler was coming to power, he took in Jewish refugees. They couldn't speak any English, but they were very kind and polite and smiling. He would introduce them to us – 'This is Carl . . . This is Emil . . . This is Gerda . . .' They left when war came. I don't know where they went. Maybe he found homes for them.

Mr Drury officiated at my confirmation. This happened when I was fifteen. We had confirmation classes in the vestry and some-times in the rectory. I think there were eight of us. He referred to the facts of life in connection with the passions. He said, 'We have passions for things. We may steal, or we may murder somebody if we hate them very much. And then, of course, there is another passion, the kind of passion between a man and a woman. We must master this. It *can* be mastered. With kindness and love it *can* be mastered.' It was absolutely muddle-headed. I think he meant kindness to the other person. All the boys sniggered and giggled. Mr Drury wasn't too pleased about this. He said, 'It's very silly to laugh because this is a very serious subject.' Somebody asked, 'How do you *do* it?' Mr Drury said, 'Your parents will tell you that.'

Then the bishop came down and confirmed us in the church. The girls wore white dresses and veils. I was very moved. I wanted to be confirmed and I did believe in God, though I don't really remember what sort of an idea of God I had. I was very religious at that time. I thought the village church and Mr Drury *were* re-ligion, you see. I believed there was a Heaven and a Hell. I could have quite easily become a nun – I was in that kind of state. But when I took communion, though it was a wonderful thing to

16

partake, I never believed that the bread and wine had anything to do with the body and blood of Christ: I never believed it was anything but bread and wine.

What Mr Drury believed *really* and what he had to say because he was the rector were two different things. You see, in class he said that it was a sacrament – none of us understood what a sacrament was – and that the bread and the wine were the body and blood of Christ but, walking around with him on a Saturday afternoon, he said that he thought it was simply that you should remember him every time you ate and drank. When, and if, Jesus said, 'As often as ye shall do this, do it in remembrance of me,' he simply meant 'As often as you eat and drink, do it in remembrance of me' – 'me' being this Good that's at the bottom of everything.

It's rather strange. When his sister died, Mr Drury went over to Ireland and brought back a bride. She was just going off to India as a missionary, so that was why he was in such a hurry to ask her to marry him. Everybody was flabbergasted, but she was an enormous success in the village. She was a very friendly person, with a sense of humour. When one of our retrievers put its nose up her skirt, she just said, 'How indelicate!' Soon after the time of my confirmation, they left the parish. We stopped going to church when the next rector came – well, not *when* he came but because of him. His name was Brayford, and he was rather Calvinistic and very dogmatic. His sermons upset the village – the wages of sin is death, and all that, and speaking against the drinking and the fornication he saw. People thought that he was getting *at* them.

My brother Tim and I were very good friends as children, just as we are today. We did things together, though he loathed other girls, and I enjoyed his company. But we used to quarrel. My mother had always wanted a boy, and there was no doubt that my brother was her favourite. I was a bit jealous, and Tim would sort of play on this by demanding to be cuddled. In retaliation I would go and take one of the china rabbits off the table in his room. Then he would come and take one of my earthenware puppies. Then I'd take something else of his. It went on and on. He had a beautiful Mickey Mouse toy, a large velvet thing that Auntie Nora, my godmother, had given him for Christmas. We were quite amicably inventing a game with this Mickey Mouse in it once, when my mother came into the room so I suddenly said, 'Oh, Mickey's very ill, you know. We shall have to see what's wrong

17

with him.' My brother was quite ready to do this, and we pretended to be doctors and put Mickey on a table and pretended that he was ill and that we were going to find out what was wrong with him. Then I said, 'You know, it's worse than I thought. The worst has happened. Mickey's turned into a girl.' Tim was so angry over that, he got his hands in my hair and pulled it out in tufts. But I think if my mother hadn't come into the room we would have gone on playing amicably. It was just this jealousy over her that always came between us.

Although I could read by the time we moved to The Long Cottage from Langton, I still enjoyed being read to. Tim also liked this, and I think we must have provided a good audience for Mother, who was an excellent reader and took pleasure in reading books to us and with us because she enjoyed them too. But it wasn't only Mother. Auntie Nora often came to see us – she had no children of her own – and she often brought a book with her. These books were always the ones that she particularly liked herself. It was she who read us *The Bad Child's Book of Beasts* and *More Beasts for Worse Children* by Hilaire Belloc, and I can still remember most of the poems. She also introduced us to *The Wind in the Willows*. This is a beauty, a book to come back to and always remember, but I can never really separate it from her voice. She read us a chapter every time she came to visit. I would never have picked it up and read it myself, and I didn't until it was time to read it to my own children. I am now looking forward to reading it to my grandchildren.

Mother's readings, which usually happened at bedtime, were usually from books that she thought we should have at the back of us, but they were delightful nonetheless. *David Copperfield*, *A Tale of Two Cities*, *The Water Babies*, *Treasure Island*, the E. Nesbit books (especially *Five Children and It*), Hans Andersen, *The Arabian Nights*. Some of them were heavy going in parts and a bit sleep-inducing, and Mother would never have abridged or skipped. But *Robinson Crusoe* nearly beat her. In the middle of a long discourse on the terrible heat of the island, she exclaimed, 'Well, if it was so hot, *why* go and wrap yourself up in goatskins?!' She didn't like being interrupted. Tim went through a phase when he was constantly stopping her to ask, 'Why?' This so exasperated her that she once forgot herself and said, 'Why?! Why?! Why?! Why?! Why not go and fry your arse in bacon fat?!'

*

18

My mother and father used to go out quite a lot. He was a Toc H member and was involved with ex-servicemen in the village, and my mother, well, she was on everything and in anything – the Women's Institute, the Mother's Union, drama. When she and Daddy were both going to be out, say, at a show in Bournemouth, Tim and I used to be sent to stay with an old lady, Martha Marshall, who'd been a parlour maid at a big house. My mother found her, I think, at a 'do' at the Women's Institute. Martha was a very dignified old lady. Beautiful she was, very upright. She always wore a black dress with a white lace front – long, right down to the ground, really out of fashion by now, but not with Martha. Next door to her was a sweet shop run by a Mrs Ford and a Miss Sturgess, probably a lesbian couple. Martha hated Mrs Ford – it was something to do with the garden fence being in the wrong place; Martha's late husband had moved it two feet over during the night. The one thing that made Mrs Ford absolutely hopping mad was anything said about Miss Sturgess, who was a dwarf with a slight hump back. Martha used to get out in the garden and sing

> There was a little nigger
> And he couldn't grow no bigger
> So they put him in a wild beast show

every time Miss Sturgess went up the path to the privy. This would bring Mrs Ford out, and she and Martha would have very *hurtful* talks, telling each other how uncharitable they were. Martha would make slanderous remarks about how Mrs Ford tricked her customers by giving short weight. Mrs Ford retaliated with quotations from the Bible in a rich contralto voice. 'Thou false tongue!' was one of her favourites.

Martha had one of those musical boxes. I wonder have you ever heard one? They have things like records with little pieces of metal sticking downwards, and there's a little needle that bangs against the metal and makes a tinkle. Oh, they're beautiful; they make a lovely sound. Some of them were vocal. We always wanted to hear 'Daisy Daisy' and 'The Bird in the Gilded Cage', though Martha preferred 'Where Is My Wandering Boy Tonight?' and 'The Old Hundred'. There was a skirt dance, too. She used to push back the big table and bring out some old lace curtains, and I used to put those round me and do the skirt dance. Tim used to watch this rather impatiently. The great thing with my brother was that he

19

always managed to get his hands entangled with Martha's hairnet. She had lovely greyish dark-brown hair, and he pulled the hairnet off to see all this hair come down. If we had to stay overnight, Martha used to make porridge in the morning. She made a pattern on it with Golden Syrup, and it tasted wonderful.

Our second Christmas at The Long Cottage, Tim and I were given Fairy cycles. We believed in Father Christmas and we'd sent the usual messages up the chimney. The living-room had a beautiful chimney for sending messages up – you could actually see the sky if you poked your head above the wide-open hearth. We used to write what we wanted on a piece of paper and then put it above the log fire so that it just wafted up the chimney. Sometimes it burned but, in any case, the draught pulled it up and then, of course, it went straight to the North Pole. So the Fairy cycles arrived on Christmas morning together with the pillowcases full of knobbly parcels and the stockings full of chocolates and oranges. Oh, it was very exciting! It was a great *event* because it meant that we could go to new places. We learned to ride them in Gravel Lane, starting at the top and free-wheeling to a grassy place where we fell off. One of our favourite bicycle rides was to a field by Little Manor which was owned by Mrs Mann. In this field was a chestnut tree with beautiful bouncy branches. We each sat on a different branch and pretended they were horses and that we were Knights of the Round Table. Mrs Mann was an eccentric old lady. She was vitriolic about cows going past her house. She was rather like that old lady in *David Copperfield* who every now and then would drop everything she was doing and say, 'Janet! Donkeys!' and she and Janet would run after the donkeys. Well, Mrs Mann was the same about cows. She was very unpopular with the local farmers because they liked to drive their cows past Little Manor down to the water meadows. Mr Bugg and Mrs Mann were at absolute daggers drawn, they hated each other. Mr Bugg was a very large, rich farmer, and if she saw his cows especially, she would immediately come out and cause a great commotion and try to drive the cows back where they came from. Of course they didn't go back where they came from: they went on across the fields to the water meadows. Once there was a court case about this, and Mrs Mann made the front page of the *Daily Mirror*. She was photographed outside her house, holding back the tide of cows like King Canute, with the caption 'They shall not pass!'

Another local character we used to see on our rides very often was Mr Seymour Portman, who lived at Charlton Manor which was a little way from Mrs Mann's. He was slightly batty and was a relation of Lord Portman who owned Bryanston House, which was afterwards turned into a public school for boys. He used to take long, vague walks across the fields and rarely spoke to anybody. He had a housekeeper who was quite well-off, and I think he would have died without her really; she waited on him hand and foot. She had a nephew at a public school, and, a little later, Tim was just the right size to wear the clothes he had grown out of. Mr Seymour Portman brought some of these to The Long Cottage in a parcel. He knocked at the door and handed this parcel to my mother, and then stood on one leg like a stork and scratched the back of it with the other foot. My mother made polite conversation and invited him in to have a cup of tea. This he refused, but he still stood there in this peculiar position. At last she said, point blank, 'Is there anything I can do for you, Mr Portman?!' and he said – he had á terrible stutter; I think that is why he rarely spoke to anybody – he said, 'I am w-w-w-waiting for the p-paper and the str-str-string.' The Portmans were millionaires.

I shall always remember my tenth birthday for the sheer *misery* of it. I had fallen in love for the second time. The Blandford Operatic Society was dominated by a very handsome man. He wasn't *really* a very handsome man. In fact, thinking of him now, he was rather seedy – you know, getting on for forty, ageing. He had a very charming manner and a lovely tenor voice, and he very often acted with my mother. I remember her playing Margery in *The Country Girl* and Angela in *Flora Dora*, and he was opposite her; and in *The Mikado* she was one of the three little maids, and he was Nanki-Poo. I fell very heavily for him. He came to the house quite a lot, and he thought it attractive to be very courteous and polite to children, he'd treat you more or less as a grown-up. And on my tenth birthday, May the 6th, which coincided with the Silver Jubilee of King George and Queen Mary, there was a terrific jamboree in the village, with a fête and a Fancy Dress Parade. I thought it was *wonderful* to have all this on my birthday, and I was just going to join the Fancy Dress Parade in the gardens of Mrs Walker, who was one of the local ladies of the manor. I was wearing a Dutch costume, a little white cap and a checked dress,

21

and carrying some artificial hyacinths, when my mother remarked quite casually, 'I say, have you heard? Alfred's engaged to Miss Moore.' Miss Moore was my brother's schoolteacher, very charming but very fat. Ooh! I shall *never* forget it! It was absolute torture to go through with that procession, knowing this. It had never occurred to me that Alfred would get engaged to somebody else. I see now, in retrospect, that he was just a vain man who had been charming in front of a child, but I was brushing away the tears as I walked in this Fancy Dress Parade. I only got Third Prize and I was sure that I should have had First Prize. It was quite unfair that they gave me Third Prize! I had this awful attack of depression, and I was sure that they were doing this on purpose!

The Miss Ainsworths, two maiden sisters who were distant relatives of Florence Nightingale, lived over the road from us. Their large house had a barn attached to it, fixed up as a theatre where my mother practised all her plays. She herself always made the clothes for these plays, and she always seemed to have a lot of multi-coloured tights, that she'd dyed for some Shakespeare production, hanging up on our washing line – tights in mauve and green and blue, and long shoes with bells on the end like the Plantagenets used to wear. The cottage was sideways on to the road, and in front of it was a little garden, and that was really the only place my mother could hang clothes. I used to feel rather ashamed about this. I thought, 'Strangers going by will think that we wear those things!'

The Ainsworths owned an island in the middle of the river and always, on November the 5th, the whole village used to congregate there to have a big bonfire with fireworks. We used to roast potatoes in the embers, and the Miss Ainsworths brought over hot soup. The village people had a love-hate relationship with the two old ladies because, although they were very excitable and interfering, they also did a lot of good. There was real poverty at that time. It was the Thirties when there was a Depression, and there was no work for a lot of the farm workers – the farms were changing over to machinery. There used to be children with bare feet, and even in winter – we thought it very rude – little girls never wore any knickers, and still only wore cotton frocks because that's all they had. The Miss Ainsworths were wonderful to these people; they did an awful lot. They used

22

to cook meals for anybody who was ill and couldn't cook for themselves, and they used to take blankets for the children, see that they got the things they needed, see that they were warm. There was a terrific lot of sickness – TB and things like whooping cough and measles and diphtheria and scarlet fever, which were very dangerous then. I was too young to feel sorry for these people at all – it was just like that – but I was old enough to feel horror, looking into a cottage and seeing there was no furniture there and just a dirt floor and rags in the corner where the family slept. I didn't often see inside such places, but sometimes my mother, like the Ainsworths, looked after such people and I waited outside.

Meanwhile my father was going back and forth to Birch Close on his motorbike in his farm clothes. He really was a working farmer now. He and Frank, the foreman, a man who'd been in the war with him, did most of the work themselves – all dairy farming; the cows were mostly Friesians. They didn't send cattle for slaughter, except, of course, the bull calves. My father never milked. There was – my goodness! they would never allow it now! – there was another man who'd been gassed in the war and got TB on top of it. He lived in a caravan on the farm and did most of the milking. I mean, a man with TB in charge of the milking! His wife and daughter, and also Frank and his wife, milked once in the early morning and once in the evening. A mistress in school once asked me, 'How many cows has your father got?' I hadn't the faintest idea, so when I went home I asked him and he said, 'Sixty.' I'd seen some calving. It was a very primitive affair compared with calving today – the cows used to just slip their calves out in the field. I never wanted to learn how to milk. In fact, I didn't want to have anything to do with the farm at all, and Tim was no more interested than I was.

My father's main rivals were the man who took over The Glebe and Mr Bugg whose farm bestrode both sides of the village, but we had the village milk round. Where their milk went I don't know, but I know that, just before the war in '39, the Milk Marketing Board took over, when it was collected by the milk train and taken to the milk factory at Baily Gate. Sam, the milkman, had retired by then. He spoke the Dorset dialect very broadly. My mother put him into a play once. It was beautiful the way he talked – 'carn for arses' meant 'corn for horses'. He and his old horse Teddy used to

23

go round with a churn and ladle, and people took out their jugs to him.

My father worked very, very hard on the farm, trying to make good all the losses, and trying to run it the proper way, and, as we were making money, coming up in the world again, Mother wanted to design a bigger house, and have it built on Birch Close, our half of the old Glebe Farm, and call it Four Winds. I can remember her sitting down with a local builder, Mr Boughton, and saying she'd seen in Bournemouth blocks of flats with corner windows – you know, there's a piece of steel comes down the corner, and you can see two ways, sort of south and west – and she'd set her heart on having these windows for the farmhouse. But Mr Boughton, the builder, said, 'You can't do it. It can't be done,' and she said, 'Well, it's there – in Bournemouth. *They*'ve got it. Why can't *I* have it?!' and he said, 'Nohow. It can't be done.' Finally he did say, 'Yes. All right. All right. Well, I'll try. I'll try. It will probably be a big mistake and you'll regret it later, but I'll try.'

She wanted corner windows upstairs and downstairs – the house was to be two storeys. Oh, she was very thrilled! She could have room for a maid and a room for herself and my father, and a room each for me and my brother (at The Long Cottage we shared), and a spare room, and, downstairs, she could have a large lounge and a dining-room and a kitchen with a modern range, a Triplex. And another thing she insisted on was a cedarwood staircase opposite the front door. Where she got the idea from I don't know, but she wanted this; she said it would always smell nice. *Again* Mr Boughton said it couldn't be done, they didn't make staircases of cedarwood, but finally she did get one. The corner windows – that was a very sad story. During the building, we went on a camping holiday to Cornwall. We were away for some weeks and, by the time we came back, the shell of the house was built and, lo and behold, Mr Boughton had built corner windows but he'd put a large block of wood at each corner instead of a small strip of steel so they were like two windows.

My mother was very annoyed, but Boughton still stuck to his story that it couldn't be done, and the windows stayed. My mother was so tired of having people always knocking on the door and always being interrupted that, when she designed Four Winds, she made the house turn its back on the road completely; she put the front door at the back, away from the road, and the downstairs bit that faced the road was a wall with a kitchen window. I always think that house *looks* like my mother. We moved there in 1935, when I was twelve and Tim was ten.

I remember, at Four Winds, the radio played a great part in our lives. In the ordinary way, Tim and I went to bed at half past seven, but on Saturday nights we listened first to 'Music Hall' at eight o'clock – later it was ITMA – and then to 'Saturday Night Theatre'. It was a very great treat and an absolute ritual and we were each given a Mars Bar. My father would put down his cowboy or detective story to listen, and Mother would go on sewing. There were those two singers, Ann Ziegler and Webster Booth, on the 'Music Hall' programmes, singing 'I'll See You Again' and sort of Straussy songs. Then there were the funny men like Gillie Potter and Claude Dampier and Leonard Henry. Gillie Potter had a very dignified style. He used to say that he'd been to the races, and tell the pedigrees of the horses – 'Mr Gillie Potter's Raspberry by Rude Boy out of Gallery' and so on. Claude Dampier had an imaginary fellow traveller called Mrs Gibson – 'Of course Mrs Gibson would never allow anything like that!' and, pretending to show her photograph, 'No, no. That's not the pavilion. That's Mrs Gibson.' Leonard Henry was more the conventional type of comic. People like Gillie Potter and Claude Dampier created a character for themselves, usually a rather silly sort of man who had some sort of an obsession. Leonard Henry was a stand-up comic who told jokes and did sketches as a dame character with a drag voice. He had a signature tune and the audience laughed uproariously when he came on, and also when he immediately said, 'Why the laughter?!' Somehow 'Why the laughter?!' was very funny because you imagined what he was dressed like.

Something I at first considered very *un*funny was the prospect of having another sibling. On a sort of autumny afternoon in October, the year we moved to Four Winds, I came home on my bicycle from school. My mother was sitting by the fire and I sat down beside her and asked if she'd seen a book of French stories that I needed the next day. She seemed a bit distant and said, No, she hadn't seen the book, she thought it must be at the school. Then she suddenly looked up and said, 'I think I'm going to have a baby.' It was an absolute shock. I cried myself to sleep that night. It seemed an *awful* thing. I don't know why I didn't want the baby. It was something I'd never thought of, never expected.

25

Perhaps at the back of my mind was the thought that it would take me even further away from my mother than ever. By the following May, though, when Felicity, always called Duffy, was born, I was tremendously enthusiastic.

My mother was again running into the servant problem. She finished up with Joan Randall, a girl of seventeen from a gypsy family, very attractive to men and with brilliant red hair. Gypsies were quite a feature of my childhood. They used to hold great gatherings for funerals in Blandford Forum, terrific occasions like wakes; they all used to get drunk and everybody else kept out of the way. A gypsy wedding is nothing; there is never any public ceremony unless the couple are 'civilised' and want a church wedding. But funerals were great occasions. Even the bereaved family joined in the party. They might grieve afterwards, but first they got drunk. Apart from the gypsies who travelled in caravans, many, like my father's family, had settled down and bought land. The Hughes family was like that. Old Mrs Hughes was a regular visitor at Four Winds. Like other gypsies who came to the door in my childhood, she sold lavender and heather and clothes-pegs and kettle-holders which she carried in a big basket, and, like the others, if you didn't give or buy anything, she spat on the door when you shut it; once, she peed on the doorstep. Joan Randall's father lived in a very small cottage on the Buggs' farm as a farmworker with his wife and ten children – how he got them all in, I don't know. Well, I *do* know because Joan talked a lot about it and told how she could watch her father and mother making love. Joan was only interested in the one, all-absorbing subject of sex, absorbing to her and absorbing to me and my brother. There was no need to question her, she just told us, chapter and verse, what she did in the fields. She came in one evening when Daddy and Mother were out and we were sitting by the fire. She was in a black coat, her hair like carrots. She came in, hardly noticing we were there, and said, 'Oh, make me worthy! Make me worthy!' then just knelt down and prayed to God to make her worthy. It gradually came out that she wanted to be worthy of Binkie, an errand boy who worked for the International Stores in Blandford. 'Oh Binkie, Binkie, Binkie! He must be the best person who ever lived in this world! Tonight we walked and we found a hedgehog, and I've brought it home, and put it in the garden, and I've called it Binkie. I shall remember this evening all my life!' So she kept the hedgehog in the garden – she was very fond of animals.

About a week later, she came in crying, and my mother was there this time but it didn't matter with Joan, she was crying, tears streaming down her face, her eyes very red and swollen, and she said, 'I've brought Binkie in with me.' This was the hedgehog. 'He's all I've got left now! Binkie says . . .' This was the errand boy. 'Binkie says we can't get married, because I went out with some-body else. He didn't say, he didn't say, he *didn't* say that we would never see each other again, but he said we've got to wait for each other, we're not old enough to get married. Well I say we *are* old enough to get married. If we've done all that we've done, we *ought* to be old enough to get married! He *could* marry me! . . .' She went on for a long time.

Joan had a lot of boys in Blandford, and she always wanted to marry whoever it was she'd been out with. She used to take walks with her sister Ruth in the evenings, and they used to stand on Blandford Bridge and wait for the sixth-formers from Bryanston School. She would tell us exactly what happened. 'It's funny, you know. I just can't help it. We get halfway up the hill and they push you against the gate and that's it, up it goes!' And, of course, she cried dreadfully when she found that they didn't want to marry her, they just wanted up-it-goes. She would allow this, but she always thought that it must mean that they wanted to marry her. She wanted desperately to get married. She said, 'When I get married, it'll be every night. He'll *have* to do it every night because I shan't want anything else and if the babies come they do. My mother had lots of babies, and she's all right . . .'

My sister, at that time, was a baby in a pram, and Joan and I used to take her for walks. Of course Joan would have an eye for any young man, usually Bryanston schoolboys. I was satisfied with simply an ogle here and there. Though I was meeting boys at children's parties given by the neighbouring farmers, and by the parents of the girls I went to school with, I wasn't particularly interested in any of them. I was too busy with my ballet at the Norman and Saxon, going there by train pretty well every night after school, back and forth, winter and summer, from Charlton Mar-shall to Bournemouth. To be kissed still seemed very, very daring, in spite of Joan, and it had only happened to me once or twice. I didn't meet my first real boyfriend till after war was declared and I was sixteen.

Holidays were always spent camping in Cornwall. We didn't have a caravan, but took tents piled on a trailer behind the car. Cornwall then was a much more lonely place than now. Sometimes we camped in the countryside or on the moors; sometimes, when we found a good beach for surfing, we camped by the sea. If we found a riding stable, we hired horses. We always packed a plentiful supply of books, borrowed from Boots Library in Blandford. I got through all the 'Herries' novels of Hugh Walpole in the warm, grass-smelling stuffiness of a closed tent, with the rain drumming on the canvas. P. G. Wodehouse was a wonderful holiday companion; I also remember laughing out loud at *The Experiences of an Irish RM*, and at a novel called *Spanish Gold*. When I ran out of my chosen books, I started on Mother's. She favoured Somerset Maugham and *The Forsyte Saga*, and biographies of various great people. Grannie had been greatly shocked when she discovered Mother read Somerset Maugham, because, she said, he picked up dirt like a vacuum cleaner.

War was declared when we were camping on Bodmin Moor. It was a Sunday morning, and we heard Chamberlain make the announcement in a very sad, tired old voice on our portable radio. I remember this specially because I felt then that I knew my father better than I did at any other moment. When that announcement was made, he cried, there were tears running down his face, and he said to my mother, 'God! We shall have to go through it all again!' That was the first time I realised what the 1914 war must have been for him; he must have gone through absolute hell. I had grown up believing that the 1914–18 war was a joke, because he would only present it as a sort of Dad's Army. He would tell stories about how the field kitchens and the baggage cars and the tanks with the latrines got lost behind the German lines, and the Germans retreated, thinking they were being attacked; how his sword got caught between his legs on parade . . . oh, various jokes. Apart from that, he would never say anything about it, except that he didn't rise above the rank of Lieutenant.

The following November, a regiment of the Royal Signals was billeted in Blandford and Charlton Marshall. Joan had a lovely time and eventually did marry. My mother chaperoned me to a dance got up for the soldiers by the Women's Institute at Charlton

Marshall Village Hall. John Wilkins, nineteen, a private only just enlisted, very good-looking, over six feet tall, came straight over to me, and we danced together all night. Though his eyes protruded and had bags under them, he had a lovely speaking voice, a natural voice with no accent at all. He came to supper the next day at Four Winds. We began to go out together and there were kisses. Finally, as I approached seventeen, the Dorset air being balmy and scented and very pleasant, there were more than kisses, he gave me a ring, and I considered myself engaged.

3

My formal education? . . . I first went to school, St Christopher's
School in Blandford, when I was five. I already knew how to read
and write, and I could speak a little French – my mother often
spoke to us in French at home, and sang French songs and nursery
rhymes. The school was run by a Mr and Mrs Phillips, who mostly
employed young girls as assistant teachers. They rarely lasted more
than a term: sometimes they lasted no more than a few weeks.
They were usually from Belgium or Scandinavia, and they couldn't
speak English properly. There were about thirty pupils altogether,
and the fees were six guineas a term. Boys left when they were
eight; girls could stay on till they were sixteen. Apart from my
brother who followed me there, I considered the boys cruel and
nasty, and had little to do with them; I didn't like them at all. Tim
wasn't a reader, and he cannot spell to this day. He went on to
Blandford Grammar School when he was eight and then, when he
was fourteen, to Shaftesbury Grammar School, which was a very
good boarding school for boys. By the time he left there, the war
was well under way, so he joined the Marines, the equivalent of
the Naval Division to which my father belonged from 1914 to
1918. Then he ran Birch Close for my father, who'd had a series
of heart attacks since being called up into the Dorsetshires. Tim
had rather fancied the idea of becoming a professional actor. He is
a *born* actor, and he's always been able to find ways of using this
talent – travelling with Mother around Cornwall in their own
group of amateur players, and, more especially, running summer
pony camps for children and adolescents, which involve trekking
across the moors with a covered wagon, everyone dressed up as

cowboys and Indians and pioneers, then telling ghost stories round the fire at night. He's even toured the States with a Medieval Jousting Pageant he devised himself, and he arranges jousting tournaments during his summer camps . . .

My first day at school was absolutely terrifying: I've never been so frightened in my life. It was like being a pygmy among a lot of giants, and the giants didn't see you, because they were looking over your head. They banged into you and knocked you down and trod on you – they probably *didn't* knock you down and tread on you, but it felt as if they did. There was Assembly, and we sang a hymn and there were one or two prayers. At Assembly, Mrs Phillips would always stand on tiptoes and roll her feet around, doing ankle exercises – she didn't like to waste time. She was very kind in an affected, superficial way but, although it was a small school, she never seemed to remember your name. I never remember seeing Mr Phillips at all, except at Assembly – he left us to the Sigrids and Mademoiselles. The older children had desks. The younger ones sat in a bare room on little chairs at tables. There weren't any toys or games to play; you just *learned*. In the afternoon we had stories and dancing and went for walks. Paper chases were also a great thing on some afternoons. A big girl started off with a bag of torn-up paper, and every now and then she dropped some and you'd have to try to catch her, following the trail of paper – I didn't like that at all.

A Miss Pratt taught ballroom dancing and a little ballet with the help of a pianist. In the kindergarten we did Ring-a-Roses and the polka step and the gallop. Of course, going already to the Norman and Saxon, I showed off. I did the splits and high kicks and curtsies and *pas de Basque* which the others couldn't do. Dancing was a great adventure in one-upmanship during my early years at school. I was streets ahead of anybody else, and this made me very pleased with myself and very unpopular. Till about the age of fourteen when I began to make a few friends, I was extremely lonely. Though the other girls couldn't help admiring what I did, my ballet training somehow excluded me. My mother would never allow me to do any homework because I had to do my hour's practice under her eye. The boys were very teasing about my dancing, they didn't like it at all. Playtimes were a nightmare. The boys pinched and punched me and pulled my plaits. Years later, I met Benita Andrews (no longer Andrews) who was one of the big girls when I was five. She said, 'You were a horrible little girl. I remember you

31

stamping on a butterfly.' I said, 'That's the *last* thing I'd do! I'd never stamp on a butterfly!' She said, 'You stamped on a butterfly. You had a little black doll with gold earrings. You used to wind it up and it used to spin round and round and round, and one day you showed several of us this doll and we all stood round and watched, and then you went and stamped on a butterfly that was sitting on the grass. We all said what a horrible little girl you were for doing it, and you said that the doll had *told* you to do it.' Well, I don't remember doing this at all, but I do remember the little doll. So what she said is probably true.

A rule of the school was that the kindergarten and the infants had to take half an hour's rest after lunch. This rest was taken in the attic in two large double beds. We all piled into these beds, boys and girls together. The attic got very hot in the summer but, in the winter, we had blankets to put over us if we wanted them. Of course we didn't sleep at all: we just lay there and talked and quarrelled and pushed each other out of bed – I usually got pushed out of bed. It still surprises me that there was no sex play. The boys usually used this period for telling rude jokes and rhymes – rather shocking things like:

> Old King Cole was a merry old soul,
> And a merry old soul was he.
> He called for a light
> In the middle of the night
> To go to the WC.

The girls would try to go one better. For example, Renée Andrews said, '*I* know a rude joke: Use our special cream for the bust. It makes mountains out of molehills.'

Another rule was that you had to wear a uniform. This was dark-green gym tunics with a braid girdle which you had to tie up, and a cream blouse. You had a bottle-green topcoat and a velour hat in winter. In summer you wore a panama. The hats had the school badge on the front. The boys wore bottle-green knicker-bockers and a cream shirt, and a blue and green tie which we also wore. In the summer we had light-green dresses with white collars and cuffs. The boys wore the same in summer, except that they wore green blazers. You bought your uniform at a shop called Cherry's.

There was a weekly ritual of story reading. The whole school piled into the largest classroom which was the kindergarten. The big ones sat on chairs, and the little ones sat on the floor, and Mrs Phillips read a story in serial form for about half an hour. She read in a very expressionless voice. A lot went over my head, but I remember *Winnie the Pooh*, which I never wanted to read myself as a child because I connected it with school; I've only just learned to value it at its true worth. I liked *The Jungle Book*, but always laboured under the delusion that Mowgli was a frog.

Under Mr and Mrs Phillips, there was a Christmas production every year. We performed in the Parish Room next to the church. The first one that I can remember was *The Frog Prince*, which included a Bee Dance in which I was a bee. Then I was an elf in *The Elves and the Shoemaker* – I had a little solo dance to do in that. I also remember dancing in *The Dance of the Hours* as Dawn. Then, when I was about nine, Miss Sayer took over as headmistress, and the parents were invited to nothing with her, there were no more productions. I liked Miss Sayer. For one thing, she abolished school dinners and we brought packed lunches instead.

Miss Sayer brought with her a lot of books, and she put carpets on the stairs and landings. I never had any relationship at all with the Phillipses, but Miss Sayer was different. She was a Scotswoman and taught a great deal of History. She went into the Scottish question very thoroughly, pointing out that Queen Elizabeth had never been the Queen of Scotland. Miss Mills, who taught Maths, was her main assistant. Miss Sayer didn't like figures herself so it was always Miss Mills who taught us Maths right up through the school. I *wouldn't* learn Geometry. I simply didn't understand it. I remember going on strike about it: I sat with an absolutely blank book. In the end, the only Maths I managed to grasp were a few bits and pieces about pounds, shillings and pence. I only began to understand Geometry when I started dancing professionally be-cause, in Modern Dance, Geometry is everything – well not quite everything, but I understood it in that context. We had a report every term. For me it was usually 'Could do better' or 'Could do much better with more concentration'. For things like History it was always 'Very good', and sometimes I got an 'Excellent' for French and English. When I left, Miss Sayer wrote, 'I have enjoyed teaching Pat. She was a very interesting child.' I think that was about the only real compliment I ever got on a report.

When Miss Sayer first came I used to go into her private garden at playtimes to avoid being pinched and punched. In the summer we took out chairs and had lessons there on the little lawn. Otherwise it was out of bounds, but I used to go in to watch the various things growing and to play by myself and explore and imagine. Now that Miss Sayer had brought so many books I would read there as well. One day, while everybody else was in the playground, I was in the garden, reading *Legends of Greece and Rome*. I was reading it avidly; I was thrilled. But someone must have told on me, because Miss Sayer came into the garden and said, 'You know, children aren't supposed to be here.' She asked what I was reading, took the book and said, 'You're not really supposed to bring books out of doors either. It's time to come in now. Put it back on the shelf.' Being found with that book was my first encounter with Miss Sayer. In a way it was significant. I *was* out of bounds and I *had* a book out of doors. Mrs Phillips would have made a row, but Miss Sayer asked what I was reading and wasn't at all cross. She used to choose books for you to read on the basis of your taste and mental age and what you'd read before. In this way, before leaving school, I'd read *Pride and Prejudice* and *Mansfield Park*, *Cranford*, *Jane Eyre*, and several novels by Sir Walter Scott, though most of all I enjoyed his long poem *Marmion*, which is thrilling.

But, next to Shakespeare – Miss Sayer loved Shakespeare, too – I loved myths and legends. There was Perseus and the Gorgon. There was Ulysses and his adventures with the Cyclops and Circe. Oh, and there was Helen of Troy. Myths are always popping up in my poems. One of my earliest – I wrote it when I was a grown woman in my thirties with children – began with the story of Oedipus. It was called 'Abortion' and was about how there is so much repercussion when any human being is killed.

Meanwhile I was progressing with my dancing. When Miss Sayer came to St Christopher's I'd have been preparing for the Fifth Grade Examination of the Royal Academy of Dancing. Oh God! How my mother used to work me up to these examinations! The Norman and Saxon School of Dancing was the only big school of dancing in the West Country, so the exams were held there. Somebody came down from the Royal Academy in London, sometimes a man, sometimes a woman. They were quite well known in the dancing world. There was Ruth French, who has written a lot of books on dancing – she came down for the Third Grade. She was elegant and rather distant. For the First Grade I had Grace Cone, a very nice, sympathetic person who still has a school at Windsor. Before the examinations I would be going to Bournemouth two or three times a week. My mother would say, 'If you don't get through this, it's all going to stop, it's going to be no more dancing!' It wasn't that I particularly *wanted* to go on dancing. It was just a part of my life. When I first went to school, I thought all girls danced; I was surprised to find that they didn't have to practise in the evenings like I did.

As regards the teaching, Miss Woodward, Madame, didn't demonstrate at all, *except* in a private lesson, and even then without putting any dancing into it. She wore a silk dress – that comes down from the Mesdames of the Russian Ballet – with a flared or pleated skirt with plenty of room and fairly long. She wore high-heeled shoes, but she had wonderful feet and legs, and you could see exactly what you had to do. Her sleeves were long and tight – again so that you could see exactly what she was doing. She had the most beautiful arm movements; I realise now that they were all but perfect. Classical ballet is a matter of position, and so she showed you what position you had to get to. She corrected while she sat. How she gave classes without demonstrating, I don't know. When *I*'ve given ballet lessons, I've had to demonstrate all the time. Perhaps it was because there were always older children with the younger ones, and the younger ones could watch those in front of them. She did all the steps with her fingers. 'Pliés in First Position!' – her hands would go beside each other. 'Second Position!' – one hand would go out because your feet were supposed to be apart.

On the day of the examination you waited in the practice room before going in to the examiner. Whereas now you wear a leotard for ordinary dancing, at that time you wore what was called a 'practice dress', which was a very short tunic with knickers. But for the exam you had a white satin bone bodice with a tutu skirt. You weren't allowed to wear blocked shoes until the Fourth Grade – before that you did everything in flat, soft leather shoes. Your mother would be pulling at your dress and picking at your hair and tying your shoes again before Miss Woodward inspected you. Then each of you would be called into the studio in turn for ten minutes, with Miss Woodward giving you another inspection at the door as you went in.

The examiner would be sitting at the end of the room on the window seat just like Miss Woodward did, and you suddenly felt it was an awful long way to get there, you felt very flat-footed and very awkward because you weren't dancing. You stood then at the *barre*, not too close to the examiner, not to crowd on top of her, but not too far away or she couldn't see you, and you might have to do three exercises to Chopin – the pianist usually played Chopin, which is wonderful for ballet practice, but it might also be Mozart, Schubert or Johann Strauss.

After your exercises at the *barre*, you'd be asked to come into the centre. 'I'd like to see an *arabesque ouverte*, *croisée* and *de face*.' This would be for the Third Grade. Now she asked some theory. 'And what is a *pas marché*?' You said parrot fashion, 'A *pas marché* is a step on the flat foot with a bent knee, preceded by a *développé*.' 'Will you *do* some *pas marchés*?' So you did some *pas marchés*. Then, 'I want to see *attitude ordinaire*, *à deux bras* and *à la Grecque*.' So you did the three *attitudes*, fortunately not falling over, because for the *attitudes* you have to stand on one leg. Then there were the more lively steps – the *ballonné composé* and the *ballonné simple*, and some *glissades* and *pas de bourrée*, and, as you did them, she – this was Ruth French – took you rather on the hop, and said, 'Yes. What is a *pas de bourrée*?' before the music for them started, and you told her, 'Three steps moving to the side preceded by a *degagé*.'

Then, after I'd done my exercises in the centre she said, 'Now will you show me your mime.' For the Fourth Grade I'd arranged 'Getting Ready for a Party', but for the Third I think it was 'Catching a Train', so I packed my suitcase and looked at my watch and did my hair and got more and more worried because it was getting late and I couldn't find my hat. 'Now can I see your dance?' This again was something you'd worked on and I remember it was the Irish Jig to the usual tune of 'The Irish Washerwoman' – *you* didn't arrange it like the mime, Miss Woodward did. And this was the end of the examination. At that point I found that the examiners called you 'dear'. 'That will be enough, dear. You can go.' No indication whether you had passed. Nothing at all. It was wonderful when, about a month later, the card came through to say that you *had* passed.

The examinations always took place in the morning, and the tradition was to go out to lunch at a restaurant with the tutu in its bag. We usually went out to lunch at Bobby's, a big shop in Bournemouth. It was a very exciting lunch with tomato soup and roast chicken. The real excitement was the sweet – ice cream or a

36

sherry trifle. There was always an orchestra at Bobby's, a little palm court orchestra. The leader must have known that there were several of us there who had been in for exams, because he played ballet pieces such as 'Les Sylphides'. Then, another excitement, my mother would take me to The Pavilion for a matinée. *Mary Stuart* it was after the Third Grade.

I'd now passed the First, Second and Third Grades, and I was happier at St Christopher's because, apart from liking Miss Sayer, I was coming into the category of the 'big ones' and it didn't seem so hostile an environment, though the fact I wasn't allowed to do homework was rather a source of grievance to my peers. I managed to get through the Fourth and Fifth Grades, which were exactly like the other exams, except that each time they got more complicated. My *bête noir* was *enchaînement*, where you had to string together a series of steps, remembering them. 'Now will you do a full *contretemps* followed by a *posé temps levé* and a *ballonné simple et composé*, then a *glissade en avant et en arrière* followed by a *brisé télémach* – twice.' I always thought I would fail on the *enchaînements*, but I never did. Now I had to do the Elementary. It was very important to me to pass this. The Norman and Saxon had a dancing display every year and, although there were a great many group dances, you couldn't have a solo until you passed your Elementary, and I wanted to get that solo.

The Elementary was different from the Grade exams, because you did it in London. I was fourteen when my mother took me. It was late June, very hot weather, and we had great difficulty getting an hotel near to the Royal Academy in Holland Park. We finally fetched up at The Winston. It was full of Germans. My mother said, 'This place has rather a sinister air. I have a feeling somehow we're in the Foreign Office.' I realise now that they were Jewish refugees.

I had the one examiner that I'd always dreaded – Mr Mac-Lennan, one of the founder members of the Royal Academy. I knew that he was very strict, and, when I faced him, I liked what I saw even less than what I'd seen of him in photographs. He had a bristly moustache, looked rather stern and smiled not at all. The little he said was in a clipped accent. I was examined much along the same lines as for the Fourth and Fifth Grades, which included point work, but it all took longer – at least half an hour instead of the usual ten minutes. You had to do a classical dance – not a character one, a classical dance which you had arranged yourself and for which you'd chosen the music. The music I used was a little waltz called 'Charmeuse'. Anyway, the upshot of the awful ordeal was that Mr MacLennan said, 'Very well. That's enough,' and I left. That night, my mother and I went to The Windmill where we saw Leonard Henry – they always had a comic at The Windmill. He was being a cockney charlady and keeping up a string of jokes, when suddenly he turned round to somebody completely invisible at the back and said, 'Well, what if I *have?*!' Somehow that was very, very funny. The rest of the show was lovely, with a can-can and various other dances, beautifully dressed and put on. There was a nude scene called 'The Nymphs of Diana'. This was the high spot of the show, but it was done behind a gauze curtain as a *tableau*, very pretty. The slogan then was not 'We never closed' but 'We never move'!

The result of my Elementary took a long time to come. It was at the end of September, I think, that I got the news that I'd passed. I was fourteen. I began at once to arrange a solo dance for the Norman and Saxon display the following summer. This was what I'd wanted to pass the Elementary *for*. Which is not to say I didn't perform it elsewhere as well. I was always dancing at social evenings and village entertainments, and charity performances in aid of this and that. No, my father never came to watch. He never had anything to do with my dancing or my schooling. I was fond of him, and I think he was fond of me, but we couldn't really talk, and there was no *rapport*. As regards schooling he was only interested in my brother at Shaftesbury, and as regards dancing, though he didn't *mind* it, he thought it all rather high-falutin'. He knew that women were silly, you see, so it was all part of feminine vapours and frippery, and, if my mother was happy that I should dance, she was to have her way. He would do anything to please my mother. She was even able to persuade him to play parts in the annual Shakespeare Festivals at Dorchester. Sometimes he was really very good, simply because he didn't know anything about it. He played Capulet in *Romeo and Juliet* in the way of a stern father. It was completely unconventional Shakespeare and yet somehow very much alive. When he told Juliet to fettle her fine joints and get off to church, he was being absolutely himself. None of the unlikely people that my mother roped in understood anything about Shakespeare or the theatre, and they played their parts exactly as themselves. Sometimes at these Festivals there were days devoted to one scene, a set scene which each village had to do, and I'd see it time after time and not be a bit bored, because everybody did it quite differently. Bert Fiander, my first great love, on whose knee I used to sit at The Glebe Farm, played Grumio in *The Taming of the Shrew* and, just by being himself, was very good and very funny.

The solo dance I arranged for the Norman and Saxon display was 'Alice in Wonderland'. I wore a blue organdie costume with a little white apron and striped socks and ballet shoes, and my hair was down loose and tied with a black band. The music I chose was a fairylike piece by Chaminade called 'Danse Callirhoe'. I started with Alice asleep beside her daisy-chain, and a tiny tot in a rabbit costume running across the stage, and Alice running after it and falling down the hole. At the trial, where Alice appeared before the King and the Queen and the jury, I folded my hands and made little nervous steps and held my neck to show I was afraid of having my head cut off. I built up a tension. You can suggest things to an audience by mime and by believing them yourself. I released the tension by pretending that everyone in court had turned into playing cards and was flying above me. Finally, as the cards fell down on stage on top of me, I woke beside my daisy-chain, wondering what on earth was happening. The dance was very popular with the audiences.

This was 1938 and, while I was studying in the winter term for what was then called the School Certificate, I managed, off my own bat, to land a job at The Pavilion Theatre, Bournemouth, in the chorus of the pantomime *Aladdin*. So, to start rehearsals in November, I said goodbye to Miss Sayer, and I never went back to St Christopher's again. I was only fifteen and a half, but I'd been in pantomime before – as Cinderella the previous Christmas in the village hall at Charlton Marshall, under the direction of my mother.

Aladdin was my first *professional* job. I was very excited. It was my first feeling of being 'on the stage'. Also, I fell in love with one of the stage hands, which was rather nice. I don't think he was much in love with *me*, but still. He was a fair-haired electrician, and we used to talk in the wings. We went to the pictures together once towards the start of the run. Towards the end of the run he asked me to go out again. I waited for him outside the stage door, and he stood me up. The ten or twelve of us in the chorus were in the one dressing-room. We each had our own place with a light over the mirror. You sweated a lot so without inhibition you just stripped everything and had a whore's wash in one of the several basins; I'd have a bath later at the South Mount Hotel where my parents were paying for me to stay. Prince Littler was the man who brought *Aladdin* to Bournemouth. The show was directed by Mr Adey, who also wrote parts of the script; a Mr Beaumont composed some of the music and conducted the orchestra. There was a terrific lot of bitchiness because Mr Adey had brought his mistress down from London and put her in the chorus without an audition.

I didn't have a solo dance, but I had a little bit in the Garden Scene with only three other geisha girls. How they found geisha girls in China I don't know, but we were supposed to be four geisha girls, and we did a little dance with fans. I had to sing, of course – all the chorus girls had to sing. We had a song with washing tubs in Aladdin's mother's laundry:

> Scrub, scrub, at the washing tub,
> Rub-a-dub, rub-a-dub all day long,
> Always working gaily, making plenty dollars,
> Scrub, scrub, at the washing tub,
> Rub-a-dub all day long.

Oh dear, for the geisha girls it was even *worse*:

> Ching-a-ring, ching-a-ring, chippy chippy chop chop,
> Chippy chippy chop chop, chow chow chow.
> Make a ring and let us sing:
> Chippy chop and ring-a-ding,
> Chippy chippy chop and ring-a-ding.

And I remember ten horrible children from London who did an acrobatic number. Before every trick, their leader would call out, 'Ready-eee?! *Roight!*'

I was paid £4 10s a week, which was a fortune. But the money I earned never meant anything. My parents, you see, were middlingly off, and my hotel and my fares and my lessons at the Norman and Saxon were being paid for. On top of that I had a ten shillings a week dress allowance, so I bought a blue silky afternoon dress with ribbons round the hem of the skirt, and a suit in a soft velvety material which I thought looked very chic.

While working for the Intermediate, I became a full-time student at the Norman and Saxon. I had a season ticket for the Bournemouth train, and knew all the guards and ticket collectors. My mother came with me one day, and we had to stop and talk to everyone. She was rather irritated. She said, 'It's like travelling with Royalty.' I worked very hard for the Intermediate, and did a lot of extra practice. It was very difficult technically, with a lot of point work – little finicking steps like beats and *entrechats* and *pas de bourrée jetés*. The exam was *gruelling*. I was most relieved when I found I'd passed it. I went with my mother to London again, and we stayed at The Regent Palace. It wasn't as exciting as when I came up for the Elementary. Austerity had begun and there was a black-out on. But we went to see Robert Morley in *The First Gentleman*, a very funny play about Prinnie, the Prince Regent, a part that exactly suited him. It was all wrong historically but it was beautifully dressed. Mrs Fitzherbert put rouge on Prinnie's cheeks and said, 'Not a little too rubicund?' Before going out of a room he would say, 'Open Sesame!' and the doors would open.

At Christmas I appeared in my second pantomime as a professional at The Pavilion – *Babes in the Wood*, again presented by Prince Littler, again directed and written by Mr Adey, and again with those horrible child acrobats. *And* it had the same principals. Kitty Prince was the principal boy and wasn't bad really – she had quite a nice voice and she *could* act. But the principal girl – oh dear! She looked *terrible*! She was a rather stout blonde with an enormous bottom. She had the most incredible flow of vile language I had ever heard. They were words you hear quite a lot now, but I hadn't heard them until then. As Maid Marion, she would come onto the stage looking the picture of innocence, very round-eyed, after saying about one of the elderly men she'd been making up to, 'I was the first virgin that ever bit him' – *that* sort of thing. Most of the men in the cast *were* elderly. Pantomime is the time when everybody gets a chance.

In *Babes in the Wood* I had two solos and was paid £5 a week. You were shown the woods and then a gypsy caravan came on and there was a fire, and I did one of my dances, a gypsy dance. Then the caravan went off and the babes came in with the robbers, comic robbers who decide to kill them and don't kill them, and the babes finally go to sleep and the birds cover them with leaves – the birds, of course, were dancers. Then there was the transformation scene into a sort of fairyland where the good fairy comes and looks after the babes. That was when I came on with some fairies and did a little classical ballet solo on the point.

*

41

It was during the run of *Babes in the Wood* that I met John Wilkins. My mother made me special clothes to look right for him. She made a taffeta dress with a tight bodice and full skirt, very brightly coloured in little squares, almost like a tartan. It had lace round the collar and cuffs, and then, as now, there was a vogue for wearing a lacy petticoat which showed underneath. To go with that dress, I had a little jet necklace. She also made a dusty-pink crêpe dress with a Peter Pan collar – again it had a full skirt, with this lacy petticoat showing underneath. But I *did* buy my own coat and some high-heeled shoes. The coat was a woollen one, bright blue, very full. When you bought a coat in those days, you always bought a hat to go with it. The hat I bought, Mother didn't like at all – it was a little blue round felt hat with brown fur on the rim and a piece of fur hanging down at the side. I still had long hair, but I began to put it up around my head, washing and drying it myself.

The day after my seventeenth birthday, May the 7th, 1940, John had to go to France. He hadn't been there long when the army was driven right back to the coast and most of the soldiers escaped from Dunkirk. But John didn't escape; he was captured at St Valéry and spent most of the war in a prison camp in Germany, I didn't know where – he wrote to me regularly, but his cards were just marked 'Stalag XXA'. It was four years later before I saw him again. I suddenly had a letter from him saying that he was at home in Reading, he had escaped from the prison camp with the help of the French Resistance, would I come to Reading to meet him and his mother. Meanwhile my mother had learned from his mother that he'd had an affair with another girl before meeting me and that he'd had a son by her. I cried when she told me this, but it was somehow because I was *expected* to feel upset; I wasn't really. I never told him in my letters that I knew, and I never *did* tell him. I was deliriously happy, I was frantic, when he returned and asked to see me again after I'd been waiting all this time.

He met me at the station, saying, 'I've been looking for a small wren!' – by then I was serving with the WRNS at Portland. We went on the river in a punt, and it was nothing but a series of awkward silences. It should have been idyllic, but we had nothing to talk to each other about at all. We were two completely different people. I tried to tell him about concert parties and play readings that I was involved in, and some stories by Katherine Mansfield

42

who I'd just discovered, *anything* to break the silence, but he was evidently bored to a frazzle – I'm always a bore when I try to make conversation, but I didn't know it then. About himself, he talked very little, and only in the way that my father talked about the Great War, as if it was all a joke.

His mother arranged a beautiful little room for me where we made love that night. But, although she wasn't hostile, I had the feeling that she thought it wasn't right because of this other girl; I even had the feeling when she said goodbye to me that she knew she wasn't going to see me again. John and I afterwards wrote one or two scrappy letters to one another. Then he told me that he was going to be married and so we mustn't meet any more. I was heartbroken. I cried. But just as I cried when I first learned he had this other girl, I think I did so because it was expected of me. My vanity was badly hurt, but at the same time I felt a certain relief. There was something a bit phoney about this tragedy, although it resulted, many years later, in one of the few love poems I've ever written. I called it 'Love Song':

> I took out insurance as green leaves uncurled,
> And my policy covered the end of the world.
> I trusted my love, but in trusting grew older;
> I doubted my wisdom and, doubting, grew bolder.
> For what can it matter one tittle or jot,
> At the end of the world, if I'm covered or not? . . .

I imagine that before I came to Reading John had already seen the girl who he eventually married, and their child, and his thoughts were on her. We no longer had anything in common except 'sex'. I don't think we'd ever had anything in common except 'sex'.

> All the lights through the fair began to move
> And the merry-go-round in the groove wailed 'Love'.
> 'Love' groaned the slow-singing merry-go-round,
> Then 'Love! Love! Love!' with a joyful sound.
> But the switch-back moved on the opposite section,
> A twentieth century modern erection
> For the perpetration
> Of sublime sensation
> With a hundred per cent protection.

43

The switch-back slowed to a groan in the groove
And the man on the steps said, 'Come aboard, love!
Come aboard with the minimum time and trouble,
Feather bed seats and each one double,
And don't imagine it's overrated,
Even if the fare's increased!
There's a carnival of animals incorporated
In the body of the two-backed beast!' . . .

That's the start of 'The Double-Back Switch-Back' which I wrote
quite recently – I think there is something of the love affair with
John in it. Really, what I write comes into two groups. In one
group is the very rhythmic type of poem which I *think* comes
directly from having been a dancer for the first part of my life. The
others don't go by rhythm or metre, but by music – piano music
as opposed to drum.

In the summer of 1940, just after John had gone to France, my
grandmother died within a few days of having a stroke. She had
fallen downstairs earlier in the year, and had never really recovered, though my mother and Auntie Nora took it in turns to
look after her with the help of her maid, a gypsy girl, a klepto-
maniac, called Olive.

Grannie's was the first dead body I had ever seen. The expression
on her face was familiar. It was the expression she wore once
when she took me on a bus ride to Glastonbury to explore an old
church, and was getting her bearings – 'Now that must be the
West Nave, and the Lady Chapel will be over there.' I felt sad but,
at that age, seventeen, I was quite sure that the 'she' that wasn't
there any more, the part of her that whispered about the carvings
on the choir stalls, was continuing somewhere else. My grandfather died a few weeks later of something they called 'pernicious
anaemia'. I felt something like a blaze of anger at his funeral –
they'd both made me think about death by dying, and as yet there
was no word from John. All I can remember about the period
immediately after that was taking the Intermediate, working for
the Advanced (which involved doing spectacular things like
fouettés, and emphasised personality and expression), performing
in a revue for a week at The Pavilion, being an usherette for a
circus in a suburb of Bournemouth called Lilliput, and pitching in
with harvesting and hay-making at Four Winds.

44

And, oh yes, about this time, we had Aunt Susan down from London to get her away from the bombing. Aunt Susan was my grandmother's sister. She was very large, and six feet tall, and nursing her husband, Uncle Will, who was in the last stages of syphilis. Uncle Will was demented. Most of the time he sat absolutely still in a wheelchair, and said nothing and did nothing. But – it was very sad really – when he *did* say something, it invariably doubled you up with laughter. He would suddenly break into conversation. Aunt Susan, like my grandmother, was a great talker: she talked non-stop. She would be talking and talking – '. . . And I suppose you know what's happened to Mrs Miller' – and suddenly Uncle Will would practically get out of his wheelchair and say, 'I do *not know* Mrs Miller!' Aunt Susan never came to grips with the idea that Uncle was saying things that were irrational. She would say, 'Oh, yes, you *do* know Mrs Miller, Will!' 'I do *not* know Mrs Miller! I have never *seen* Mrs Miller!' 'Yes, you *have*. She has a *geranium* in her hat!' 'I have *not* seen Mrs Miller! I do not *wish* to see Mrs Miller! I shall *never* see Mrs Miller, even if she comes before me!' 'Will, you know Mrs Miller very well! . . .' This would go on for a long time, until Uncle subsided again into absolute silence and nothingness.

My Aunt Susan – partly because of these interruptions to her talk – got to dislike my uncle more and more. In the end, she wouldn't allow him linen sheets because he was incontinent; she put him simply between two rubber ones. My mother tried to protest and said, 'It's very cold for him,' but Aunt Susan said, 'Oh, they soon get warm. He'll get used to it.' Her conversation was one-sided, but, unlike my grandmother's which was straightforward scandal, hers, possibly because she lived with my uncle who was going madder and madder, was illogical. She would talk like this: 'You know that shop, Peggy?' My mother was always called Peggy. 'You remember that shop, that beautiful good-class shop? . . . You know, you remember it. It was there in Old Compton Street. It was the shop where we got the marrons glacés. Do you remember that shop, Peggy? Well, it's gone. And, of course, you must remember Mildred. Well, my *dear*! Mildred – you know she's suffered for years from gallstones – she sat on a hatpin. And Mrs Asselford the other day, it was most sad – she dropped her false teeth on the stairs, and Mr Asselford was running up behind her . . .' My mother didn't know or remember any of the people or things she talked about. She used to sit with her sewing, and I

45

could see her shutting off in just the same way as I did with my grandmother.

I think Aunt Susan and Uncle Will had been very much in love, and she was angry with him now for being mad. She would say, 'Will, will you stop looking so vacant!' And, of course, he *couldn't* stop looking vacant. But she would go on talking. 'I don't know what's happening to young people these days. Will and I would *never* have behaved like that. We enjoyed ourselves, we certainly enjoyed ourselves –' Then Will would suddenly break in: 'I knew Marie Lloyd!' 'Will, you did *not* know Marie Lloyd! She was a very famous woman.' 'Oh yes, I did! I did know Marie Lloyd! I was a masher, I was!' 'Will, you did not know Marie Lloyd! *How* could you have known Marie Lloyd?!' 'I took her out to dinner.' 'Oh well, then, you took her out to dinner. You took her out to dinner. I think it's time you went to bed, Will.' Actually, he *had* known Marie Lloyd.

Finally Uncle Will had a seizure at Four Winds and died, and Aunt Susan went back to London, bombs or not, to have him cremated. Later, when my mother went up to see her, she found her crying in the Garden of Remembrance at Golders Green. She said, 'You must come back to Four Winds. Uncle Will is preying on your mind too much.' 'Yes,' said Aunt Susan. 'He *does* prey on my mind. I wish he had a grave. I can't believe that the ashes don't get mixed up.'

So back Aunt Susan came to Dorset. We tried to interest her in the doings of the neighbourhood – assembling gasmasks, making camouflage nets. She nearly went back to London over those camouflage nets. They were made of horse and cow hair, and mud had to be teased out of it. In the end she went on strike; she said that the mud was dung, it made her sick to touch it. Anyway, she stayed on until my father, now a Captain, was invalided out of the Dorsetshire Regiment because of his heart attack. My mother was running the farm on her own, with the help of Frank, my father's right-hand man, and having to nurse my father into the bargain. When Aunt Susan offered to help her with the nursing, my mother became frantic. 'I've had a terrific lot of nursing experience with Will,' was the last straw; my mother knew how she had treated Uncle Will. She said, 'I'm sorry. You'll have to go back to London.' Aunt Susan couldn't understand this, knowing my mother needed help. Eventually she went to Uncle Leonard's over the jeweller's shop, but she drove them crazy there too, with her constant flow of talk, and finally she did go back to London.

My mother went to see her in about 1950 when she was dying. She confessed on her death-bed that she had spent a weekend in Brighton with Uncle Will before they were married. My mother said, 'That was in the Victorian Age! Whatever made you *do* such a thing?!' She said, 'Well, you see, he knew so many actresses I had to do something about it. My mother came down too, and then the three of us came back to London on the coach, and Will and I had to get married at once. I feel much happier now that I've confessed this to you' – and then she died.

In 1941, I decided to train with The Anglo-Polish Ballet, who had a temporary studio in Lansdowne Road, Bournemouth. While there, I got an inkling of what the war was really about. Most of the dancers were Polish refugees. They couldn't speak a lot of English but you did hear about concentration camps, about beatings in the streets, about people being arrested and shot for just being what they were. Some of the Poles were saying that we shouldn't be dancing, we should be doing something more active. I got this bug very badly. I thought 'I can't be boot dancing and wiggling around on my toes during this. I'll have to go and do something a bit more useful. I've got to get into the war. I'll leave the Anglo-Poles and I'll drop my classes for the Advanced Norman and Saxon and I'll try nursing.'

After applying to several hospitals, I eventually got in at the Royal Hampshire Infirmary, Winchester. I have never spent such a miserable six months in my life. The Royal Hants was run by a very elderly Matron and elderly Sisters, most of them unmarried, all of them staid. The training there was one of the strictest and most conventional in the country. I couldn't *take* this. The first three months you were in the PTS, the Preliminary Training School, under a Sister Tutor. Apart from a little practical chemistry, this was almost entirely bookwork. You had to do papers on Dietetics and Anatomy and Physiology, none of which I'd done anything about at school. I was completely at sea, but I did get through at the end. After that three months you went onto the wards. You were still in the PTS, but you had to do I think it was a year before you were finally accepted as a First Year Student Nurse. Well, I'd never done much in the way of housework at home, and I was always forgetting to dust ledges. When I did sluicing I'd always be sick – sluicing is removing the solids from the sheets before they go to the laundry.

Then, making beds. I really wasn't any good at it. The ward had a long row of beds down each side – I suppose there'd be about twenty altogether. I could move the patients and I got along all right with them, but I held the other nurse up when I was bed-making because I did it much more slowly. I hadn't the hands for it; I was always in the wrong place. It took me ages to make a bed, whereas it would take somebody else ten seconds. I was more or less all right at taking temperatures but, after a while, you had to give injections and do enemas and bladder wash-outs. And again I was no good. I never knew where to get the syringe *in*. I'd get it wrong and have to try again, and it was awful for a patient. This really happened to all the student nurses, but I got more and more depressed because I thought it was only me.

And then, of course, there were the Sisters. They were the great bugbear. They constantly carped about everything you did, and I couldn't take it. I was used to discipline. Dancing is a very rigorous discipline, but it's a different kind of discipline, and I could not work in this atmosphere of disapproval and it made me *ill*; I felt constantly sick. It wasn't the blood or disgust at the various things I had to do – I was pretty bold about that. It was just this awful sort of cold atmosphere with these elderly Sisters coming down on you. I think they turned out good *nurses*, but it wasn't a discipline that I could take to or be happy in. The patients in the Men's Surgical Ward always tried to keep their urine bottles at night, and the Sister was very adamant that they shouldn't. She used to go round searching for these and was furious with me because I could never find the wretched things. After a while, I got tired of being told off and I said, 'Oh, come on! Give them to me! I know you've got them somewhere!' One old man said, 'Come on, Fred! Render unto Caesar!' You see, that was the thing. I mean, we used to be told off for not finding these bottles and I minded. In the end, I left by mutual consent and went back to Four Winds. The Matron said, 'I don't think you're happy, are you?' and I said, 'No, I'm not. I would like to finish.'

My only real contributions to the war effort were while I was in the WRNS. I applied to join soon after I left the hospital. I was called to Portsmouth for an interview after a few months, and was finally stationed as a domestic steward, at HMS St Vincent, which

48

was a shore base at Gosport, in the WRNS Officers' Quarters. It was like being a maid in a private house. I did the best I could. The girls I worked with were very sweet. I learned a great deal from them. They could have been very nasty to me because I knew far less than they did about how to light fires, how to cook, how to peel potatoes quickly, how to clean saucepans. They were from very poor families in Portsmouth and *knew* all this, and instead of ostracising me for not pulling my weight, they were very nice and did a lot of my work for me and showed me how to do things. They even showed me how to wash and iron collars. The girl who helped me most was called Eileen. Ei was very puritanical about boys. She was rather pretty, and they were always mistaking her for a tart, and she was quite the opposite – *very* puritanical, and saving up everything until she got married.

The First Officer and the Second Officer and the Nursing Sister from the Sick Bay lived in a house by themselves, and we had to serve them. The First Officer looked like a man in drag. She had to have prunes for breakfast and insisted they were cooked so they didn't stick to the stones. The Nursing Sister, tall and dark and with long hair, a very romantic lady, was having an affair with the Commander, or so it was rumoured. His nickname was Crash, because he couldn't navigate (another rumour) – that was why he commanded a shore base. While we were serving dinner they went on talking as though we weren't there – how So and So was good at her work, and another a blinking nuisance and another a lesbian and another going to have a baby. We were very discreet; we didn't spread the gossip.

But I wasn't much good as a steward, so they put me into office work – as a messenger in the Signals Office. All I had to do was walk about the base with little bits of paper. Signals were the orders that came in from the Commanders-in-Chief. Some went to the Captain's Office, some to the Navigation Block to the people in charge of training, because St Vincent's was a base training the Fleet Air Arm. Some went to the Commander's Office, some were orders for the Sick Bay. Then there were the signals from the Captain's Office to the Yeoman of Signals, from the WRNS Officers' Office to the First Lieutenant's Office. I was just somebody who had to walk all the time. There was no other way of getting these bits of paper from place to place.

At St Vincent I liked the people I worked with and most of the people I worked *for*. And, though I was writing to John and thought of him as the most important thing, I did have quite a lot of men friends. I was pretty, and sailors and sometimes officers would invite me to ship's dances or for a meal. Because of rationing, the food would be very plain – you know, stew. The fashionable thing to drink was gin and lime. You wore black Pusser stockings and long black regulation Pusser knickers – black-outs – to go with your uniform. I like women less than men – it's only one now and again that I really like – but I got friendly with a girl called Kathleen Cheeseman who I met at a ship's dance. She was a VAD in the Sick Bay. She was rather interesting because she was a graduate and had been to Europe. She thought the war was an absolute waste of her time. I could honestly say that I was enjoying it. Lady Rushborough, a tiny little woman, was a messenger in the same dormitory as me. We called her Lady 'Washborough' because she couldn't pronounce her 'r's. When she first came into the dormitory, she put a damp towel under her bed. She said, 'There must be so many germs floating about with a lot of people sleeping in one room like this. A damp towel will collect them.' The Queen's Hotel was the big hotel in Portsmouth, and she said to me once, 'I spend most of my off-duty time at The Queen's. It's a second home.' I said, 'Isn't that very expensive for you?' She said, 'My dear, don't be so ridiculous! You can't live on your *pay*!' Which was true – we had less than a pound a week, and you had to buy things like stockings and toothpaste and make-up, and it was the thing to do to go to the pictures in town.

Oh yes, I did make a *great* friend at St Vincent, and that was Vicky. She was the ship's cinema operator. She was widely read, and we used to talk a lot; it was a very close friendship. When I went to dances she didn't like it when I made dates with male partners. She wanted a lesbian relationship but, although I liked her very much, I wasn't tempted.

There were one or two boys that, if it hadn't been for John, I *could* have been fond of. I met one of them when I was down in the Navigation Block delivering signals. His name was Len Murray, and he was training at St Vincent as a Fleet Air Arm pilot. I always wonder now when I see Len Murray, the Trades Union leader, on television whether it is the same man. I think, 'Well, the features are the same. The voice is the same. The accent is the same. But is it or isn't it the same Len Murray? He's certainly not the Len Murray *I* knew, but then he wouldn't be.' He asked me to go out with him, and we went to dances together. He liked, strangely enough, the same poets as I did – Kipling and Shakespeare. He was crazy about Omar Khayyam and could quote from his poetry, though Omar Khayyam was unpopular then and everybody laughed at him and called him OK. But the usual thing happened. The Fleet Air Arm pilots had to go to a base in America to do their final training and get their commission. We wrote to one another for a while until, gradually, the letters petered out.

Len had seen me in one or two concert parties. Though I wasn't an ENSA performer, someone had found out that I was trained as a dancer, so I arranged solo dances for concert parties that went out to various shore bases. I'd amassed a lot of costumes to do with displays at the Norman and Saxon, and danced something I called 'The Glow-Worm Gavotte', in a high-waisted Regency costume, and a gypsy dance, some classical ballet to the music of Chopin and a dramatic piece called 'The Flight' about an escaping refugee.

The First Lieutenant, Jimmy the One, was a kindly old gentleman always on the look-out for talent for these amateur entertainments. He was delighted to hear that I had ballet costumes which he said would 'brighten things up'. He told me there was a linen cupboard next to his cabin where I could keep them. After a while, it began to puzzle me that, when I came to take them out, they were occasionally torn and had splodges of make-up on them which I hadn't put there. One evening I was amazed to see a cadet disappearing into Jimmie the One's cabin clad in a tutu of mine which he was wearing rather askew because he couldn't get the bodice done up. I made a complaint that someone was borrowing my costumes, and after that the borrowing stopped.

My job as a messenger didn't entail night duty; I just worked from nine to five. When you were on duty, you didn't go to the shelters during a raid. The raids didn't frighten me. You're rather silly when you're young; you don't have the imagination, or the fear of consequences. You resented the lack of sleep when the raids took place at night, but there wasn't any panic; it was just a matter of going to the shelter and coming out again. We were told at some time that it was likely that the Germans would invade and that we were a prime target. I'd been in this little ballet company with the Poles and I knew what was being done on the other side of the Channel and I knew what would be done if the Germans got here. *That* was the fear at the back of my mind: it was not the air-raids. We were given a lecture on how a revolver was fired and

51

told that, if the Germans came, we could go to a certain place and take a revolver to defend ourselves. I doubt whether I could ever have fired a revolver, and I was very glad the Germans didn't come.

By 1944, though, our armament factories were at full blast and there was a lot of talk of us invading France in answer to the people in Europe's call for a Second Front. Of course someone such as myself wasn't told whether there was to be an invasion or not, but I was sent as a telephonist to one of the network of little signal stations all along the coast. I was with three other telephonists in a pillbox specially added to an old fort by Lee-on-Solent. We ate and slept in a cottage called Cottage By The Sea near the village of Alverstoke, and worked in three watches.

During the bombing at night it was rather hairy, stuck out in this little signal station on the cliff; the place used to rock sometimes. We were the only people who were allowed to show a light. Our code name was Turko, so we had a T on top to show our aircraft where we were. The trouble was the Germans could see this light as well. Also the men flashing signals from the roof could be seen, though of course they didn't signal during an actual raid: all signalling stopped till the all-clear when the air-raid siren sounded. Signals were sent by lights at night, and by flags during the day, to and from the Commander-in-Chief who had to be in contact with the ships in Portsmouth Harbour. When the ships wanted to send messages to the Commander-in-Chief – berthing instructions, orders for supplies, news of anything wrong on board – they signalled to our man on top, down the tube on a form came the message to us and we would telephone it to the Commander-in-Chief's Office. For instance, 'Commander-in-Chief's Office. I have a signal for you. "To Commander-in-Chief's Office from HMS *Grey Hare* (a code name). I am arriving at 09.00 hours. May I have berthing instructions?" ' Then the Commander-in-Chief's Office might ring back 'From Commander-in-Chief to HMS *Grey Hare*, Your signal received. Berth at 569 Berth Portsmouth Harbour' or 'Stay put. No berth available but accommodation being arranged', and you would write this down and send it up to the man on the roof. I suppose all this was necessary because wireless messages could have been intercepted. Everything depended on secrecy and surprise, so it was vital that the Germans didn't know what ships were coming and going, and how they were being supplied.

We were completely confined to the pillbox and The Cottage.

Social life was nil. No, I didn't smoke – except with my mother when on leave. She was bitterly disappointed when I dropped dancing to become a nurse, but when I came home on leave, we were better friends than we'd ever been. She was a chain-smoker; she would always offer me a cigarette, a Craven A, and say, 'Oh, come on! *Do* have one! I don't like smoking on my own.'

Like Mother, Daphne Gravett, a fellow telephonist, was someone I could really talk to. There are only certain people I can talk to – you're one of them. It's always been like that. Daphne Gravett *gave* me something. She'd been an art student before the war, and was married to Guy, a painter who was now a pilot. She was a very mature person. She talked very frankly about sex, but not in the way, for instance, that Joan talked frankly: she talked about it because she was interested. She *hated* the war, hated the life in the WRNS. She said, 'I've been in this hole for so long now without seeing Guy, I don't know whether I could rise to the occasion.' She said she'd had a very painful growing-up because, although she was attracted to men and was really rather highly sexed, she was not content simply to settle for sex, she wanted somebody she could literally sleep with. She'd gone through a lot of unsatisfactory affairs at Art School and looked back on them as a rather sordid form of pornography. She didn't think she could ever again go to bed with somebody that she didn't particularly like and have an affinity with, and she did have this affinity with Guy. She knew about John, and she said, 'You shouldn't put somebody into cold storage like that. He was nineteen when he went away, and he can't possibly be the same person when he comes back.' She was quite right, but he was writing to me from the prison camp and depending on my letters in return.

Above all, at Lee-on-Solent, I felt the need of books, but at first I hadn't any, except a little copy of *The Rubaiyat of Omar Khayyam* which I think Len Murray had given me. Nobody else seemed to read anything but magazines, and we couldn't get to a library. However, for meals, when we were off duty, we went to a large house in Alverstoke which had been taken over by the Navy, and there I found a bookshelf. It contained poetry and a set of novels by D. H. Lawrence. I read the novels one after the other. I wouldn't read them now, but there's one *poem* that remains with me, a poem called 'The Snake'.

As the invasion of France approached, more and more ships crowded into the Solent, and there were dozens of exercises with motor-torpedo and flat-bottomed boats. All that was left of the French Fleet was in Portsmouth harbour, and I got a lot of messages from the French ships because I was listed as a French speaker. The Germans must have known about all this furious activity, but, whether it was the fault of their Intelligence, when we did actually invade, they were completely unready. I remember the fleet went out once and then came back again because they'd got a wrong weather report. My poem 'Two Minutes Silence' contains a description of the final sailing:

> But the grey ghosts that sailed from Pompey harbour,
> Those I remember well by flag and light.
> They slipped away on a sly tail end of the dog watch,
> Before the sea flung back the sheen of a pearl
> Into a mist of shining mermaid's hair.
> Hand on my shoulder, whose I can't remember, –
> 'Is it important? Does the Solent care?'

After the D-Day landing, I was redundant. I was sent to Portland Bill, where I was given a job as a receptionist in the Officers' Ward Room. I sat at the front of the Ward Room in a little box. All the officers lived in the Ward Room, you see, and you booked them in and out and you arranged that they could have a meal if they wanted one that wasn't at a regular time. Lieutenant Allen, one of the officers on the base, was an actor in civilian life, and I joined his play-reading group and appeared in a revue for which he wrote some sketches – our costumes were made of dyed surgical gauze and parachute silk. I also danced in several more ship's concerts which we took around the coast with some help from ENSA. It was at this period, waiting for demobilisation, that I went to see John in Reading.

One day, I received a flustered call from my mother saying that she'd had a visit from Leonard Montefiore, a family friend, and he was on his way to Portland to ask me to marry him; I must be very careful as he was obviously as nutty as a fruitcake. He was now about twenty-five. I originally met him on a camping holiday in Cornwall and, as soon as war broke out, he had joined the RAF. He telephoned me at the Ward Room, and we met in Weymouth at a tea-shop called The Clinton. He was thin, almost emaciated, and he wore an open-necked shirt and khaki shorts and sandals. He weighed in at once with a formal proposal of marriage because

54

God had told him to come down to Portland and marry me. He hastened to add that he probably would have done this anyway. Did I believe in God? I said I did, but I didn't think He told you who you ought to marry. Leonard was a small, dark man, rather like a gnome. If the year had been '83 instead of '44, I might have told him plainly, 'I don't fancy you.' As it was, I had to resort to 'reeling and writhing and fainting in coils': I said we shouldn't be happy, I wasn't a very religious person and, anyway, I had a career to think about. He went away saying that I was too young to understand, but he was sure that God was not mistaken. I haven't seen or heard of him since.

We were beginning to think of demobilisation, and I was called for an interview with the Captain of the ship . . . Oh, haven't I already explained? A naval shore base is run as a ship and you call it a ship. The Captain of the ship and my First Officer, a WRNS officer, interviewed me about what I wanted to do after I was demobbed. I said, of course, 'Get back to dancing.' 'What sort of dancing?' 'Modern Dance.' I was a completely different person by now. The war was a matter of getting your hands dirty and finding out what other people's lives were. It brought you down to reality. I couldn't go back to classical ballet – it seemed to me pure phantasy. They suggested I talk to Lieutenant Allen.

Now, the only Modern Dance company in England at that time was The Ballet Jooss. Kurt Jooss, a Dutchman, a pupil of Rudolf von Laban, had a school in Frankfurt before the war, and I saw his company performing *A Ball in Old Vienna*, *The Prodigal Son* and *The Green Table* at the Bournemouth Pavilion soon after I left St Christopher's. The company came into being on the strength of *The Green Table*, which won a competition. It was about war and peace, and the great feature of it was a very beautiful, stylised dance of politicians around a conference table. They did it so well that you could see, through the dancing, what each one was trying to argue. Jooss himself danced the part of Death, most expressively. I said to Lieutenant Allen that I would very much like to join The Ballet Jooss. He said, 'I know Margaret Leona, who has danced with The Ballet Jooss. She's holding a Summer School at Dartington Hall. Would you like a letter of introduction?'

So in September '44, after demobilisation, I went to see Margaret Leona at Dartington Hall. She took me by the hand as we went down the passage to her room, and this somehow made me feel very happy. I explained that classical ballet was simply a technique that I'd learned, something I'd grown up with and accepted as part of life because of Mother's insistence, and that I wanted something more which I thought The Ballet Jooss could give. She got me an audition at The Pavilion where, by a stroke of good luck, the company was appearing again at the end of November.

The audition was given between the matinée and evening performances. The theatre was dark and echoing as empty theatres are. Tall and grey-haired and sharp-sighted, Kurt Jooss represented something exotic that I had hardly met before. Wearing my dark-blue practice dress and without a pianist, I danced three dances for him to records I brought with me and played on my own wind-up gramophone. To the music of 'The Skaters' Waltz' and the overture to *Prince Igor* and Gigli singing 'La Danza', I danced a skater's dance, a sad slow Russian gypsy dance and a tarantella. This man was an artist; you felt that he could see every flaw of artistry in what you did. His verdict? Very clever little dances, but I was still basing them on a classical technique. 'With more training you will be a modern dancer. The body stands in the upright position, the feet are on the end of the legs, the head sits correctly upon the shoulders. There is no reason why you shouldn't dance.' At the end of his present tour he was going to Buenos Aires where the company had been offered a permanent theatre. He could not engage another dancer, but I should apply for a place at The Art of Movement Studio in Manchester, which was run by von Laban, Sylvia Bodmer, his own former dancing partner, and Lisa Ullman, a teacher he praised to the skies. He would write them a letter; the government would assist me with a grant.

In January 1945, with the blessing of my parents, to Manchester I went. I was twenty-one.

4

I stayed a night in London with Aunt Susan. Next morning, I travelled by Tube from Golders Green to Paddington and from there to Crewe. Between Crewe and Manchester, sleeping opposite me in the same compartment, sat a beautiful creature in African dress. She was the first black person I had ever encountered. The image was indelible:

> She carried her parcels tied in a red bandana.
> On this she rests her head as the lumbering train,
> Mumbling and murmuring rumours of destination,
> Cradles the pouting child
> Trapped in a stoic journey of long endurance.
>
> Her coat was bought in haste at a church bazaar,
> For she had not learned that the sun
> Would not, of necessity, rise, or would ever be cold
> As Mehdani who searches all night through the hills
> For the drum-throbbing fingers of darkness.
>
> Her cotton skirts, voluminous, loosely draped
> In the manner of Caesar's wife, and above suspicion,
> Are touched with the colours that flame in a parakeet's tail.
> She can never have learned that so great a profusion of colours
> Will lower prestige . . .

Her mood was infectious, and *I* went to sleep. When I woke at Manchester, I saw a black porter. For a moment I couldn't believe it! But there were many black people in Manchester, and they fascinated me. I would soon go with other students from the Art of

Movement Studio to a little club called The Cotton Club where Africans and West Indians congregated, where I saw *dancing*, wild and free.

My appointment with Lisa Ullman was for three o'clock. I left my luggage at the station, and took a taxi to her flat in Fallowfield. Ivor Novello and Vanessa Lee were in the taxi queue – they were about to open in *The Dancing Years* at The Palace Theatre. She was talking in a loud and terrible way: 'Why didn't you *tell* me to wear boots and a fur?! I've never been so cold in my life! . . . That bloody Midland Hotel is *always* awful! . . .' She was in that kind of a mood. And she was such an *appealing* actress and singer! I'd already seen *The Dancing Years* at Drury Lane. A friend from the Norman and Saxon was in the chorus.

It *was* bitterly cold, *and* foggy, but Lisa Ullman's flat, where she lived with Laban, was warm and pretty in complete contrast. For me, just out of the WRNS, the atmosphere seemed rather rarified. She offered me coffee and little almond cakes in a sitting-room with lovely pictures and a lute and tambourines and castanets with ribbons on the walls. And it wasn't just dancing that she talked about: it was painting, the theatre, books . . . all the things that I liked. She was a small woman, very relaxed and serene. Her movements were like a cat's, controlled, deliberate, with no be-ginning and no end. Her hair, as I would see it so often, was hidden under a silk scarf, draped turbanwise, its dull red and yellow stripes exactly suiting her sallow skin. There was nothing about her face to suggest how old she might be. Was she thirty? Was she forty? When I last saw her, about fifteen years later at Laban's funeral in Weybridge, she looked sixty, but by then she was putting on weight, and she was stricken with grief.

I was to discover that, under her catlike serenity, lay the German capacity for work, together with complete dedication and ruthless efficiency and love of order. She did most of the real teaching at the Studio because Sylvia Bodmer was over fifty and Laban, who was seventy, only gave a master class every now and then. She also organised movement 'choirs' – sort of 'keep fit' classes in church halls where she divided her pupils into high dancers and low dancers, sopranos and contraltos, made them improvise one against another. And she went to country houses to give summer schools and courses, and she did the paperwork for the Studio in her spare time . . .

Anyway, she gave me the whereabouts of the Art of Movement Studio in All Saints and told me to be there by nine o'clock next morning, which I was, after spending the night in a bed and breakfast hotel.

The Studio wasn't a studio as *I* knew them. It was a basement, very dark, with no windows; we could only see by electric light, and we danced on a stone floor covered by a thin carpet. There was no heating, and we literally warmed ourselves by dancing, by keeping moving. I was wearing my Norman and Saxon practice dress, which was almost knee length. The two boys wore tights, but the other girls – there were four or five of them – were in very short tunics that clung and were much more revealing, showed every movement. Girls went bare-legged, but later we decided to have tights because we thought that whatever you did in Modern Dance, as in ballet, needed something to contain the muscles of the legs to keep them in shape.

We stayed at that studio for about six months without even a pianist, and I always think it was a great tour de force on Lisa's part that she was able to galvanise us into work and keep us interested with only a tambour to beat out the rhythms. Her classes were wonderful, and we all enjoyed them. The warming-up class, pretty well all exercises, lasted till about eleven. Then we had a break. Then we had a class which was more 'dance' till twelve when we had a long continental break till three. We used to go over for hot soup and rolls to a snack bar called Paulden's on the other side of the road. Then we'd have another warm-up and dance till about five when we went home on the tram.

In Modern Dance every class is different; it's not like ballet which is repetition. There are a thousand exercises, though no work of course, at the *barre*. You'd do exercises for feet and ankles and go right through to waist, shoulders and arms. You'd even do head movements. And there were even exercises for fingers, and for eyes and expression, how to move the face. Very often after that, in the second session, we worked in an icosahedron fitted together from a bundle of canes. To get your right direction in space you did various movements towards points of this icosahedron, with different parts of the body, moving quickly or slowly, directly or indirectly. The ways you can move to the points of an icosahedron are infinity. Sometimes you'll go directly to all the points with a *strong* movement – you'll thrust or you'll flick to A, B, C, D . . .

59

You see, Laban's technique evolved from his own theory that there were four elements of movement – time, space, energy (strong or light) and flow. Time, of course, was how *quickly* you did something. Space was *how* you got somewhere – in ballet it's the position and position and position, but with Laban it's the movement *in between* positions that matter, whether you get to them directly or indirectly, with a floating movement or with a strong one. Energy was *effort* used in floating, gliding, thrusting, flicking, pressing, slashing . . . Flow was continuity. If you slash, you do a quick movement in time, it's indirect in space, it's strong in energy, and the flow would be how you go, say, from a slash to a flick.

Most of the other students were young, just out of school and too young to have been in the war. There was Mausreen Myers, a Jewish girl who I thought very promising – she had terrific vitality. My best friend was Mary Elding, who had been to Art School and had been a painter and a sculptress. Though she called herself by her maiden name, she was already married to Elios Cabrerizo, a Frenchman from the Basque country who had come from France and joined General de Gaulle's Free French Army. He was now at his home in the Pyrenees, trying to piece together some sort of life for himself, while she was in Manchester, alone, waiting for him to write and say that he had a job and a house for her to go to. They wrote to each other regularly, but she wasn't at all sure that she actually would ever start a life with him. That was really how the war was. All relationships were affected by the war, and people got into situations that would never have happened in peace-time. She went to Paris eventually to live with him, but they were divorced a few months later.

Manchester was very badly scarred by war: bomb sites were everywhere, making huge gaps in the architecture. Everything seemed drab and dirty, and a great many prostitutes walked about, untroubled by convention or authority. Rain spat on you from black lowering clouds. The war with Japan wasn't over, and austerity was still very evident – restaurants and cafés had very little to offer; rationing seemed to be worse than ever. At last I discovered that a Mrs Clayton ran a guest house in the quiet suburb of Didsbury and was prepared to take boarders at £2 a week. Mrs Clayton – I afterwards knew her as Nancy – opened the door of her gabled, white-painted house herself, a dark, small birdlike woman in a brightly coloured overall. She showed me a room on

60

the first floor – a very pretty room with flowered curtains and bedspread, and a big window overlooking the front garden. She told me that the £2 included breakfast and meal at night and a hot drink at bedtime, but that baths would cost me a shilling extra each.

I went to live there. Staying with me were two girl students at the University and a fifty-year-old woman who complained incessantly and took most of her meals alone in her room. The rest of us ate together. For breakfast I had toast and marmalade and coffee; the others had cereal and dried eggs as well. Evening meals were stews and ragouts, with a cake or a bun instead of pudding. At ten o'clock you came down to collect a hot-water bottle and a mug of Ovaltine or Horlicks made with water. All over the house were little brightly coloured ornaments – birds, flowers, musical boxes – and little pictures and things made of shells. Many of these were from the East.

I didn't know until later that all this brisk brightness hid a very unhappy woman. Nancy had been born in Bombay and had married a commercial traveller there called Harry Clayton. He was much older than she, and fatter and not very exciting. She wanted more children, but couldn't have any after the first, which had died almost at birth. She couldn't understand why Harry had been rich selling electrical goods in India but, doing the same here in Manchester, couldn't afford servants or a car. She looked back on India as a kind of paradise. She seemed to think that, if only she could get back there, it would all be waiting for her – her mother, the dances, the parties, the pretty dresses, the frills. She hated Manchester. She said, 'The sun never gets up here!' Harry was away a lot on business, and that was why she had started the boarding house – to have people to talk to, because she couldn't bear to be alone. Whenever Harry came home, they used to have the most hair-raising rows. She threw saucepans, and shouted, 'Old stick-in-the-mud!' The main trouble was jealousy; she was always quite sure he had another woman tucked away somewhere. I felt sorry for Harry. I really think she was wrong about his *affaires*.

Though I was behind the others at the studio because I'd never done any Modern Dance before, I could do more with my body than they, because they hadn't been trained, as I had, from childhood. Modern Dance had a completely different psychology

61

from classical ballet; it was a much freer thing, a much more intellectual thing. In classical ballet there had always been the set steps which you were given by word of mouth to do, and you did them to the best of your ability and made them into a dance. Modern Dance was a matter of taking a theme or a character, improvising upon it and evolving appropriate movements. It took me a year to learn to make my own dances in this way. My forte was dancing. Most of the other students hoped to be teachers, but Lisa said I would never make a teacher: she said, 'No. You are a performer.' Lisa had got it into her head who were going to be teachers and who performers. Only one teacher I've heard of since became a *well-known* teacher, and that is Geraldine Stephenson. She specialised in antique dances, and I very often see her name on television. This was another thing we did at the studio – antique dances. Laban had an enormous respect for antique dances, so we did the minuet, the pavane and the jig. He regretted that the old dancing masters had only written in *words* that a certain figure had a certain number of steps and how the head had to be carried erect and so on. That was why he actually evolved a means of writing down dance like a musical score. Hence his book *Labanotation*. He used the two staves as you have – in music. The top stave was for the top half of the body – you could even notate movements of fingers and eyes. Knees, legs, thighs and hips were on the second stave. Square blocks were put on the correct lines. He often gave us talks – as did Lisa Ullman; as did Sylvia Bodmer, who did it ad infinitum. The Modern Dance movement stems almost entirely from him.

Laban was born into a rich Bohemian family and travelled with the Russian Ballet. He gave special lessons to Pavlova and took ideas from Nijinsky and Isadora Duncan, but these people were artists and dancers themselves and did not have the right kind of minds to evolve a new system. His new technique, though, caught on in Germany. There were Labanschules all over Germany before the war. The Nazis didn't like them, and labelled them as communist. He was ballet master at the Vienna State Opera when the Nazis came to power in Austria, so he had to leave in a hurry. The Art of Movement Studio in Manchester was his first school in England. One of his pupils in Germany was Mary Wigman, who pioneered Modern Dance in the USA.

I remember him as a large, round-headed man with grey hair, a moustache and very bright, lively eyes, sometimes blue, sometimes grey or greenish. In the studio he wore brightly coloured shirts – soft collared, open neck – and grey flannel trousers. He had a very strong German accent – 'Ve shall begin'; 'Feet like buns! . . . Back like dough!' 'Hop/ Dahn! Hop! Dahn!'; '*Now* vill you learn to bend ze knee!' As he was over seventy, he didn't demonstrate much, but he had an almost magical way of showing the movement he wanted with hands, fingers, head, face, even voice.

Sylvia Bodmer was a Swiss, a buxom pink and white lady married to a doctor. She was a good teacher but rather long-winded, with many admonitions such as, 'Be breathtaking!' We did not look forward to her classes, but she was a kind, rather motherly presence, and the fact that she was fallible and a little boring made her more human than the other two. She had a great belief in not being too single-minded about dancing. Lisa and Laban were entirely concerned with dancing, but she was very keen that we should go to concerts, go to art exhibitions. She took us to an exhibition of Picasso and Matisse. It was an absolute revelation. I hadn't seen modern art before and I didn't understand it at all; I hardly knew Picasso by name, certainly not Matisse at all. But Sylvia was very enthusiastic and took us round this exhibition and kept saying, 'Look! Look! *Movement! Movement!* See how it *moves!*' My enjoyment of modern pictures I owe entirely to Sylvia Bodmer, because she forced us to see the pictures in this exhibition.

After one of Sylvia's classes where she said, 'You should not be confined to the studio. You should go out to experience pictures, music, *life!*' I remember one of the girls saying, 'Well, what do we experience when we get out of here? Our *landladies!*' And I really think that was mostly it, though some of us used to go to The Cotton Club and to hear the Hallé – to plays also, especially if *advised* by Sylvia Bodmer. I do now see what Sylvia meant. I think of poetry as a continuation of dancing.

But it was the workaholic Lisa Ullman who inspired me above all. She would keep you at it *beyond* exhaustion – when she had completely exhausted you, that was when you must start work. 'Now, let's see. Who can do the best interpretation of a circle?', and each of us would have to go out and give our intepretation. Thereby hangs a tale. In the Sixties I read a poem of mine called 'Line, Circle and Spiral' to a group organised by Edward Lucie-Smith. It was a poem about which everyone was very enthusiastic, and it went right back to this time when I was working with Laban in Manchester. Laban said that there were only three shapes in the universe – the line, the circle and the spiral – and that, if any of us could find another shape, he would give us £100. Well, we would sit up night after night scribbling things on bits of paper and trying to find another shape which, of course, we never could because there are only three shapes in the universe. This is not really correct geometrically but, from a dancing point of view, and we were all completely concerned with dancing at that time, from a dancing point of view it *is* correct: there is no other shape. A straight line is a shape in dancing because it is a different experience from a curve, and a spiral is something different again. All dancing is based on these three universal shapes. So, many years afterwards, I wrote this poem:

> See there, in the line of the river,
> How the spine of the Venus flows softly –
> The spirals that rise,
> In the shimmer of light,
> In the dance of the gnats,
> In the song of the reeds,
> In the rise of the grasses,
> The flight of the fledgling,
> The sigh of a faun, and the laugh of a dryad –
> The spirals go turning, go turning for ever –
>
> Around them goes turning the wheel of the circle –
> The cattle that drink will be slaughtered tomorrow,
> The grasses be mown, and the bird turned to silence,
> The water boil dry to be drawn to the cloud
> That will break to the earth, that will filter the furrow,
> Through waters of Styx to be sprung to the light,
> That the circle may turn, and go turning for ever –
>
> The spirals may rise to contend with the circle,
> May rise to deny and defy with the circle,
> May blend and transcend, make an end of the circle –
> And there, though they shimmer and shine,
> The spirals we hold, in the winter's white teeth,
> Can be governed at last by the line.
> So love, the all-conquering master of death.
> At the height of its glory may be
> Sucked down to the bones and the boulders of life,
> And be tumbled away to the sea –

May be tumbled away to the sea, my love,
And then, if the sea boil dry,
Line, circle and spiral might sometime agree
In the formless mirage of the sky.

When I'd read this, Alan Brownjohn said, 'Well, I think you won your £100, Patricia. The poem proves there *is* a fourth shape, which is the shape of the sky which is nothingness.'

In September 1945, the Art of Movement Studio moved to a new address. It was still at All Saints, but it was a *real* studio – a long room on the second floor, with windows and a polished wooden surface to dance on. There was heating and a proper cloakroom and showers – the first time I ever *saw* a shower after a class or a performance was at this new studio in Manchester! Really, it seemed like heaven. We even had a studio pianist. Whatever was her name? And, by this time, we were becoming a group. We'd formed a relationship that came entirely from dancing. It was group movement; it was telepathy; you moved together and your minds began to work together so that you knew exactly what the person next to you was going to do. To begin with we'd done little that you would call creative or dramatic – it was mostly a matter of exercise and getting the body to work in the right way. Now we were working more on *dances*, and Ronnie Curran had joined us.

Ronnie was only sixteen and he came from Scotland. He'd done Highland Dancing and he looked like being something quite out of the ordinary. He *added* something; he had enormous life. Because of him, we began to do more and more in the way of the dramatic. We didn't all want to be stage performers but, by the end of that year, out of about twenty students, three girls and a boy, who had wanted to be Modern Dance teachers, somehow got drawn with me and Ronnie into this feeling of artistry and imagination. We began to make our own ballets. Laban said he wasn't teaching us how to become professional dancers, but he could see that some of us had talent, and that we might form a small ballet company, like a chamber orchestra, which was related to modern life. I was elated. I was reaching towards a peak and I knew that I was exactly the right size and shape for professional dancing. I'm just under five feet two, and my legs are about as long as my head to the base of my spine, which makes for a good proportion and looks all right

65

on a stage. How hard I worked, despite the aches and pains! One day, in dance, your instep hurts; the next day your ankle hurts; then it's your knee.

Jomo Kenyatta at this period was lecturing at Manchester University, where they'd created a department specially for him called The Department of African Studies. He was a great character about the city; you couldn't miss him because he was very large and flamboyant, and went around in a chauffeur-driven limousine and wore a fur coat and always carried a cane with a silver top. He had an office, the Pan African Club, almost opposite our studio in All Saints. The Pan African Club helped any Africans who had arrived in the city, and printed a lot of leaflets and campaigned against the colour bar and so forth.

Mary Elding and I were so impressed with the dancing that we'd seen at The Cotton Club that we wanted to know whether Jomo would come and give some lectures on African dancing at the studio and perhaps bring some dancers to demonstrate. We bearded the great man in his den, boldly told him that we were very interested in his African studies and that we were from The Art of Movement Studio. 'Oh yes,' he said. 'Well you would want to know about marriage customs and women's talk, of course.' I was a bit nonplussed by this, and I looked round to consult Mary and all I saw was her back going out of the door – she was furious. So I said, 'That wasn't quite what we had in mind. We're interested in drum rhythm.' He wouldn't accept this at all: 'Oh yes?! Oh yes?! Oh yes?!'

In the end, *I* turned my back and went out. Perhaps we'd come there in too casual a way, and he wanted to be treated with more respect. But he came to the studio with some drummers and dancers after Lisa Ullman wrote to him seeking advice as to how to obtain a demonstration. He told us how the drums were still used in Africa as a means of communication to tap out messages from one village to another where there were no letters or telephones. There were various revolutionary societies including The Leopard Society to which he belonged, that killed anyone who didn't believe in the emancipation of the African. These societies found the drums very useful because the white man couldn't understand what the drums said. It was very sophisticated, really – even the villagers didn't understand what, say, The Leopard Society was communicating to its members all over the continent, sometimes thousands of miles apart.

*

So we went on, day after exciting day, made all the more exciting for *me* by the arrival on the scene of my future husband. For some reason, at the guest house in Didsbury, my little electric iron never worked properly. It would go for a time and then it would sort of blow up and fuse all the lights in the house. I would take it back to the shop where they would do something to it and say it was mended and then, when I took it home, it would fuse the lights again. Finally Harry Clayton had a look at it and said it needed a new plug. I didn't really know how to fix a plug to an iron, but I attached one very gingerly and for a while it was successful. I usually had lunch at Nancy's on a Saturday because we didn't go to the studio on that day but, one Saturday in April, Nancy said we would have to hurry and there would only be salted pancakes and a cake for lunch because her brother Philippe [pronounced Philip] was coming to visit her and she was going to the station to meet him – he was a sailor and his ship had docked at Grimsby. Next day I was using my little iron and it did its usual little trick and fused the lights. Nancy rushed up the stairs, her brother with her, and said I must never use the iron again. But her brother said, 'Let me see if I can do anything with it,' and stayed behind with me and mended it.

I found Philippe attractive immediately. He was five years older than me, and very good-looking. He was slim, about a head taller than I am, and he was wearing an open-neck white shirt and flannel trousers, and a plaid jacket bought in Canada with a zip up the front and a fur collar. He was a petty officer, a freelance engineer of some kind in the Merchant Navy, and what he'd come to Manchester to do was get through the hundred pounds that he'd earned on his last ship before joining another. He looked like a Welshman – he had brown eyes, his colouring was dark and his hair was thick black. He even *sounded* Welsh, with a faint sing-song accent. He was fiddling around with this iron and he said, 'I've been in Montreal. Everything seems to be muddy and foggy here. I find Manchester very dull. What is there to *do* in Manchester? Where do people go at night?' I didn't yet realise that what he would probably like to do best would be to go into pubs and clubs to find girls, so I didn't mention The Cotton Club, where the dancing was wonderful but the clientèle were mostly girl-hunters and it could all be rather rowdy with a lot of drinking and throwing of bottles. I said, 'There are theatres and cinemas.' He said, 'Somehow I don't feel like going to places like that on my own.' I said, 'You've only just come. I expect you'll find things to do.'

He said, 'What are *you* doing here, anyway?' I told him about the Art of Movement Studio. Where had I come from? How was it I had no accent? I described Four Winds and how my parents had no accent, except my father who could drop into the Dorset dialect very easily, having one accent for the corn merchant and another for, say, Henry, one of our cowmen: ' 'Ow be ee this mornin', 'En?' 'O, all ri', Mas Bob.' ' 'Ow be'est Vi'let get on? Be she gone down yet?' 'Na, ark'ard sod, she b'aint. She be up over Long Wood in the carner.' ... He asked me would I go out with him somewhere during the week and, as I remember it, we went to a Chinese restaurant – the Chinese were always able to give you a good meal, even with the austerity rationing. Over a bottle of wine and an excellent dinner we became friends. I began the process of gradually falling in love.

Philippe's full name was Louis Philippe Kass. His father was a Bavarian, a ship's captain who always sailed on British ships, with a house in Bombay. His mother was born in Mauritius. He himself was born in 1918 at Belgaum, where all the family was interned because his father was German. He considered himself to be English. His father never spoke German and he learned no French from his mother. He ran away from home at sixteen and joined a circus as a mechanic though, after a while, he was promoted to book-keeper. When the Second World War broke out he joined the army but couldn't get a commission so pretended to be ill and was demobilised. He then joined the Merchant Navy, obtained an engineer's ticket somewhere along the line, and that's how he spent the rest of his war – working on ships. He could be very gay, but I was aware that he was deeply unhappy and very bitter. The sun in Manchester never *shone* properly. People in England wore dull clothes. The world was unjust and only for the rich.

Because of this sense of injustice, which was like a sore which he kept licking like a dog, he took me to hear Harry Pollitt, the communist leader, speaking at Belle Vue. He sometimes got angry with me because I wasn't discontented enough, I was too complacent. But, in spite of all this, the friendship grew into a romance, we relaxed. We laughed together as we walked in Victoria Park. He said to me once, 'You mustn't bother too much about me! It's just this Mother Country. I've been told about it all my life, and it appears that my mother won't look after the likes of me.' In time, his attitude seemed to soften, he seemed to be more contented. He called me Fairybird. Boggart Hole Clough became one of our favourite places – a boggart is a fairy. Around this hill with a cave in it, ran little paths among clumps of trees and gorse bushes and grass where you came across sheep. 'Fairybird, please may I kiss you?'

> 'May I kiss you?' he said.
> Answer: A lifetime of unsolved equations.
> And, oh, the questing lips, the probing tongues,
> The thirst for knowledge,
> Flavour of high adventure!

He asked me to marry him. He was going away on another ship to earn more money, but would I marry him first?

I hesitated because of what was against it. Firstly, though I'd mentioned him once or twice in letters, my family had never seen him. Secondly, and more important, I was a dancer and I was very deep in plans for the new ballet company. This wouldn't do for Philippe: he wanted to get married *now*; and what was to stop me dancing? Anyhow, he'd soon be away for about a year. If I ever wanted to marry him – he knew that I loved him – I must make immediate preparations.

So I decided to telephone my mother. One evening, after we'd finished at the studio, I said to Mary Elding, 'Will you come with me to a public telephone box? I've got to make a call to my family and it'll be a bit of an ordeal. I've to tell them I'm going to get married.' Mary was very scathing. She said marriage was the last thing I should consider at the moment. I was making a career for myself; I should concentrate on that. I had some talent and I should think about using it. And, when I telephoned my mother as I had to do in order to face Philippe, when I said to her quickly, to get it over, 'I have some news for you. I'm going to get married,' she raised the roof. She said she'd never seen this man and who was he anyway and, of course, what about my career? She then called my father, who repeated all that she had said because, although dancing didn't matter to him, all he ever wanted was for Mother to get her own way. I had to promise then and there that I wouldn't marry Philippe without first bringing him to Four Winds. Before he went to sea in October, I persuaded Philippe that this was only fair.

*

69

We were doing a lot of things now *outside* the studio. Lisa or von Laban would come with us to factories and point out how people were handling things wrongly, how they could lift enormous weights without hurting themselves if they did it in a certain way, how they were forced to move unnaturally to the rhythm of their machines, how they could avoid various illnesses and disabilities by using tools and lifting and moving according to the techniques of Modern Dance. Our nucleus of a modern dance company which we had decided to call The Young Dancers' Group was hammering out one or two dances which we showed in schools and old theatres and church halls at places like Edale, Borrowdale and Bolton to adult education groups and to acting groups interested in incorporating 'movement' into their drama. Mary had done dressmaking, and she taught us how to do needlework and how to make costumes on a shoestring. Props were minimal. One dance required a bus stop, so we had a bus stop with just the usual black curtains around.

Laban did most of our choreography, and a man by the name of Eric Hudes played the piano – he composed a lot of the music himself, though he also used Beethoven, Scriabin, Scott Joplin and the blues. We did quite a lot of these shows in the studio. Lisa hired chairs and put up posters, and people paid to come in. *The Forest* was the name of one of the ballets we produced as a studio performance. It was a very avant-garde, almost abstract work about the life-cycle of a forest. Insects came into it. There was a sequence with flowers growing and water lilies coming up through some water. To show how messages were transmitted we used the drum rhythms that we'd learned from Jomo Kenyatta. There was a nightmare sequence where we were horrible monsters who made their own noises – in those days it was a great shock for an audience to hear dancers making noises. In one scene, Maureen Myers and Ronnie Curran and I were acrobatic little tree sprites. Some of the scenes had no music, but that one did have. The music grew with the dancing. Eric Hudes improvised as we improvised and then, eventually, as the dance was set, the music was set, a very exciting process.

Lisa had invited Joan Littlewood and her husband, Ewan McColl, the folk singer, from Theatre Workshop. Joan Littlewood was very enthusiastic and made a speech to the audience begging for money to take the ballet to the 1947 International Festival of Dancing to be held in Copenhagen in August. She said she would like to add a

70

scene using hefty woodcutters which could be provided by Theatre Workshop. We were in full agreement, and the scene was added with a great deal of attention to 'work movement' and work songs written by Ewan McColl. Although *we* weren't expected to be hefty woodcutters, we had to join in the exercises at rehearsal. These were taught by McColl, and it was all rather odd. Theatre Workshop was based on 'the Method' as evolved by Stanislavsky, and I remember moving round in a circle grunting, and shouting occasionally, 'Poyé mayo!' which we were told was a Lesotho word used for calling cattle.

Joan Littlewood struck me as a very strong, enormously tolerant woman. She would even tolerate bad acting until it could be improved. She herself was a marvellous actress. I saw her as Mother Courage, and in a play by Molière, and also in Lorca's *The Shoemaker's Wife*, at the Unity Theatre. She had lovely hand movements and a strong low-pitched voice. She was more interested in directing than acting, and, perhaps, more in political sociology than either. With Lancashire people she would drop into a Northern accent. This dual speech reminded me of my father.

The Forest didn't win a prize at the festival, but it got a special recommendation for originality. The ballet that won was *La Cellule*. It was performed by a French company and it anticipated much of what was to be done much later by John Cranko and Lindsay Kemp. It was frightening and very sad, about a man condemned for murder. At the time we called it 'existentialist', a word coined by Sartre, but I'm still not quite sure what it means.

The Danes were absolutely wonderful to us. Denmark had been liberated and we were allies. We didn't need to book hotels – they opened their houses to us, quarrelling with one another because they all wanted some English. Mary and I had a studio in a large house put at our disposal by the owners. We ate and slept and did some practice there. Rehearsals and performances were at The König Theatre, the largest theatre in Copenhagen. And, in the second week, after *The Forest* had been staged and while we were still there to see the rest of the festival, a sort of miracle took place. I still can't really believe it happened. Philippe's ship, a Canadian ship, docked in Copenhagen on a trip back from Kotka! Mary tactfully went and lived elsewhere and left the studio to us. We went together to other ballets, we went to a nightclub, we went to the Tivoli Gardens, we slept together for the first time. Then we had to split up again because I was returning to Manchester with the company and he had to continue on board ship until the autumn.

By the time he came home, he had saved about £500, and £500 in those days was a considerable sum of money. He'd also bought me in anticipation a wedding ring made of Russian gold. We moved to a room in Sloane Street – a dark little street of old back-to-back millworkers' houses in Moss Side – so we could live together. The frail old landlady only charged us £1 10s a week, including use of kitchen.

5

Philippe wanted to be a married in a church, any church but a Roman Catholic one. He and his six sisters and brothers had been brought up as Catholics. As I've said, his father was a Bavarian, and, of course, the Bavarians *are* Catholic, and very religious by all accounts. But Philippe, when he ran away from home, finished with his religion, though he still had what I can only call a reverence for it born of fear; while his whole intelligence seemed to be geared towards disapproving of it, while he *said* that nothing would happen to you if you broke the Catholic laws, yet he somehow believed in them – it was a peculiar sort of relationship. I was quite prepared for him to suggest a quiet ceremony in a Registry Office, but he picked the Walley Range Methodist Chapel, perhaps because it was the one thing that his Catholic teachers would have hated most.

I took Philippe down to Four Winds for Christmas '47. We arrived on Christmas Eve and the Christmas festivities passed off fairly well. My sister Felicity, who was now twelve, was there. My brother Tim was there with his Swedish fiancée, Birgitta. Philippe seemed to be welcome and there was a lot of superficial bonhomie. One of the things we had to do was to visit Auntie Nellie, my great-aunt who lived in Salisbury Street, Blandford. She received us magnificently dressed, as usual, in sombre satins and velvets, her white hair piled high on her head. Her nephew, Louis Strange, the aviator who had flown with Blériot, and trained pilots in both wars, was one of her great admirers. He said that he couldn't bear the thought of Blandford without Auntie Nellie, so, if she died, he was going to have her stuffed. She offered us a 'little glass of sherry', and fetched

73

a large yellow chamberpot which she placed in the corner of the room, telling Philippe that of course, being a sailor, he would need a spittoon. I don't think she gave a monkey's whether Philippe and I got married or not, and she was the only member of the family that he really liked.

Tim had plenty to talk to him about because he had been stationed in India with the Indian Army during the war, coming out as a sergeant. He had acquired a stray dog once while on the march, and this had given him an insight into the caste system. He couldn't feed it himself because that 'wasn't done', and he couldn't find an Indian prepared to do it either because that was 'unclean'. He was also very much attracted by the Sikh women; he said they were the most beautiful he had ever seen. It was such a waste, because so many of the Sikh men were homosexual ... For some reason Philippe thought Tim was talking *down* to him.

It was after Christmas that the real fun began. My parents were horrified when they discovered that Philippe's father was a German. They both had a block against Germans – my mother because of her French connections, and my father because he had fought them in two world wars. That Captain Kass only worked for British companies and never spoke German to his children and brought them up as English made no difference – Philippe, on his father's side, was *German*. The fact that his mother was French should have pleased my mother, but when he happened to let slip that he was born in Mauritius, she raised the objection that he might have Indian blood, our marriage might be a mixed one. She said she knew about the relationships French families in Mauritius had with the indigenous population; the French colonists never had a colour bar like the English in India, and they married the local women and settled down with them.

These racial objections seemed *obscene*. I was now *determined* to marry Philippe, and at once. Possibly if my parents had allowed me to take a long cool look at the situation on the basis of their more rational objections such as lack of money and throwing away my career I might have changed my mind. But, as so often when disagreeing with another person, I went too far in the other direction. Their remarks about his temperament, about his clothes, about the cruel manner in which he whipped Felicity's pony, Robin, when we went out riding, seemed silly and trivial and symptoms of a deep prejudice which I detested. I was in a fury – Philippe was in a fury – even the kindly Birgitta hurt him because

74

she was approved of. Announcing that we would now get married without any question, we returned to Manchester a week before we originally intended. Mother wrote to me saying, 'You will have to take the consequences. If you think I'm going to pull your chestnuts out of the fire, you're wrong.' She enclosed a letter from my father who said he couldn't forgive me for what I was doing and that I no longer fitted in with the West Country way of life. This seemed to me a bit muddle-headed. I hadn't been aware that there was any particular way of life in the West Country but, if there was, it shouldn't have included my parents' behaviour. I knew that the real crime I had committed in my father's eyes was to upset my mother, a crime which he wouldn't allow at any price. Back at the studio, Mary Elding was very interested in the situation when I told her about it. She said, 'Supposing Philippe *is* an Indian, would it make any difference to you?' I said, 'No, it wouldn't. I can't see that it's important.'

So we were married in February 1948. We walked from Sloane Street to the chapel. The minister was a dear little man. Philippe wore a grey suit and I wore a blue dress and carried a bouquet of blue flowers. My parents had said they wouldn't come but, as we entered the chapel, Nancy whispered to me that my mother was there. Sure enough, there she was, sitting in a pew, and there she remained for the whole of the service after which she simply disappeared. All the Art of Movement students were present, too, and Harry Clayton gave me away and witnessed our signatures in the vestry along with Ronnie Curran. Philippe had ordered a barrel of beer for the reception at the studio afterwards. I remember our elderly landlady getting very drunk indeed, and singing loudly, dancing by herself, being sick, passing out and having to be carried home. Ronnie did some Highland dancing in his stockinged feet, which is supposed to be very lucky at a wedding. Years later I saw him in a revue in the West End of London. He still had that 'thing' we had in The Young Dancers' Group, but somehow it was all covered over with a veneer of slickness and commercialism, all the life had been knocked out of it. I've often wondered what happened to Ronnie since then. I have never seen anybody perform the Highland dances with such grace and beauty. Philippe was extremely reserved with Ronnie and my other friends. I was to learn that he was jealous of my friends, that he didn't like other people to be friendly with me at all.

We continued to live in our little room in Sloane Street. Philippe decided never to go back to sea. That was his French side – French sailors, once they're married, always settle down if they can, preferably to run a chicken farm, a French sailor's dream. He got a job as a sheet-metal worker in a factory – I think it was Rolls Royce. I was a dancer and a housewife. The cooking and the housework were a nightmare. Philippe had to take over most of the cooking. Meat in the North had special names. If you merely asked for 'steak', butchers palmed off dreadful things on you. Our landlady helped me to say things like, 'I want two pounds exactly of chuck steak and trim off the fat.' And, in about April, any sort of food began to make me feel sick and I became very tired and couldn't get through classes. For a while, what was wrong didn't register; it didn't yet occur to me that Philippe's preventative measures were haphazard and that I was pregnant. Even when I realised this, I struggled on at the studio until one day I collapsed in class and burst into tears and admitted to everyone that I was going to have a baby and that soon I would have to give up dancing completely because it would begin to show.

There was an awful feeling of having let everybody down. I wanted the baby dreadfully because I was in love with Philippe and he wanted it too, but I was a king pin in our little company and I knew the consequences if one of so small a number of dancers dropped out. Also I knew that I had a talent, something to contribute which gave the group a kind of life, and I was taking that away. Not only would I have to leave the studio, I would have to leave Manchester. We couldn't find cheap alternative accommodation there suitable for bringing up a baby, and Philippe had given notice at work; he was drawing the dole, and wouldn't go back to work in another factory. He had lost his temper with the foreman – this was to happen again and again – and called him a louse and a bastard, and said that, anyway, he loathed the men he worked with because they always talked about sex in such a disgusting way. Needless to say, my parents had cut off my allowance once we were married, so we began to look at advertisements in *Reynolds News* and *The Manchester Guardian* to find a job for him, any job that would get us out of Manchester.

In May, we saw an advertisement in *The Manchester Guardian* – a lady and her mother, a Miss and Mrs Canvin of Ivy Cottage, Beeston Castle in Cheshire, needed a couple to run their small house as cook and butler. Well, Philippe said he would do the

76

cooking, if I would do the butlering; we could sort of manage the house as a team effort. It was still as much as I could do to cook eggs and bacon, and, without much success, he was trying to teach me how to make Indian curries and Indian sweets and crêpes suzettes. After many drafts, we concocted a letter explaining that I was expecting a baby, which was our reason for wanting to be in the country. Mary Elding provided the most glowing reference. She presented herself as a very rich lady whom we had worked for in Manchester for many years and signed herself with a great flourish as Mary Cabrerizo, her married name. She was very professional: she wrote at the top 'To whom it may concern' and explained how we had been faithful servants and were honest and clean. Back came a charming letter from Miss Canvin, saying she would love to have a baby in the house. We didn't realise till afterwards that she was surprised to get an answer to the advertisement at all! Like my mother when I was a child, she and Mrs Canvin were right out in the country and couldn't get anybody else to work for them.

We packed our possessions into two suitcases which Philippe carried one in each hand, and said goodbye to Manchester. We said goodbye to our landlady, who was in floods of tears because she felt we were her children. We said goodbye, or rather I did, to the students and to Lisa Ullman. Lisa Ullman was not too keen on me just now. She had given permission for the wedding reception at the studio, but hadn't known about the opposition of my parents; she thought that she was conniving, in some way, at an abduction.

Miss Canvin fetched us from the small railway station at Beeston Castle in her car. She was in her forties and worked as a physiotherapist at the hospital in Nantwich about ten miles away. Our main task was to look after her mother whenever she was at the hospital. Otherwise we had to provide them with tea and toast for breakfast and cook their dinner at night. Mrs Canvin, who was very old indeed, had to be *persuaded* to eat lunch. We used to say, 'Well, you must eat something. You must keep your strength up.' 'Well, I think I *will*! You know, you're so persuasive I think I *will* have a tomato!' And this tomato, cut in half, had to be served on a special plate, and the table laid with two knives and two forks and a spoon and fork and a glass and the condiments. Though we were only paid £4 10s a week between us, the same amount as I received years ago in pantomime, we were happy to begin with. Miss Canvin did the shopping for us and we had our own room overlooking a large garden at the back. We arrived in late June and, one morning, I looked out of our window and saw a stoat jumping up and down and turning somersaults on the lawn – stoats do this to attract the birds. It was dancing on this square of lawn with roses and clematis and jasmine growing all around, and it looked like a magic, fairy thing.

Oh, another of our jobs was to spy on Tom, the gardener. Every day, Mrs Canvin used to make it her business to find out whether Tom had actually put in his two hours of work. 'Now, when did he arrive? ... Ah, yes ... And did you see him go? ... No. Well, you must be very careful about that because, you see, he *will* cut the time and we cannot afford that, we cannot afford to pay somebody for time that they do not put in. Now, what has he actually *done* this morning?' 'Well, I don't know, Mrs Canvin. We were rather busy.' 'Well, you must keep an eye on him, you see. I mean it's no good his coming and then sitting on his spade.' Sometimes Tom didn't turn up at all, we told Mrs Canvin. But if he happened to come late or go early or sit on his spade, we didn't betray him. We liked Tom. Apart from Aunt Nellie, he was one of the very few people that my husband ever took to. He was a very simple country man. When he came in to drink a cup of coffee with us in the morning he showed a great interest about life in the town because he had never lived there. We'd tell him about Manchester and he'd sit there going 'Oooh! Oooh!' like an owl.

I said just now that Philippe and I were happy at the Canvins' to begin with. I should have said 'fairly happy', because we were always hungry. Sometimes Miss Canvin left us only one egg each to last the day. Philippe complained. One evening when she came in from work he said, 'We've nothing in the house. You've brought the meat for tomorrow, but we've no bread, we're out of sugar. You like marmalade for your breakfast and you've pots of marmalade and jam in the cupboard in your bedroom, but there's none for anybody else! You must bring in more food! You're bringing in just enough for yourself and your mother, and very often we have nothing for ourselves!' Miss Canvin flared up over this. She said that she'd had many maids working for her and they'd left for one reason or the other; certainly they'd left from loneliness, but they'd never complained about the food; the food she was buying was quite sufficient and she wouldn't change the catering. In the end, we had to go to the village shop past a little line of cottages and buy our own supplies. But even this had often to be out of Philippe's savings, because we weren't being paid regularly: Miss Canvin would say, 'Oh, I haven't been to the bank this week,' and we would have to wait.

One day, in the middle of July, Mrs Canvin called us into the dining-room while she was having a lunchtime tomato. She addressed herself to Philippe. She said, 'Tell me, Mr Kass, do you consider yourself to be paid enough money here?' He said, 'The pay isn't much but we are content for the moment.' She said, 'Well, I've lost a most valuable ring. It's been in my family for a considerable time. It was in my bedroom last night on the table beside my bed. It's not there now. I am *most* careful about where I put things.' She wasn't at all careful. When Philippe realised that she was accusing us of stealing this ring, he flew into a temper and shouted, 'How dare you talk to us like this! You and your kind think you're ladies and gentlemen, don't you?! Well, you aren't! You're the scum of the earth! You and your bloody daughter! You think you've nothing to do but sit on your arses while the rest of us were made to bloody work for you! . . .' He went on in this vein for quite a while; feelings about social injustice had been bottled up inside him for years. Mrs Canvin couldn't get a word in edgeways. In the end she said, 'Will you kindly leave the room,'Mr Kass!' Philippe left the room, and I followed him. To my knowledge, the incident wasn't mentioned to Miss Canvin. I think Mrs Canvin found the ring and didn't want to admit she'd lost it.

But, as time went on, there were other rows in the *presence* of Miss Canvin, who was absolutely horrified when Philippe swore and inveighed against the idle rich who sat upon their arses, and one day towards the end of August I heard a terrific row. I don't know *exactly* what was said because I was elsewhere being sick, but Philippe had cornered Miss Canvin before she went to work and was demanding our wages, which hadn't been paid for a fortnight, and demanding that they be increased as well. I know that we never did get those wages and that we walked out the following Saturday. Philippe wanted to walk out at once and leave the old lady to her own devices, but I said we must wait till Saturday, when Miss Canvin wouldn't be at the hospital.

On Saturday Miss Canvin called me to join her for morning coffee and proceeded to tell me what a terrible man my husband was. Had I considered leaving him? No, I said, I hadn't. She was

79

frightened of her mother being left on her own so, if Philippe left, would *I* be prepared to stay? I said I couldn't think of splitting up, especially as the baby was due in October. She said this would be quite all right; she was a trained nurse and knew exactly how to look after babies; we could look after the baby between us. 'No,' I said. 'It wouldn't do at all.' I was still in love with Philippe. With all his outbursts, you see, she thought I couldn't be.

Philippe was sitting in the kitchen having coffee with Tom. He said, 'What was all *that* about?' I was in two minds whether to tell him or not, but tell him I did. He said, 'That settles it! We're leaving!' and we left the same afternoon.

We had simply what we stood up in and our suitcases. We didn't even know where we were going. We walked down the drive and, at the gate, we actually tossed a coin as to whether we should go right, in which case we'd arrive at Nantwich, or go left, which would take us to Crewe. Well, Crewe won, and we just set off on a bus to Crewe. I always think that's rather significant, because they were two opposites, Crewe and Nantwich; they represented two completely different ways of life. Crewe was a big industrial town growing very fast, with a busy railway junction and people pouring in to find work in the new factories. Nantwich was a prim little country town built in what they call the 'magpie' style – white houses with black gables and oak beams.

I never knew what a roller mill was, but every Bed and Breakfast place we tried in Crewe was full because of the extra people who had come into the town to work in this new roller mill. We were walking around Crewe, and oh it was hot, *frantically* hot. I was wearing a yellow maternity smock and quite a thick skirt, and I was just so hot I couldn't breathe. Late in the evening, a sympathetic woman, who could see what my state was, directed us to a Mr Lawrence, 'Everybody calls him "Lol".'

Now, Lol was a down-to-earth spiv, a Lancashire man on the make, who had turned his large home into a boarding house for about twenty men workers and was running it himself with the help of his mother-in-law and wife and daughter. We knocked on the door, and Lol, fair, stocky, in rolled-up shirtsleeves, answered us. 'Sorry,' he said. 'Full up. We've got nowhere.' He then looked me over and thought again. 'Well, I don't feel I can send you out on the streets tonight in that state. Come in and have a cup of tea.' We went in gratefully and we had this cup of tea and, if you have a cup of tea in the North, there's always something with it, so we had bread and butter and slices of ham as well. He said, 'We've an old wash house we don't use. I'll put a mattress in there and at least it'll give you somewhere to sleep. You can eat with the family. I won't charge you until you find your feet.' It was incredible. I think Lol, with his round blue eyes, was basically a romantic, a romantic who couldn't help using you to his own advantage when he got to know you. He had battery hens and he knew them as individuals and let them out to scratch. Anyhow, for about a fortnight, we slept in this wash house where the 'grey flies' picked on me and stung me and I itched.

During the first week Philippe found a factory job and, thanks to Lol, by the end of the second we owned, and were living in, our own house, a semi-detached with two large bedrooms and a box room, a bathroom and a lavatory upstairs, and a living-room, a dining-room and a kitchen down! – 19, Derrington Avenue, Crewe. Lol, because he couldn't really think in any other way, had discovered how he could put the accident of our arrival to use. 'I've a friend Frankie who lives at 19, Derrington Avenue. He needs a down payment for another property and he's desperate to sell. He wants fifteen hundred but, though he's a mean little bugger, he'll come down I'm pretty sure. You can get a mortgage.' 'How can I get a mortgage?!' said Philippe. 'I've only just got a job and they keep a week in hand!' 'You'll get a mortgage,' said Lol. 'I know the man at The 'Alifax, and you won't even have to put any money down. We'll knock Frankie down from fifteen to thirteen hundred, fake it that you've paid two hundred as your down payment.' And that's what happened. Frankie agreed to the arrangement, The 'Alifax decided to lend us the money and Lol got a rake-off, and Philippe and I were soon busy buying bits and pieces of furniture and making ready to turn 19, Derrington Avenue into a guest house after the birth of our baby, to be called Louis if it was a boy, Tansy if it was a girl.

The local doctor – everybody called her Dr Annie – booked me a bed in the Barony Hospital. I packed a case. I followed the drill. When I woke in great pain one night, Philippe went out to a taxi rank and brought me to the hospital. I've had three children altogether and that confinement was the worst. The Barony was an emergency hospital, a very old one. They didn't agree with having analgesics. They believed that pain was *necessary* to a birth;

81

it was the pain somehow that attached you to the baby; you wouldn't be so fond of the baby if you didn't suffer pain. So I had the most dreadful time. I've never actually contemplated suicide, but there have been times in my life when I didn't care if I lived or died, and at that time, I would have been quite happy to die just to get rid of the pain. It was a terrible thing, and it went on for two days and two nights in that October of 1948.

The baby was eventually born in the morning of the second night. The pain had suddenly stopped; I couldn't think of anything except that this pain had stopped; that was the only thing that mattered. It was only a little afterwards that I thought of the baby. I said to the old midwife, 'Where's the baby?' I was thinking, 'The baby ought to cry. There ought to be some noise, and it isn't crying.' The old midwife said, 'Shh! You've got to get some rest now. You've got to get some rest.' I said, 'But where *is* it?!' She said, 'Now never mind about the baby. You get some rest.' I said, 'It's dead, isn't it? It's not crying.' She didn't like to tell a lie, she said, 'Yes. But we mustn't worry about it now. You must get some rest or you will die, too.'

I *did* go off to sleep after that, and it wasn't until I woke from that sleep that the enormity of the baby dying hit me. So many *dreadful* things are happening in the world, a still-born baby isn't *really* a dreadful tragedy, but the thing is you've worked up to having this baby, for nine months your whole body has been preparing for it, and I was very much, how do you say?, I was very much *attuned* to the things which were going on inside my body because of the dancing – in dancing the body is the instrument that you play on. Because of this, losing my baby seemed like the end of the world. There should have been something there to love, and there wasn't, there was nothing there at all. And I never did see Tansy. They showed her to Philippe. The first thing he said to me when he came to take me home was, 'Oh, darling! You had a *lovely* baby!' I said, 'I'd like to see it.' But they wouldn't show it to me. They thought that if you never saw the baby you wouldn't miss it, but I did just the same. The girl in the bed next to me, she was only a teenager, and she had an illegitimate baby and her baby lived, and, strangely enough, I didn't feel any resentment, I felt interested in it, I felt a kind of affection for it, I felt I hadn't quite lost the baby I *had* lost. My poem 'Still Birth' is a combination, as is all poetry. It is *my* story, it is how *I* felt, but it also has in it this teenage girl in the bed next to me with her illegitimate baby:

82

I'll have to stop crying. They're right, no doubt.
If only I knew what I'm crying about!

. . . .

What monster mother of waste or wild
Has given no love to a first-born child?!
But how can I love what I only knew
As a dancing flutter and pain come true?
No love for the hands that will never be kissed;
No love for a face that will never exist,
My brave little ghost who went away
Without word or cry, without time to stay.
And the worst of all, when she fought for air,
It might have hurt her – How can I care?! . . .

6

I don't really think that Philippe was much bothered about the
loss of the baby. We were in rather a tight corner and, with me
running the guest house, a baby would have meant more re-
sponsibility, and I wouldn't have had enough time for it. But he
could see I was upset and, for a while, the experience drew us
closer together. He was very anxious that I shouldn't work too
hard. He even became over-protective. This over-protectiveness,
which was connected with his jealousy of my friendships with other
people, was to become a bone of contention between us. I didn't
want to be protected. The day after I got home from the hospital,
the woman at the corner shop where I usually bought the groceries
came in to say how sorry she was that I'd lost the baby, and I
burst into tears. Philippe started a terrific tirade: 'Can't you see
what you've done to her? How *dare* you talk about the baby! Why
stick your nose in where it's not wanted?! You're an interfering
woman! . . .' I kept trying to tell him that the woman was only
being kind. In the end *she* went off in tears.

Despite Philippe's anxiety, I worked very hard getting the house
ready for our first boarders. I was *determined* to make a success of
something at last. With the loss of the baby had come a sense of
failure. You know, I sort of felt I couldn't do anything properly: I
couldn't dance any more; I couldn't cook; I couldn't keep a house;
I couldn't even have a baby. We put a card in the window and
waited and, for about a month, all we got was Mr Taylor. Mr
Taylor was a little, middle-aged man who'd come to Crewe from
Bolton to find work as a joiner, and he considered himself tremendously lucky to be the only tenant in a boarding house and to

find the work he wanted. He settled himself in and was very regular with his rent. In fact, for that month, he was our prop and mainstay. Our terms were £2 a week for bed and breakfast and evening meal and supper at nine, with lunch on Saturdays and Sundays.

I don't know how much Philippe's wage was – he never told me how much he learned – but I know it wasn't enough to cover the £5 weekly for Hire Purchase for the furniture and the £2 weekly for the mortgage. He would give me £5 now and again to buy food and, when that was gone, I would ask for more. Having only what Philippe gave me and not a penny from my parents who I didn't write to and only knew about through Tim and Birgitta, I was walking about in my yellow maternity smock as I couldn't afford new clothes – and there didn't seem to be jumble sales and second-hand shops as there are now. Though we also put cards in newsagents, they resulted in no new boarders. It seemed a hopeless situation. Philippe and I were still very much in love but, partly due to extra worry and partly due to his temperament, he was subject to frightening rages. If, say, I upset anything on the floor, this would send him white with anger. He would say how stupid I was and – his usual theme – that I was one of the idle rich who'd never done a hand's turn in her life.

Philippe's rages were definitely, I think, a legacy from his father. His mother had died when he was nine, worn out and depressed by his father's constant rages and bullying. The Lascar crews that his father commanded were the toughest of the tough, and I think he treated his family in exactly the same way that he treated them. Because of his hatred for his father, because of his love for his mother whose solace before her death was brandy and water which Philippe would take to her room when he was a little boy, he had a kind of aversion to birthday cele-brations because of the memories they stirred. He never cele-brated *my* birthday in any way. His birthday was the same as my brother's, October the 20th, and I would say 'Happy Birth-day!' when he got up in the morning, but he was always furious if I attempted to do anything about it. I gave him some cuff-links before we were married, but he made it known that in future he didn't want any 'silly presents'. Though he did celebrate Christmas and Easter, and always cooked the Christmas dinner himself, they were very bad times for him and he would shout at everybody with whom he came in contact. He sort of felt that he *ought* to celebrate these times but, because of his hatred of the Catholic religion, he was unhappy doing so.

I don't think Lol liked either Philippe or me, but our *situation* rather moved him when he came down one day in the new year with his wife, Maggie, and his little daughter to see how we were getting on. He said, 'I don't understand it. I've to keep turning people away. Anybody I've to turn away from now on, I'll give them your address.' We were always full after that: the four beds in each of the two bedrooms were always occupied, and the one big table in the dining room, the front room, would just about seat eight. People needed beds so badly that once or twice we let them doss on the floor without a mattress.

Most of the guests were very rough. A lot of them never thought they were getting enough for their £2. The majority had just come over from Ireland, probably from Irish farms where they could get a much better deal. You see, the war was over but there was still rationing. I had to take their ration books, and they used to complain about the scrambled eggs I made for them out of dried egg powder. They said my menu was limited, and it's a fact that I was always making stews or liver and bacon, and salads for lunch on Saturdays. Philippe wouldn't eat this plain English food at all – I'd to make him curries and ragouts and pots au feu separately. There was one lodger, a man by the name of McNally, who refused the dried eggs, so all he was getting for breakfast was porridge and bread and marmalade. One morning I took these in and he said, 'I've had stuff like this, I've had it all right, but I've had it *before* I've had me breakfast!' and he threw the plate of porridge on the floor. One morning, I went up to make the beds, and surprised him with a lady. I asked him to go. To bring a woman in and sleep with her, with three other men in the room, seemed to me an obscenity.

We had two *very* attractive brothers from a tinker family – the Hanraghans. One was dark with thick curly hair and grey eyes and a beautiful smile, and the other was blond, rather like a Viking. They had beautifully soft voices and their manners were perfect, but they were absolute devils; they were always together and they got into everything under the sun. They were labourers, I think, on the roads, and they used to bring their pickaxes in and put them in the hall and cover the hall with mud. They used to get drunk and fall up the stairs, and their beds always seemed to have earth or hay in them. I suppose you would say they were really very bad lodgers and yet, every time you thought, 'The Han-raghans must go!', they would somehow argue themselves out of it; they were always such nice, smiling people that you *couldn't* throw them out.

Later, I wrote a poem about the Hanraghans. I called it 'The Hanraghan Brothers – A Landlady's Complaint to the Probation Officer'. They were always having trouble with the police. Not that they were thieves in the professional sense but, when they got drunk, they would go and steal things for fun. For instance, they would raid the Methodist Chapel and take what they could find, the most *unlikely* things – things, say, collected as prizes for a Whist Drive. The police called and said they thought the Han-raghans were taking things and asked if we'd seen any stolen goods in the house. I said, No, we hadn't. They went away and sent back a plain clothes man who said that he would have to search the house. He went up to the Hanraghans' chest of drawers and he pulled out things they could *never* have wanted – tablecloths, alarm clocks, china dogs and sets of spoons. So I wrote a poem about the Hanraghans:

> As soon as the Hanraghans entered the door
> There were nettles grew up through the cracks in the floor
> There was hay in the beds and a pick in the hall
> And they'll mop it all up for it's nothing at all
> But the Hanraghans' mopping is worse than the mud
> And they're running a greyhound the bad-tempered bitch
> No fathers nor mothers
> The Hanraghan brothers
> Just somehow crawled out of a bit of a ditch
>
> And the women come round no accounting for tastes
> So they've borrowed ten bob for they're honest as prastes
> They've alarm clocks and tablecloths stuffed in the drawer
> And it's what they knocked off from the chapel next door
> So I tell them to go but they blarney it out
> They'd a fight on the step with a devil called Flynn
> Oh Mister Carruthers
> The Hanraghan brothers
> Would drive a psychiatrist into the bin . . .

One of their favourite phrases was 'Honest as prastes'. For in-stance, when they wanted to borrow money they would always say, 'I'll let you have it back, for we're honest as prastes.' Anyway, the upshot was that the blond Hanraghan had a terrific fight outside in the street one night. I looked out of the window, and he was sitting in the middle of the road among a lot of broken bottles. I suppose I should have taken him in, because he certainly didn't look as if he knew what he was doing, but I just shut the window and left him to it; I thought, 'You've got a key. You'll come in if you want to.' And I never saw him again. The police must have collected him, because he didn't come back though his brother paid his rent. Perhaps he went inside. His brother became silent and sad, and, in a little while, he disappeared too.

On Midsummer's Eve 1949, my brother Tim married Birgitta, his Swedish fiancée, on the Island of Öland. Birgitta was very rich and very lovely. She had come to England as an agricultural student, and Tim had met her at a Young Farmers' Dance. Her father, Papa Sten Rudberg, was a very well known factory owner, a manufacturer of wooden houses. Though she was highly strung and a little unstable, Birgitta and I were always good friends. The marriage was on the current Swedish formula that neither Tim nor she demanded fidelity from the other, and they were always having *affaires*. The Swedes are a peculiar mixture. On the one hand, they're completely amoral. On the other, they have a terrific family feeling, a feeling that the home is the centre of everything, so the two of them kept their *affaires* out of the home, away from the family – they had four children: Peter, Wendy, Bonnie and Josephine – and the family was the focal point of their lives.

To jump ahead, in '78 I had a terrible letter from Birgitta saying that Tim had overstepped the mark by having an *affaire* with someone, today his wife, Meg, who, along with her two children, they'd allowed to live with them because her husband had left them and they'd nowhere to go. Tim had brought this relationship into the house, which she thought was unforgivable; she didn't know what to do. I realised this was a very distraught and one-sided account of the situation, but the relationship preyed on her mind so much that, in the winter of '79, she took the car up onto Bodmin Moor in a violent snow storm and, with a flex from a vacuum cleaner, directed the exhaust fumes into the inside of the car and committed suicide.

Why choose Bodmin Moor? Because, while Philippe and I were

working for the Canvins, my father, due to ill health, agreed with my mother to sell Four Winds and to move with her and my sister, Felicity, and Tim and Birgitta to Treworra, a low-lying, six-hundred-acre farm in North Cornwall on the edge of Bodmin Moor, where they'd have no dairy cattle but would just buy some steers for beef, which wouldn't require so much organisation and hard labour. My father was a very sick man indeed. My mother was quite prepared to go on running the dairy farm with the help of Frank, the foreman, as she had done when my father was in the army, but he was a very awkward patient, he *would* go out and direct things himself. The idea was that Tim would run the new farm as long as Daddy was alive, take over afterwards and look after my mother, and perhaps, after a little while, sell up and go to Sweden with Birgitta. Papa Sten had offered to take Tim into his business. He sent one of his wooden houses over to Tim and Birgitta as a wedding present, for assembling on Treworra. They called it Owl's Gate because they saw an owl sitting on the gate which led into the field where they decided to build.

Treworra itself is lovely – a large grey stone farmhouse with a strangely Gothic appearance. The film *Tom Jones* was made there, and several horror films due to a general creepiness. It's wet and cold – the wind just sweeps across the vast moor of Bodmin, and the scattered oaks, beeches and larch of the parkland cannot hold it back.

At the end of summer '49 I discovered that I was pregnant again. I'd written to my mother to tell her of the loss of my first baby, but I didn't write to tell her this one was coming for fear of losing it, too – I wanted, if possible, to present her and Daddy with a *fait accompli*. This time I was more organised. I got hold of Dr Annie right away, and she looked after me very well. The hospital I went to before was more an emergency hospital. Now she booked me in at Linden Grange Maternity Home, a beautiful place with beautiful grounds.

A short time before I was due to go in, in May, I received this telegram: 'Daddy died early yesterday morning – Be brave – Love Mother.' I telephoned her at once. She sounded completely shattered. He had died of a heart attack at Treworra after returning from a farm sale. I had never been close to him, and my mind was geared to birth rather than death. I knew the heart attacks were painful and he couldn't walk far, which made him angry – I was

89

glad there wouldn't be any more of that. There were a few tears, but I think they were mostly for my mother. There were still barriers caused by their treatment of Philippe, but no real resentment or anger; I was merely ashamed that they should think the way they did, and hurt because I had hurt them; I knew they couldn't be anyhow else, but neither could I.

I began to get the pain one afternoon, while Philippe was at work. I figured that the men would be coming in for their meal so I went on cooking. When Philippe came home I said, 'It's no good. I've prepared the men's food but I shall have to go to the hospital,' so he went out and got a taxi and took me there. It was still a very *slow* delivery, but not nearly as bad as before because I was given gas and air and, every time I got a pain, I just grabbed the mask and put it over my face and breathed into it, which would send the pain off for a little while. And that was Louis. Louis arrived at about eight o'clock on a beautiful spring morning, Saturday the 8th of May, 1950, just two days after my own birthday. I could hear the birds singing and, oh, it was just wonderful because I was so happy that this baby was alive; I'd half expected it would be the same as the last time, but he was alive. I was kept in hospital for a full fortnight and I thoroughly enjoyed that fortnight in spite of a strict old Scottish nurse who accused me of not feeding the child – his weight didn't always go up after his feed because he would often fall asleep at my breast.

Philippe, when he visited, showed no interest in the baby at all. All he would say was, 'It's got no chin.' I explained that babies when they are born very often *do* look as though they haven't got a chin, but his mind wandered to a pretty nurse. He made a row, caused rather a nasty atmosphere, when he came to take me home. He thought that *I* should have ordered the taxi; he said that the fact *he* had to order it showed I didn't want to return home. But, when we finally got into the taxi, he insisted on taking the baby and, from that moment, he was completely captivated by it.

We were not living the kind of life that Philippe envisaged for the son who was all-important to him now. He began to talk about running a farm, the matelot's dream. At first he'd been glad to have lodgers to make some money out of them, but now he resented them; once or twice he quarrelled with them very violently indeed. Then he had a bust-up with Management at the factory, where he was a shop steward, and he had to change to another firm. I thought, 'If he gets a farm and he's his own boss, at least there won't be all these rows.'

Under my father's will, Treworra went to Tim and I got a third share in the rent from some water meadows which, by the way, have recently been sold, but there was a clause which said that, if either my sister or I wished to borrow money from the estate for any project of our own, Tim was to lend it. I asked Tim if he could lend us some money so that we could try for a small farm. He was very chary but said if we found a suitable property he would advance £2,000. Philippe decided that he wanted to do dairying – Jersey cattle and pigs – and, on the advice of Lol who nevertheless pooh-poohed the idea, we began to read the advertisements in *The Farmers' Weekly* and *The Farmer and Stockbreeder* for farms in Wales where land was cheap. We noticed that, the further over the River Teifi you went, the cheaper and cheaper it became.

When the baby was six months we decided to have him christened Louis after Philippe, who was Louis Philippe, and after Auntie Nellie's nephew, my Uncle Louis Strange, who flew the Channel with Blériot. Now, Philippe was very definite that he didn't want Louis to be brought up as a Catholic. In fact, he didn't want him to be brought up with any religion, because he thought religion a terrific sham, a sort of drug to tell people they would be happy after they were dead so it didn't matter how poor and miserable they were while they were alive. But, for some reason, he *did* want a christening service, and we met the minister from the Baptist church nearby and both liked him very much. He told us Baptists didn't immerse small children, they did that to you when you were older, but they did have a service rather like a christening service, which welcomed children into the Church. Well, he didn't say what church and I was pretty sure that Louis wasn't going to be a Baptist, but it seemed rather nice to me, the way he put it. He said it was very much a matter of going to the church and declaring that you would do your best to bring the child up as a good human being. That really sounded attractive, though I liked the christening service of the Church of England best, and I still do. When you translate its olden language, all it means is that you know you've got a dangerous animal here and that you will do your best to let it do as little damage as possible. To be able to go to a public place and say this is something important.

Many people argue against the christening service because it says that a child is evil and is born into sin. But then a child *is* born into a sinful world and, with the first drop of mother's milk that it takes, it condones all the wars that have been fought, all the animals that have had to be killed, all the violence and cruelty that have gone before in order to get that little drop of milk there. And it seems to me that the child, even if it *knew* about this, couldn't possibly help it; it would have to eat to survive, and that in itself is a sinful thing if you accept that there is such a thing as sin. So I don't have any quarrel with this idea of a child being born evil and into a sinful world, because that's how it is. Anyway, Louis was taken to a Baptist church and christened Louis Dominic – why the Dominic, I can't remember – and it was a very nice little service with everybody crowding round and wanting to cuddle and hold this very beautiful baby. My mother and Aunt Nora came up to Crewe for the occasion and stayed in an hotel. Philippe avoided my mother and wouldn't speak to her.

By Christmas, our first with Louis, Philippe had found the farm he wanted – Parke Farm, Llanarth, near Aberaeron, Cardiganshire, now Dyfed. He had made Aberaeron the centre of his search for a farm, because his youngest sister, Marie Louise, lived there, and he could stay with her. 'Parke' was pronounced 'parquet' like the flooring. Louis was born in May; he was christened in October . . . I think it was in February '51 that we sold 19, Derrington Avenue and put down a deposit on Parke. I'm hazy about the dates. I'm rather like the nurse in *Romeo and Juliet* calculating that Juliet was fourteen:

> 'Tis since the earthquake now eleven years;
> And she was wean'd, I never shall forget it.
> Of all the days of the year, upon that day;
> For I had then laid wormwood to my dug.

Yes, we sold 19, Derrington Avenue in February, '51. Due to the outstanding mortgage and Hire Purchase Payments we only made a profit of about £100. The farm, fifty acres, cost £1,000. We intended to pay £500 out of Tim's loan and raise the rest by means of a mortgage. The balance of Tim's loan would be needed for initial machinery and stock – two cows, two heifers in calf, two sows in pig, a tractor, a trailer and a milking machine. While the deal was going through, we stayed with Marie Louise, Philippe's youngest sister, at her Council flat in Aberaeron.

There were ecstatic greetings – Marie was Philippe's favourite sister. But, by the end of the month or so that we were there, the relationship between brother and sister had worn very thin. I got quite friendly with Marie, you see, and this was like a red rag to a bull: anybody who was friendly with me, he would automatically turn against. There were the most terrific rows. 'Why are you so late, Philippe?! Dinner's been waiting half an hour!' 'I'll come in when I feel like it, not when you've decided when I ought to have dinner! And, anyway, what *is* there for dinner?! It's always the same. You only have English food here and it's a lot of shit!' 'Well, you're in Wales now. You·must eat English food.' 'But not sitting next to a belching woman like you!' And so on. Then he would stamp out of the house.

Marie Louise was married with a toddler of three. Thereby hangs a tale. Her husband, Ron, was a paraplegic in a wheelchair. He'd recently returned from hospital, having broken his back in a motorcycle accident. The extraordinary thing was that Ron, when he became a paraplegic, attracted a great many women. He was a very brave man, because he had a lot of pain, particularly in his arms, but he wouldn't have the nerve killed in case he lost the use of them. Marie installed him in a room of his own downstairs, and it took all her strength to get him into bed. But, as I say, ladies liked him. He would visit them in his wheelchair and, later, in one of those little invalid cars – he was very independent. A coolness developed between him and Marie though they never have actually divorced.

I was in two minds about taking Parke. From Llanarth on the Aberystwyth to Cardigan Road you had to walk two miles uphill along the Lampeter Road, then turn right through a farm, Nant-y-Meddal, which belonged to a Mrs Bradley, then cross a field and wade ankle-deep over a stream, a tributary of the Aeron, then climb a steep half-mile to this grey stone cottage with a cowshed attached and a barn with a farmyard at the front. The cottage was only two up and two down: a room with an Elsan bucket-loo and a sitting-room with larder and an alcove large enough to hold a marble slab for curing a pig downstairs, and, upstairs, two bedrooms with one tiny window in each. On the other hand, because they had never been farmed very rigorously, the fields were a riot of daffodils, violets, primroses and cowslips, to be succeeded by bluebells, wild roses and purple orchids. From the well, about ten minutes from the house, you looked down a long valley between two wooded hills to a triangle of bright electric blue which was Cardigan Bay, due to its sand clay bed the bluest water I've ever seen.

The particular corner of the bay that could be seen from Parke was New Quay, a village built on a steep slope under wooded cliffs under which was a little beach which you approached by a path that had a Welsh name meaning Little Milking Lane. When I first saw Dylan Thomas's *Under Milk Wood*, I was sure it must have been written about New Quay, it was so exactly right. But people kept saying, 'No! No! Llareggub, if it was based on anywhere, was based on Laugharne where he used to live.' Later, I discovered that my first instinct was right. He *was* living at New Quay when *Under Milk Wood* was written. New Quay has nothing to do with Llareggub now, except that Mrs Ogmore-Pritchard, the landlady, has taken over completely. The place is populated by guest houses and holiday homes that stare at you with vacant emptiness all winter. The name Llareggub spelt backwards is truer to the Thomas intention than ever.

When we'd finally climbed up to Parke and I saw it that first time, it looked absolutely derelict. I thought, 'It's certainly high enough to qualify for a hill farm subsidy, but we can't possibly take it.' The then owners, Mr and Mrs Beynon, truly frightened me. They were both *wild*-looking. She came to the door in bare feet and her black hair was unkempt and standing on end; her black dress was ragged at the hem. He was sitting on a settle in front of the fire in wellingtons, and he was *another* wild-looking character, with long black shaggy hair and stubbly cheeks and chin. There was a dresser in the corner and, over the fire with its big open chimney, hung a large kettle on a hook – I got to know that chimney very well: you had to have a fire at Parke all the year round. They offered us tea. If ever you go into a house in Wales, in Cardiganshire at any rate, you're offered a cup of tea, and it always runs to the same formula: the woman stands at the table and cuts slices of bread, and butters them as she talks; when you've finished what she's handed you, she automatically cuts another slice and butters it and hands it to you, and this goes on unless you tell her to stop.

Except a few chickens there were no animals that I could see. The well – there was no running water let alone electric light or telephone – was two fields away. Tradesmen's vans could only get as far as Nant-y-Meddal because of the stream, so we would have to collect our goods from there. We looked at the various fields and the boundaries and, though I was half despairing, the land seemed pretty good. That night we talked hard and long. By the end of the following morning we'd instructed Willy Lewis, an auctioneer in Aberaeron, to complete the purchase.

In April 1951, we moved up to Parke. The Beynons had taken their dresser, but they left us a settle and a bed. Louis slept in his pram for quite a while, and then we bought a cot for him from Marie Louise because her boy was getting too big for it. Gradually we bought chairs and things from a second-hand shop in Aber-aeron and brought them back by tractor and trailer which we had to get very early. We bathed in a tin bath. I drew water from the well in buckets and heated it in a large olden Welsh cauldron hung over the fire which I lit every morning. At first we didn't have any paraffin, but Eileen had taught me in the WRNS that furniture or shoe polish is very inflammable, so I smeared these on sticks. We burned a mixture of logs and coal which came by lorry to Nant-y-Meddal from where we collected them. Some of the logs were from apple trees on the farm which weren't bearing any more. Tradesmen such as the grocer, the butcher and the baker came as far as Nant-y-Meddal, and I'd go down for our supplies with a large sack. We seemed to eat nothing but rabbit. We lived on rabbits to such an extent at Parke that I can't look them in the face now, I simply can't eat them. Philippe trapped them with wire snares – you'd hear them screaming in the night – and then he wrung their necks. Day in, day out, we lived on rabbit.

The first winter was an absolute devil. The well froze over every winter and you had to bang it but, this one, it was also blocked up with snow which I'd to shovel into buckets and put to melt by the fire – a whole bucketful of snow would make less than a quarter of a bucket of water. It was a lonely life. The Welsh are very hospitable to strangers, but they don't really *like* them, and it was a struggle for them to speak English. The Bradleys of Nant-y-Meddal were English, but Philippe had a row with Mrs Bradley during our first week. A couple of collies and a young Alsatian rushed at you whenever you went through, and the Alsatian bit my left thigh and Philippe was very angry. He said, 'Those dogs ought to be killed!' I wasn't lonely consciously. There were cottages along the Lampeter Road and I used to pass the time of day with people and very often they would ask me in for a cup of tea when I came past.

95

I soon realised I should learn a little Welsh. But there was no *time* for lessons in Welsh just yet: I was too busy.

For light, Philippe hung a Tilly lamp on a hook in the ceiling. I never learned to light it; I simply couldn't master the technique; I used a candle if I was by myself. The Elsan bucket-loo we moved to the barn and I used that little room for washing clothes. The new loo in the barn was rather nice. We built it with bales of straw and left a gap for the door and put waterproof sheeting over the top. The bucket we still emptied into the cess pit in the yard.

We bought two sows at the market in Lampeter. Our two cows and two heifers we bought from people around. We made sure the cattle were tuberculin-tested so as to get more money for the milk though, for some reason, the cows in Cardiganshire did not get tuberculosis. I always think they should have researched this more – I think it was something to do with the soil. The two heifers and one of the cows were pedigree Jerseys – Philippe had decided to have a TT Jersey herd, and he always bought heifers in calf, hoping to build up the herd in that way. Thereby hangs a tale. All the time we were at Parke we only had one female calf. Now, Jersey bull calves are no good at all; they're no good even to raise for beef. You just had to send them to the market, where they went for next to nothing and were slaughtered for veal. It really seemed that there was something against us because all the calves born at Parke were bulls. All except one. We were very excited when this little heifer calf was born. But the blasted cow – Vedas was her name – must needs go and stand in the river to have the calf, and it nearly got drowned. We managed to rescue it just in time; we happened to see it in the river and we got it out and dried it and carried it home, almost dead. We got it on its feet, we got it eating, and then, for no reason at all, it started to shiver, and the next day it was dead. We called it Perdita. Perdita was the only heifer calf we had, and it died. It really seemed as if there was a jinx on Philippe's idea of building up a Jersey herd. Finally he hit on the idea of getting some bull Friesians and Welsh Blacks for beef. He was rather good at picking these at market, and we did sell one or two at a profit.

Two things on the farm I never took to – hoeing the turnips and the mangels and the carrots, and killing pigs. You had to keep weeding the root crops every day while they were growing, and the housework didn't get done, the cooking didn't get done and the washing didn't get washed. Then a sow would have a litter of seven or eight pigs, you'd bring them up, and off they'd go to market except one which you killed for your own use. Will Davies, the farmer from next door, showed us how to kill a pig. I hated the process. You just stuck a knife in its throat and let the blood come out. I could not watch this and, although you could shut out the sight, you couldn't shut out the noise. It was like a huge squeaking balloon gradually going down, fainter and fainter. When the pig was killed we laid it out on the marble slab in the larder and salted it for bacon after eating quite a lot of pork first. The salted joints were hung up on hooks in the ceiling and, whatever else you didn't have, you always had bacon to eat and could cut off bits as you wanted them.

It was the cheques from the Milk Marketing Board which were really keeping us alive. Milk was the only thing that was really making money. Though almost all of it went into the churn, I did make a little butter sometimes because butter was expensive. I had an old pickle jar, and I used to just shake and shake and shake the milk till it turned into butter which I then salted. I also made a little cheese, cottage cheese, very primitive, just a matter of milk curd that the moisture had dropped out of, through muslin hanging up outside the door.

In Cardiganshire there was a system of communal farming which Philippe wouldn't at first fall in with. The group of farmers that you belonged to would all turn up and help you at busy times. But, for haymaking and harvest, there was a definite code of practice – the oldest among the farmers had the privilege of cutting first. People did try to warn him – they said, 'Willy New Georgia has got first cut.' But he went ahead and cut the hay because it seemed the right moment to do it and, when he asked anyone to come and help stack it, they wouldn't, they stayed in their houses and didn't come. I then went round myself and asked them to come. They were perfectly courteous, but each one had an excuse. One said, 'I can't because, you see, I've got to visit my mother today. I always visit my mother today. It's something I can't break.' Another one said, 'Oh, I've got some business to settle in Aber-aeron.' Philippe had only cut one field and we raked that up and stacked it ourselves somehow, but the rest of the hay we lost completely. When it came to corn harvest, he followed the code, so others were prepared to cut and stack and thrash. From then on, Philippe was *forced* to give way.

*

97

Louis – we called him Dommy till we learned that 'dom' in Welsh means cow dung – was growing up, toddling about, though not quite able to walk. He learned the languages of animals long before he learned to talk English. He could make the exact noises of birds – curlews he was *very* good at. We didn't have any horses but, over one hedge, there was a woman who kept horses for riding and he could imitate her horses. And cows ... If a cow was outside in the yard sort of blaring, he would do the same, it was really as if they were talking to each other. He also talked with Bess, a Welsh sheepdog we had as a puppy from the Bradleys.

Bobby, my third child, was born on May the 13th, 1952. On learning that I was pregnant, Philippe had accused me of sleeping with his nephew, his sister Sophie's son who came to see us while we were staying with Marie Louise in Aberaeron. 'It's not my child!' he raged. 'It's Jimmy's child!' Well, Jimmy was fourteen! Philippe's rages were becoming almost schizophrenic. One day Bess hadn't come to heel and he gave her a thrashing with his hand and tied her up in the yard. Later I heard her howling. I said, 'It's very cold out there. We'll have to let her in tonight.' 'Oh, no,' said Philippe. 'Let her stay there. She's got to learn.' I didn't see that she'd to learn like that so, after a while, I said, 'She needs to be fed anyway. Or at least give her some water.' He said, 'No. She's all right. Leave her.' Well, later on, when he was sitting in front of the fire, dozing, I thought, 'I must give that dog some water,' and I went out to her. Bess had been tied with a slip-knot and was nearly strangled: she had pulled and pulled, and was nearly dead. I rushed in and got a knife and cut the rope – otherwise I couldn't have got it off, it was so tight. I was furious with Philippe. I woke him up and said, 'Whatever have you done to that dog?! You tied a slip-knot! It was choking!' He said, 'Oh? I didn't know I made a slip-knot.' It was something very strange that was going on.

While I was pregnant, Dr James of New Quay came to see me at least once a week and gave me special vitamin tablets; he was used to dealing with smallholders, and knew that the sort of food we ate lacked vitamins. Bobby was a very awkward baby – he *would* lie crossways or with his feet down. In the end, Dr James said I would have to go in to Aberystwyth Maternity Hospital a fortnight before the baby was due. So Tim came and took Louis to Treworra, and an ambulance took me to Aberystwyth. It helped enormously that I went to hospital early. I've always thought this ought to be studied more because, by the time the baby was actually born, I knew the surroundings, I knew the people, I was confident of where the loo was, it was all familiar and I'd relaxed. There was no sort of newness, and I'm sure that was why there was no pain with that baby, a breech baby, and why the delivery was all over in a couple of hours.

About a mile down the Lampeter Road from Parke was a public telephone kiosk. Philippe, having just delivered a cow of a calf, and with Bess about to have puppies, went down to the kiosk and rang the hospital. When he heard that the baby had been born, he jumped on a bus to Aberystwyth and came to see us in an orgy of maternity. He didn't come again for about three days, which I understood because he was so very busy. But, when he did come, he was in a terrible temper and he was late. At the end of visiting time, he had a quarrel with the nurse. He said he didn't see why he should be shut out, and why couldn't he see his wife, wasn't his wife his own wife and, anyway, why wasn't she coming home as there was a lot of work to do on the farm and he was having to manage it all himself? In the end, he turned his back and went off in a huff, and I didn't see him till he came to collect us in a taxi at the end of the fortnight prescribed. As a result, I used to cry and cry.

Nevertheless, this long spell in hospital not only provided a rest – the woman in the next bed, who had come in to have her eighth, said she regarded it as her annual holiday – it gave me a chance to read something again. The hospital boasted a book trolley. It was like a very small library that whizzed round the ward every now and then. Most of the books were either in Welsh or about Wales. I found some poems by Dylan Thomas, and a book that told me something about the Welsh poets from very early times to the moderns, and then I discovered a book consisting of a single long poem called *Taliesin through Logres* by a poet whose name I can't remember. 'Merlin ran through Logres in the wolf-month . . . hair caked with dung . . .' – so it began. Logres was King Arthur's legendary kingdom after the Romans left Britain. Taliesin was a real poet who is believed to have been a bard at King Arthur's Court, but there are two Taliesins, and it's not always easy to separate King Arthur's bard from the later one. I knew I would be frantically busy when I left hospital, but I made up my mind that, by hook or by crook, I would learn some Welsh and I would read the Welsh poets.

As with Louis, Philippe seemed at first to take no interest in Bobby at all, except to look at him and say he was ugly. But, when we got out of the taxi at Nant-y-Meddal and he actually held him before carrying him up the hill, his attitude completely changed. This is a moment I always look back to as a happy moment. It was a most lovely spring day, very warm, and, oh, there were foxgloves by the stream, and everything was pretty, the laburnum was out and there were still primroses and there were daisies. It was just a beautiful spring day, and we walked up to the house and Bobby became a member of the family. When he got a bit older, he was rather mischievous and, if he was doing anything he knew he shouldn't, he would shut his eyes because he thought that, if he shut his eyes, we couldn't see him. One day when he was, oh, not much more than a year old, he pulled himself up off his chair and took some steak I had specially cooked for Philippe and, hot as it was, began to eat it. When Philippe came in, he put it back on the plate and shut his eyes!

My mother, not Tim, brought Louis back from Treworra because she wanted to see the new baby. She didn't stay the night, as Auntie Nora, who was with her, wanted to see Aberystwyth, where they stayed at an hotel. She was absolutely shocked at the primitive state of Parke and she showed it, above all after visiting the loo in the barn. Philippe was hurt and, therefore, furious because I put up with her. When she'd gone, he kept me and the two babies awake most of the night, shouting and spitting – I've hesitated to mention it up to now but, whenever he was angry with me, he used to spit in my face, or on my head. A few days later, I had a letter from Mother advising me to take a firm line with him; something *must* be done about the way we lived; I was 'too sweet, too patient, too enduring.' This was the last straw. My sweet endurance snapped with a nasty little twang, and I wrote at once telling her that I was perfectly happy – a thumping lie! – that she had already caused a great deal of trouble, and would she please leave us in peace. She replied with a very short little note that she would, and I didn't see her again for several years.

Later, during the summer, Vicky, the cinema projectionist on HMS *St Vincent* who I'd kept up with by letter since our days in the WRNS and who was now a telephone operator for the GPO in

London, came to Parke with the intention of staying for a fortnight. Philippe had raised no objection when I told him she wanted to come but, once she arrived, he found reasons for not liking her. He said, 'Why must you *always* have visitors?!' Well, apart from the fleeting visits of Tim and Mother and Auntie Nora, Vicky was the only visitor I ever had! Unfortunately, Vicky chose to come at the very time Philippe had decided to clear out the barn and put all the corn and mash and so forth in mouse-proof containers. As there wasn't anything very much for the mice and rats to eat, they all invaded the house. It was really terrible: the mice were running all over the beds. One night, a mouse ran right over Vicky's face when she was asleep in bed, and woke her up. Next morning – she'd only been with us a week – she said, 'I'm very sorry, I cannot stay. I just can't stand the mice!' Philippe laughed fit to bust. He didn't say goodbye to her, and he was glad that she went.

7

I've always thought of mice as a symbol of freedom. A mouse is an animal that goes through all sorts of machinations to stay alive and to be free. I prize freedom tremendously. The trap for a human being is not to be free, to lose the ability to know what you want for yourself. Right from the time I was at school, I never wanted to believe what other people told me, I always wanted to test it out. I never questioned the authority of my mother or my father or my teachers, but I always thought that you had to preserve your freedom underneath all their demands. I felt the same about Philippe. He was a paranoiac: there were times when he hated everybody, and he used a rampant Bolshie politics to justify this. Some of what he said had a lot of truth in it, but I felt very strongly that I had to keep a balance, otherwise I would suck this in, I would actually be brainwashed. It was politics without a heart, communism without the real reasons for communism. It appeared to me that people whose lives were completely governed by politics or the extremes of religion had to tell themselves a lot of lies to make their theories come right. After Bobby was born, I began to write poems and then stories. This, I'm sure, was due to a strong need for an underneath freedom from Philippe's particular madness. What gave me confidence to begin to write was something Laban had said to me when I wrote for him once an essay on movement. I brought into it what I knew about life on the farm at Birch Close and how animals moved in different ways, and he told me, 'This is really good. You ought to write.' My first story, not the poems, was the result of an irritation at Philippe's talking about writing a novel and never writing it. Ever since coming ashore he had been planning to write a book, and jotting down in a notebook snippets of conversation he overheard.

We had no books of our own at Parke except Webster's Dictionary, and a large tome that Philippe had carried around the world with him as a kind of Bible – Ludwig's *Life of Napoleon*, from which he would sometimes read to me aloud. He had never read any novels by Somerset Maugham, though he read them all later, but, aboard ship, he had read some short stories including 'Rain' and 'The Letter', and also a book of criticism. On the strength of this, he had decided that ·Maugham was King, second only to Napoleon who was Emperor. He would talk about Maugham's ideas on 'the novel' by the hour. This would have been enjoyable if it had been conversation, but it wasn't: I was never more than a sounding board.

Mostly, however, he talked about his own novel, about the various characters and the plot, and about the politics he wanted to expose. The central figure would be a girl. An innocent, but silly and weak, she would spend a lot of her time in a pub where most of the action would take place. Her parents would be very religious, and they'd show up all the rottenness of religion. She would fall in love with a negro who would be disgusted by her, and he'd say, 'Leave me!' and she would go mad and start screaming, 'What a bloody set-up!' and all the people in the pub would show how rotten and greedy and bigoted they were. The heroine would be called Yvonne and the negro, the only good character in the novel, would be called Indigo. The novel would hold up a mirror to show people what they were really like, but they'd enjoy it because they wouldn't recognise themselves, they'd just think it was everybody else.

Writing 'The Fisherman's Tale', my first short story, was a tremendous relief. In a way it was an argument against the 'everybody's rotten' theory, and the fact that it was solid and finished may have been what made Philippe throw it back at me and call it 'crap'. He never liked me to write anything afterwards, and was always telling me to stop wasting my time 'writing shit'. From then on, he hardly seemed to me a lover, let alone a friend. My poem 'To a Lost Lover in Spring' is one of the few poems written at Parke that I've kept:

> You should have known
> That, if you plant

103

Those of my hybrid genre
In late October,
They surface in spring.
You were never a gardener?
Then, shall we say, you dropped me?
That, after all is no more than a manner of planting –
The way of the birds.
And what have I done with the winter?
I think I've been growing;
I burrowed and dived with the bayonet frost at my heels
Till I stumbled on bedrock,
And there I slept,
And from sleeping came dreaming,
And, waking, the dreams became words.
What novels lie locked in the dark of the daffodil bulbs?
What poetry pushes the fingers that feel for the light?
And what are the tales in the rattling sticks
That are somehow connected with roses?
Now they would be something.

If comparisons count,
It was little enough I could say,
But an essence of growing.

It says in the Prayer Book that service is perfect freedom. With
Philippe I was never physically free. In the service of writing I
would always be able to retain my freedom.

'The Fisherman's Tale' was very much a mixture of Wales and
Cornwall and legends. I wrote it in a loose-leaf notebook which I
bought in Aberaeron – I hadn't seen a notebook like that before: I
thought it would be very convenient to tear out pages when I
wanted and I've used loose-leaf notebooks and school exercise
books ever since. The story was about a Seal Princess who turns
into a perfectly nice little human being, and it ended with what, in
Cornwall, we used to call the Furry Dance or the Floral Dance and
everybody dancing through each other's houses. I doubt whether
it will ever be published, but it seems to me to have some sort of
merit. It has the disadvantage of not being completely a children's
tale and yet being really too naive for grown-ups. My second story,
which I *drafted* at Parke, was called 'The Voyage' and has the
same disadvantage. I was interested in the Indian boy that

Shakespeare mentions in *A Midsummer Night's Dream*, a change-ling, 'a lovely boy, stolen from an Indian king'. I made out that this boy was actually Sinbad the Sailor and I described his voyage back to El Basra and then to Baghdad and the Caliph Harun Al Rashid.

Most of the poems I wrote in Wales, I've torn up because they were pretty awful. Marie Louise's brother-in-law was the local travel-ling librarian. He went round with books in a van and would come to the bottom of the hill and sound his horn, and I used to go down to see what I could find. I was trying to learn Welsh, and I pestered him for books of Welsh poetry instead of the books of sermons which he provided for the farmers. An interest in Welsh poetry was something he didn't cater for, so I went to the Public Library in Aberaeron instead. There I found poems by Dafydd ap Gwilym, the fourteenth-century troubadour, and by Taliesin and the other Welsh bards, with the Welsh originals on one side and English prose translations on the other. What I wrote under their influence was archaic and very pretentious. I wrote one poem that began:

> And Courage? Hast thou Courage, voyager,
> Searching the land with grave, bewildered eye?

It went on in this vein, and there were lines worse than that! I mean, the ideas may have been praiseworthy, I don't know, but the style is not acceptable.

I consider that most of my poems which came from Wales were like very bad Tolkien, although I hadn't read Tolkien at that time. When I left Parke, I was still inclined to think of the Welsh bards, and I was wary of writing like them because I realised their magic, their very dignified and beautiful merman style, wouldn't fit today.

I wrote, at Parke, by the fire at night. Philippe very often didn't come back till late. Sometimes he went to the village pubs down at Llanarth – The Pen-y-Bont or The Llanina Arms. Sometimes he would go out contracting – working for a farmer who hasn't got the implements – and perhaps he would be asked to stay to supper. I believe that he was then being faithful to me.

As I wrote, I could hear the rabbits screaming in the traps. Often I would hear cats screaming, too. Philippe used to trap the cats from round about that had gone wild because they took our chickens. A cat caught in a trap makes an awful noise and, when

105

he heard it, he would go out and wring its neck as he did a rabbit's. I couldn't do that. Philippe never really *cared* for animals. Dogs would never obey him because he shouted at them and, the more he shouted, the more frightened they got and the less tractable they were. No, I'm wrong. There were one or two animals that he did like. One or two of the black and white Friesians which the children played with, he took a special fancy to himself. There was one that he'd brought up from a tiny calf, and he got so fond of it that he was distressed for a whole day when it finally had to go to market. He couldn't bear it: he kept saying, 'He trusted me! He trusted me!'

There was an incident with one of these calves which shows *me* in a bad light, but I think it needs to be said because it does show the rift that was coming between us. We were feeding a calf on a quarter of a bucket of milk three times a day – you had to milk the cow and keep some of the milk back for that calf to be fed. It was supposed to be fed in the morning and then at one o'clock and then again in the evening. Well, one day, I didn't get the one o'clock feed in because I was very busy with other things. I fed it at about three o'clock instead. Philippe came home at six and said he would feed the calf. He went to this little calf and came back in a frightful temper and said it wouldn't drink. I knew that this was because I fed it late, but I was so frightened of Philippe's rages which by now usually ended in physical violence, that I was afraid to explain. I said, 'Leave it a little bit longer. It will probably be hungry later.' He wouldn't do this. He said, 'No. It's got to be fed at six o'clock and it's nearly half past six now.' So he got out the baby's feeding bottle that we used for very small calves – small pigs, too – and he took it to the barn and he force-fed the calf, and it died. He had a terrible guilt feeling about this calf because he thought he'd killed it, which he had, though it was my fault. And, of course, his guilt came out for a time in rages at every little thing that went wrong – rages at the children, rages at me, rages at the animals – and I just couldn't tell him why the death had happened, I let him take the blame. I've always felt bad about that. But, you see, you somehow behaved like the dogs he shouted at behaved – you were so nervous that you became more disobedient than ever. Perhaps 'disobedient' is the wrong word. It was more that I couldn't be entirely frank with him and share the thoughts that mattered.

Very late, our third Christmas Eve at Parke, Philippe was at the pub and the children were in bed and I was making mince pies like you make griddle cakes, in a frying pan over the fire. I remember that I looked at the time and it was exactly twelve o'clock. There is a legend that at twelve o'clock on Christmas Eve the cattle in the stalls go down on their knees. I thought, 'I just wonder if it could possibly be true!' So I tiptoed out – I somehow thought that if the cattle *were* on their knees they mustn't know I was there – I tiptoed out, and I got as far as the cowshed door when I was struck by an absolute terror. I realised that if it was true, if the cattle actually *were* on their knees, it would be something so terrible, so supernatural, that I would be completely shattered. I didn't go into that cowshed; I couldn't. I went back to the fire and the mince pies. When Philippe came home from the pub, very maudlin, very drunk, I didn't tell him what had happened. You see, let's face it, I was by now downright afraid of Philippe, and of what he might say or do. And I was beginning to realise that there had *never* been much between us except a very strong physical attraction, a mutual physical attraction. He had decided to live in England and he didn't get on with Nancy and he felt very much alone, very insecure, and his grab at me was a grab at security – there was this strong physical attraction on both sides but, on his side, there was also a feeling that, if he married me, he would marry the country that he wanted to live in. When he hit me, he would be terribly sorry afterwards and he would cry and say, 'I didn't mean it! I don't know what came over me! You know how I am!' Well, I *did* know how he was.

I'd had a religious upbringing and, at first, I thought that I loved Philippe and that this was something that should be for ever – I counted the physical as love then, and I still count it as love, but not the whole of love. I'd learned that love lasted for ever and that, if it didn't, if it could be and then die, either I hadn't loved him at all or there wasn't any such thing as love, in which case there was no such thing as God. I've since come to think that it's the capacity for love in general that counts. If you have the capacity for love, as long as that remains, then you are alive spiritually and can believe that there is a God. At Parke my belief was wavering. Philippe's rages were, I knew, partly due to worry over the Jersey herd and the harvests and the fact that milk cheques, contracting and the sale of steers didn't cover the mortgage payments and our food and the food for the cattle and the fuel for the tractor and all our other expenses. But when he began to hit not only me but

107

Louis, how could I be sure the God I had been taught was love?

Philippe first hit Louis when he was only two, the year that Bobby was born and I was thirty. Louis was sitting on the trailer at the back of the tractor while Philippe was driving it and, for some reason, he jumped off. Philippe thought that he'd gone under the wheels of the trailer and he was frightened and he gave him an almighty hiding; the baby came home with bruises all over his face, and there were bruises on his neck which made him look as if he had been half strangled. Philippe wouldn't admit to having hurt him at all, but I knew that those bruises couldn't have been caused by just a fall.

I wonder if it was because of my religious doubts that I delayed over having Bobby christened. Strangely, it was Philippe who urged *me* to go and see the Church of England rector in Llanarth about a christening when Bobby was a year old. It so happened that the rector was out and I spoke to his wife instead. She said, 'How dangerous! You've left it rather late! If anything had happened to him! . . .', and Bobby was christened, Easter 1953, in Llanarth Parish Church. Marie Louise and her husband, Ron, were godparents.

As regards the contracting, we put advertisements in the local paper and they brought in no replies at all because the Welsh farmers would not write letters – if they wanted a contractor to plough or cut hay or harvest for them, they always used the telephone and we didn't have a telephone. So we put in an advertisement with the telephone number of the kiosk on the Lampeter Road – 'Monday to Friday between the hours of 9 and 12' – and I was deputised to go to this kiosk and stay there during those times in case the telephone rang with a contracting job. Louis would walk down with me, and I'd take Bobby in the pushchair. If it was fine they used to play around on the grass beside the kiosk; if it was wet they would have to come *into* the kiosk with me.

Because we had to spend three hours there every morning, I managed to educate the children in the way that my mother had educated me. You see, she'd taught me to read and write before I went to school and, in this three hours every morning, I taught them both to read and to make their letters and to write after a fashion.

In the spring of 1954 I was shopping in Llanarth in the post office cum village shop, and Tudor Owen Post Office introduced me to the village schoolmistress, and she said she would take Louis into her school. The lessons were given in Welsh, and a little boy who knew some English was supposed to translate for him because, otherwise, the lessons would go over his head. Louis would get some very strange versions of the lessons. I remember him coming home one day and saying, 'We had a good story today. It was about Joseph. Joseph was a nice little boy, but his brothers were a rotten lot of buggers who put him in a hole . . .'

Louis' formal Welsh education didn't last long because we had to leave Parke the following September. Philippe was worried crazy. For two successive years the hay and the corn had been beaten down by rain, rain, rain. The harvest of 1954 wasn't too bad, but by then we weren't being able to sell much milk because the cows had gone out of milk and some of the inseminations hadn't taken and so we hadn't got anything to replace them with, there were no young heifers coming on. We were having to sell the beef steers too young. We were having to sell the Jersey heifers at knock-down prices because they were without calf at heel. We made plans to go.

Philippe looked in *The Farmers' Weekly* and *The Farmer and Stockbreeder* for advertisements for a farm manager, and very soon got a job running a farm in Lincolnshire, a few miles from a market town called Bourne. We had a farm sale. There wasn't much to sell. We sold the geese and chickens and a few pigs and the few cows that were left and some farm implements. None of it fetched very much. We tried to sell the farm itself. One or two people came to look, but nobody would buy as it was so inaccessible. In the end, after finding a home for Bess, we just left, and I imagine that Willy Lewis, the auctioneer, took the place over and foreclosed the mortgage. We had bought our thrasher on Hire Purchase. We left that behind. Whether the Hire Purchase company collected it, we never knew.

We left Parke in blinding sleet and rain – the weather hadn't finished with us yet. Philippe hired a lorry from a driver recommended by Dan Soar. It was really too small to load furniture, even the little we had. We hadn't gone very far before a motorist drew level, making frantic signs, and shouting at the driver, 'Couple of bags fell off 'bout a mile back!' We went back, but could find no trace of the lost property – pots and pans and wellington

109

boots loaded on at the last minute. The weather was so awful that we didn't look for long, and set off again. A few miles further on, there was a crash. 'The lot's fell off now,' said the driver calmly. We climbed out again, and surveyed the chaotic mess in the road. Philippe turned to the driver: 'You bloody –!' He didn't get any further. He must have heard a noise from me, because I was laughing helplessly and I *couldn't* stop. It seemed to be Parke's final send-off. For once Philippe saw the funny side, too, and, even when we were loading the lorry again in driving rain, neither of us could stop laughing. If only we could have laughed together more often.

The farm we went to was a very large arable farm, and the cottage we lived in seemed really like heaven after Parke. We were able to furnish it with our few bits and pieces, and it had running water and electric light, and you could heat the water in an old-fashioned copper. Although I had a permanent sort of cold because of the distemper on the walls, I lost a lot of the weight I'd put on having the children, and this made me quite pleased. Though our neighbours were a very closed, narrow little community settled round a Wesleyan Chapel and I couldn't talk with them, the children could play in the cottage garden, and I had more time on my hands and could now tidy up my poems and short stories, *assess* them.

The farmer Philippe worked for had syphilis and had to be looked after by his wife. Philippe didn't do too badly as manager until the usual thing happened. It was a very large farm and he had several men under him who he had to direct, and if they made the slightest mistake he went right up in the air and swore at them and called them names. In the end – we only stayed about six months – the farmer had to sack him. I wasn't sorry, because he had a daughter who was a nyphomaniac. She used to lie in wait for the farm workers – they had all slept with her. Of course she made a dead set at Philippe. She had a peculiar, slant-eyed look and used to hide in the garden at night and peer in through the windows. But I don't *think* Philippe ever slept with her. Anyway, we left there – I think Philippe had a month's notice – so he could manage a dairy farm near the village of Dennington in Suffolk. We lived in a derelict manor house very like Langton Farm which, though it was impossible to heat, gave us plenty of space, and there was a very large garden where the children could play without going out into the fields – farms in the mechanical age are really very dangerous places for children; quite apart from the animals, there are so many things such as tractors and cutters which can hurt them.

We stayed there for about nine months. Philippe got on with the men and he liked having a herd of Friesians and using milking machines, but the farmer, a Mr Camberley, considered himself a gentleman. That sort of man can be dealt with, but certainly not by people like Philippe. Philippe asked for more pay as soon as we arrived, and Mr Camberley said, 'No. That is not possible. You get quite enough. Anyway, what is there to spend your money *on* around here?!' Philippe had the idea that he was talking down to him, and he was definitely a man who expected you to touch your forelock and take off your cap. In the end, Philippe went on strike and wouldn't go to work at all. He sent a message to Mr Camberley through one of the cowmen, asking would Mr Camberley come to the house. Well, Mr Camberley did come to the house, but he wasn't very pleased about being summoned in that way and, when he came, Philippe managed to treat him as if *he* were the farm worker and he, Philippe, the employer. He said, 'You need me to work for you, don't you? But do you ever get off your arse yourself? You think you can run a farm by sitting in your own house and looking after your wife and daughter. Well, you can't! *You* have to come into it, too! Now, if I'm going to stay here, you'll have to pay me more, and the farm will have to be completely reorganised . . .' The upshot was that Mr Camberley still refused to pay him more and said he wasn't going to reorganise the farm and that Philippe had better take a month's notice, which he did.

This time, he only landed a job as ordinary cowman for a farmer in High Wycombe. The cowman he was to replace was still working and was living in the cottage which would eventually be ours, but Philippe could live, meanwhile, in a room in the farmhouse and store our furniture in the dry barn. We decided that, because we had to leave our present home to make way for a new manager, I had better go with the children to the Claytons' house in Didsbury, Manchester, where Philippe and I had first met. I had never been separated from Philippe before, and I expected to join him in High Wycombe very soon. This was November 1955, and, as things turned out, we didn't meet again till the following February.

*

111

Since our marriage, Marie Antoinette, another of Philippe's sisters, who had married a German engineer high up in the Krupp works and had spent all the war trapped in Germany, had left her husband and elder boy, Manfred, and come with Egon, her younger boy, a toddler, to live with Nancy and Harry in Manchester. Unfortunately, Nancy, who welcomed her at first, got it into her head that Marie Antoinette and Harry were having an *affaire*. They denied it, but Nancy went berserk and left the house, leaving Marie Antoinette to look after the boarders. Harry then left in search of Nancy and found her living in a seaside guest house, near Blackpool, where she died soon afterwards. Harry had never returned to the house in Didsbury which he let to Marie Antoinette, who was surviving as best she could, using the methods she had learned to survive by in Germany, namely prostitution and theft. The house wasn't really a boarding house any more because Marie Antoinette was just living there with her lover, a student at the university who got an allowance from his mother. So now there were me, Louis, Bobby, Egon, Marie Antoinette, her lover, and Peter, their child, whose legs didn't work because she'd tried to get rid of him when she was pregnant. We agreed that I should pay £1 a week until Philippe sent me money from High Wycombe, when I would pay a proper rent.

Philippe, meanwhile, went to High Wycombe and stayed with the farmer and stored our furniture in the barn, and waited and waited for the cowman he was replacing to leave his cottage. But not only did the cowman not leave the cottage, he didn't leave his job either, so Philippe was stuck there without a job, without pay and without his own home for at least a fortnight. He wrote to me and said he had begun to write a play instead of a novel, he was giving up farming and he was off to London to find work there. He left our furniture in this barn in High Wycombe – it's still there as far as I know – and went to London and, after a while, wrote to me from a hostel in the region of Notting Hill Gate, asking could I send him some money. I had a Post Office Book with about £5 left in it and I nearly sent that, but Marie said, 'If anybody has that money, *I* want it. You're not to send it. He shouldn't ask for it in the first place and, anyhow, he's left you, he doesn't want you to rejoin him at all.' I was pretty sure he did want me to rejoin him, especially because he was fond of the children, but, as she was now keeping the three of us for nothing, I said to her, 'I'll write to him and see exactly what he needs the money *for*.'

So I wrote, and the letter was sent back 'Gone Away' and Marie, of course, said this proved her point. She said, 'You'll have to choose. Either go to London with the children and find Philippe, or stay here and throw in your lot with me. I could do with a partner. Especially for shoplifting. Shoplifting's much easier if you've got a partner.' She was stealing the daily groceries and the sort of things which can be sold to second-hand shops, and at night she sometimes went out on the game. I said that I didn't *want* to go on the game and that I shouldn't be any *good* at shoplifting, I was completely unlucky and unfitted for it and I'd be caught first time. She said, 'Very well. You'll have to leave. I suggest you take your children and go to London and find Philippe.' I didn't see what else I could do. The money in my Post Office Book was just enough to pay for overnight coach fares from Didsbury to London, and would give us a couple of nights' bed and breakfast if necessary. Armed with the clue of Philippe's last address, we travelled to London the next night.

8

It was pouring wet and very cold when we arrived in London. We walked from Victoria Coach Station to the Underground. The pushchair was in High Wycombe with the furniture, but the children could walk with me – Bobby and Louis were rising four and six. I was carrying a suitcase. Something in me kept saying, 'Don't panic!' In situations like this an icy calm descends, and I don't panic. I knew that our chances of finding Philippe were slim, and, if we did find him, what then? And how would he receive us? Would *he* panic?

We went straight to Philippe's last known address. It was a place very much like the one we ran in Crewe, where men slept in dormitories. The man in charge told us Philippe was again staying there, and would be back from work at around six thirty, so we hung around in shops and in an Italian café till then. I remember it was Italian because there was ravioli on the menu and I didn't know what ravioli was. All I could afford was some milk for the children, a cup of coffee for myself and a buttered roll each. When we returned to the hostel, Philippe seemed genuinely glad to see us. He said to Bobby, 'My goodness, I hardly know you, Bob! You've changed!' and Bobby said, 'People grow, you know!'

As I say, it was *pouring* with rain – we were wearing macs and gumboots. Philippe couldn't have us at the hostel, but he asked if he could bring us in for a minute to dry the children's hair and dry me. So we went in and dried up a bit. Philippe had left the hostel before because he hadn't any money, but he'd sold his watch and so he could afford to come back. I never did ask where he stayed meanwhile. He now had a job as a sheet-metal worker with

114

a firm called Napiers' in Acton, but he hadn't yet been paid because they had this system of keeping a week's money in hand. He lent us his umbrella and came with us till we found a bed and breakfast place nearby to stay the night.

Next day I filled in forms so that my eight shillings a week Family Allowance money could be transferred from Manchester, and I spent the day looking for a cheap room for me and the children. Now that I knew where Philippe was, I decided not to bother him as I knew he was already worried sick. But I found out that, once people realised you had children, the only way to get a room or a flat was to put down about £300 key money. We had to spend our second night in the bed and breakfast place again. One nice thing, though, did surprise me. When I bought rolls and milk for the children in cafés, I found that, several times, complete strangers came over and offered unexpected kindness. One man bought the children a bar of chocolate. Another, when Louis was asking for a milk shake and I kept saying, 'We can't afford it!', bought us *all* a milk shake. It surprised me very much. Really, I wouldn't have thought . . . you know . . . I mean we were a drop in the bucket in a big city.

On the third day a newsagent advised me to go with the children to Camden Town; he said Camden Town was the place to look, I'd probably get something there. We went by Tube to Camden Town. No luck at all, and it was getting late. I saw a policeman standing on a corner. I said, 'I've got these children, and I've simply no place for them to sleep tonight. I don't know what I'm going to do. We shall have to sleep on the streets.' He said, 'Well, you can't do that. You're not allowed to do it. If you do that, your children will be taken away from you.' I said, 'What can I do?! Can *you* recommend anything?' He said, 'Have you any money?' I said, 'About five shillings.' He said, 'Yes, well . . . it's not enough for a night's lodging. I can recommend you a hostel, but it's right on the other side of town. It's in Westmoreland Road and, to get there, you'll have to go to the Borough Tube Station. It's Newington Lodge and it's a hostel for mothers with children, but,' he said, 'I warn you – if you try to keep the children out on the streets all night, you'll be arrested and the children will be taken into care.'

We went immediately on the Underground to the Borough. It was dark when we came out of the station. None of the street names was the one I wanted. I wasn't very good at reading the

115

A–Z Philippe had given me. Eventually, I asked a man did he know Westmoreland Road. He said, 'We-ell, um, yes, let me see . . . It's a bit difficult to tell you, but I'll take you there,' and, with that, he picked up Bobby and walked on. I thought, 'What a kind man!' He said, 'Why do you want Westmoreland Road?' I said, 'Well, there's a hostel there – Newington Lodge. We're hoping to get a place for the night.' He said, 'Don't go there! It's dreadful! Come home with me!' I said, 'Really, I can't.'

You see, I realised by now that he thought I was a tart. I said, 'I have a husband, and he certainly wouldn't like it if I came home with you.' He said, 'I don't think you *have* a husband! You come home with me!' and – he had Bobby in one arm – he took hold of me with his free hand and *propelled* me in the direction he wanted us to go. I broke away. I said, 'I can't! It would cause a *great* deal of trouble. My husband would really be very angry if he found that I had accepted hospitality from a stranger.' So he argued a bit more, then put Bobby down and said, 'Oh, get the hell out of it, you bitch! Westmoreland Road's that road, there!'

Well, it was dark and I couldn't see the road signs, and it was completely the wrong road. We walked up this road for ages, and it was raining, and it wasn't Westmoreland Road at all, we were a long way from it. Again I told myself not to panic. We were in an unlit road and there were no people about. The children were getting very tired. I kept talking to them and telling them we were nearly there, and then Bobby began to cry. I stopped, thinking I'd have to carry him for a while, but all he said was, 'You're *squeezing* my hand!' and I realised I was applying the old cure for stage-fright, the trick of putting all the tension into one place – a finger, a toe, an arm, an elbow – so that the rest of you can dance quite lightheartedly. Poor Bobby was getting the full force of all my submerged panic. Finally, I met a woman, and I asked *her* to direct me, which she did. Her directions were long and tortuous but, by dint of asking several other people, we did get to Newington Lodge in the end.

It was after ten o'clock. The words 'Newington Lodge' were on the door, and there was a bell. I rang the bell, and a man looked out from a little sort of spyhole. I told him the story and how the police had directed us and how we'd had a lot of trouble getting there. I think it was the word 'police' which persuaded him to open up in the end. A woman came to meet us. She was dressed in a nurse's uniform, a very dirty and dilapidated nurse's uniform.

116

She was a cockney, but she was very nice, very kind. She said, 'You're pretty late, and I don't know if there's any soup left,' but she went to the kitchen and said, 'Oh yes, well, at least have some soup before you go to bed because I expect you're hungry.' We were so glad to get this soup that I really could have kissed her.

Then she showed us into the dormitory, which was a very congested place. The beds were . . . well, I thought they were right up against each other, but actually they weren't. You see, everybody had their luggage and prams and various possessions in all the available spaces. The woman said, 'I'd like to give the children a bed to themselves – they could sleep one each end – but we simply only *have* one bed, so you will all have to sleep together.' I said that I was so tired I didn't give a damn where we slept, and I didn't. She gave us a couple of blankets, and I put the children in at one end, and I got in the other. There were no sheets, and I discovered afterwards that the blankets were seldom changed; you slept in blankets that had been slept in for the last six months by a lot of people.

In the morning we went into the next room for breakfast, which was tea and thick slices of bread and butter. I was told I'd have to see the Warden at nine o'clock and then, after I'd seen the Warden, we would have to go out with everyone else and not come back till seven at night. A lot of us were marshalled up a long staircase to the Warden's office and sat outside on a bench till our name was called. A very officious woman was in charge of us. I came to really dislike her. I suppose she'd had a lot of rough people to deal with, but she treated you as if you were going to cause trouble. 'Well, sit there! – there's plenty of room! . . . Well, the children don't need to sit down! – they've got strong enough legs! . . . Now, when you go in to the Warden, don't waste his time with any silly complaints, because this is all we can do for you! . . .' I didn't like that one at all!

So I took the children in with me to see the Warden, and he *was* a *very* nice man. Somehow that made a lot of difference. He couldn't do anything for us, he couldn't alter the awful situation that we were in, but somehow it was nice to be talked to as a human being. It was sort of on an equal footing – you know, he was quite friendly and relaxed, and not in a uniform. He said, 'I understand you came in late last night. How did that happen?' and I told him that we'd been directed by the police and then

117

misdirected. He said, 'It was a terrible night, wasn't it? I suppose the children were wet when you got them in. It must have been awful.' Then he said, 'How do you come to be *in* this position?' I told him how Philippe and I had run a farm which failed in Wales and so on, and that we couldn't find anywhere to live as a family in London at a price we could afford. He seemed to be very sorry. He said, 'And what do you intend to do now?' I said, 'As soon as I go out this morning, I'm going to go on looking for a place to live.' He said, 'That's what everyone here is doing but, if you've come from outside London, I can't even put you on the Housing List because you haven't lived in London long enough to be entitled. Well,' he said, 'at least you've got a roof over your head now. Stay here as long as you like but, meanwhile, do everything you possibly can to find accommodation.' This was somehow – it was just the way he said it, I think – it was somehow very encouraging.

Newington Lodge was a place where they sent homeless women who had children, because it *is* against the law to keep children on the streets at night; men and women on their own can take their chance. I came across women there in all *sorts* of situations. There was a girl with two most beautiful little Chinese children – they were like little dolls. *She* wasn't Chinese, she was Irish, but she was very pretty and she had lovely dresses. While we were waiting to go to sleep on my second night, she told me that she'd been living with a Chinese student and that he had suddenly got a letter from his father in Hong Kong saying that he had found a bride for him and that he was to go home at once. Of course, he had to go, because what his father said meant everything to him and, not only that, if he'd stayed here his allowance would have been stopped. The story seemed like *Madame Butterfly* in reverse. She said, 'He had plenty of money while he was here, but we spent it all. He cried when he went away, and said, "Whatever you do, don't give up the children, don't give up the children!" We had a very expensive flat, but I couldn't pay for it any more, so we were out on the street with nowhere to go.' The three of them looked so *completely* defenceless. They were so beautifully dressed, and you felt that those clothes would very soon turn to rags.

After that first morning, I didn't have to see the Warden again. You had to be out all day, and just left at nine o'clock and came back at seven. The first couple of days were awful, because I had literally no money till the eight shillings Family Allowance money

118

came through. This hostel didn't cost any money if you had none, but we only had this bread and butter and tea to go out on. I managed to take some extra bread and butter so I had something to give the children at midday but, apart from that, we had nothing except soup and bread at night. I took the children into shops and into a big public library nearby where I showed them books, all the ones I remembered – the fairy tales, *Alice*, Edward Lear, *The Wind in the Willows* . . . It rained a lot, and the time small children will stay quiet in a shop or a library is limited.

Later when this eight shillings a week came through, we used to go down into the Underground and go round and round on the Circle Line or right to the end of a line and back again. The children loved that; they were warm and dry, and always quiet and happy as long as they could count the stations and watch the people getting on and off. We went to art galleries, and we used to go to Trafalgar Square to feed the pigeons. And, oh, we went to all the parks – Hyde Park, Green Park, Holland Park . . . The fine days were quite easy.

Although I didn't really miss Wales, and although the children had Welsh accents, I missed Welsh voices tremendously. London voices seemed very harsh. A group of drunken Welshmen on the Underground inspired this poem, 'Three Welshmen Sang':

> Three Welshmen sang in the Underground.
> They were drunk, of course,
> And they sang in the underground way of the Welsh,
> With a soaring lift of the harp
> From a subterranean lake of sound
> That erupts in a fountain of sunlight,
> Warm from the throb of the fiery heart
> Entombed in its coffin of coal . . .

I didn't see Philippe at all to begin with. I could write to him and telephone him, but he couldn't do the same. Letters couldn't be delivered to Newington Lodge – it's dreadful, it's unthinkable. When I did contact him again, we used to meet in a nasty little café in Whitehall at weekends. He gave me some money and that did make things easier. I remember I tried to get a job at Guy's Hospital, which was near the hostel – domestic work. I would have had to have the children with me while I did the work, and that wasn't any impediment, they were prepared to countenance that, but No. When I went for the interview, the Almoner said, 'We can't possibly employ you from that address.'

Philippe wasn't looking for a place for us to live, but I was looking all the time. One very wet day, I had some flats to see. I knew pretty well that it would be fruitless, but at least they were advertised, and I had to try everything. I thought, 'Well, I *can't* drag the children about in this rain,' so I went to the nearest vicarage and I said to the vicar's wife, 'I want to ask you a terrific favour. We can't find a place to live, and I have these addresses to go to. Could you possibly have the children while I go and look for them? There's just a chance.' She said, 'No. That's quite impossible. A lot of people come here. I'm afraid we can't help you.' And that was that.

For about a month I was travelling around looking for a home. Then, one night, when I took the children back to the hostel at about seven, they didn't want their soup. They should have been hungry because we'd been walking about all day, but they just wouldn't eat anything, and they were both very sick in the night. By the morning, I could feel that they both had temperatures, so I went to the awful woman. I said, 'The children are ill! I don't know what to do! Shall I take them to the hospital?' She said, 'You must take them to the Warden first, and report that they're ill, and say the symptoms. *Then* you'd better go to the hospital.' This was Guy's, where I'd tried to get a job.

It was dreadful getting them there, because neither of them were in a fit state to walk, they were really quite ill. Needless to say, the awful woman, after putting her hand to their foreheads and feeling their pulse, had said, 'There's nothing much wrong with them at all!' At the hospital, I'd to wait all morning while a doctor took the children away for tests. When he returned, he said, 'The children will have to stay here. They've got a type of dysentery. What have they been eating?' I said, 'In cafés they usually have milk and rolls of some sort. But I rather suspect the soup at Newington Lodge – they do have it there every night and it isn't very good.' It had cabbage and things floating in it, and sometimes it had a peculiar taste to it and it smelt that sort of sour smell when soup has been ... you know ... you can't put green vegetables into a stock pot and keep them indefinitely because they will go sour; they have to be put in fresh every day. Anyway, the doctor said, 'The children will have to stay here. In fact, as we don't know exactly what this germ is they've caught, they will have to be taken to the isolation hospital. You can come with them in the ambulance if you like, but you'll have to get back by yourself.'

So I went with the children in the ambulance out into the country, to somewhere near Epsom, and came back by train on my own. I hated leaving them, and the nurse said, 'It's better if you don't say goodbye.' I could see the sense of that. I was to wish the parents at Paray House, the school where I eventually became a teacher, would understand it, too. She said, 'Just go,' so I turned my back and left them to complete strangers, which was awful, but I had to do it. It was Mothering Sunday. When I came out of the isolation hospital, I went to the nearest church, where there was a special children's service going on. I sat through this service, and cried and cried. Afterwards, the vicar was organising a sort of picnic for the children on the lawn, and giving them all flowers. He must have seen me coming out in floods of tears, but he probably thought I was moved by the service and he didn't say anything except, 'Oh, do come into the garden. There's some very nice cake.'

The hospital said that the children would be there for about a fortnight – it did prove to be a kind of dysentery – and that I wasn't to visit them, I was just to telephone. Now this left me really free to search for accommodation. And the very first thing I did the next day was to get a job – you could get a job in Central London at the drop of a hat in those days. I worked at The Omelette Bar in Leicester Square. There, at least, I had enough to eat, far too much really, and also I could earn a little money. I didn't tell them it was only temporary, otherwise they wouldn't have taken me. We were paid by the week, and they didn't make you go a week in hand. It was a late night place, and you worked in shifts – one day you had the afternoon off, the next the morning. I was washing up at first, but then one of the waitresses left and I went on the tables. I was there with a girl from the hostel whose children had been taken into care. As waitresses we wore black dresses with a little lacy apron and a cap. By not saying the work was temporary, we managed to get a room together in Camden Town.

I rang the isolation hospital every day. It was nearly a month before the children were ready to come out and, meanwhile, I found a room in a house in Ferdinand Street, Chalk Farm, where Philippe could visit me and I thought I might be able to get them in later. The room was at the top of the house, and it was fairly

121

big with a large double bed. The landlady lived on the ground floor, and I was completely alone in the house except for her. Gradually I talked to her about my children and having nowhere for them to go when they came out of isolation. I paid my rent regularly and we got to like each other, and she said, 'Well, yes. You can bring them here.' And this is what I did, and we all slept in the large double bed.

The day I finally fetched them out of the hospital was a very traumatic time. I rang up the hospital one morning, and they said, 'You can fetch them this afternoon.' I said, 'Could I possibly leave it till tomorrow? For one thing I'm on duty this afternoon at my place of work and, for another, nothing's ready for them where I live.' But they were absolutely adamant, they said, 'No. You can't leave them another day. We want the beds. It'll have to be this afternoon.' It was all very bad. I saw the proprietor of The Omelette Bar at lunchtime, and explained. I said, 'I just can't come to work any more. I've *got* to get my children out of hospital this afternoon and look after them. They've sprung it on me very suddenly.' He was very angry because I hadn't told him the situation. I said, 'Well, what would *you* have done?! I had to do something! I had to get some money somehow!' He calmed down a bit but he sacked me there and then, and I didn't get paid for the work I'd done that week.

We lived in Chalk Farm for perhaps two months, and Philippe visited us quite often. He was still in the men's hostel at Notting Hill Gate and he was earning money, and only occasionally did he burst into one of his rages. We got Louis into a school for a few weeks – he had his sixth birthday there. I used to take him, with Bobby, straight from school onto Primrose Hill, where they used to play for a while, and afterwards go round the back of the Zoo, where you could see the animals but didn't have to pay to go in.

Then something dreadful happened. The old lady fell ill and had to be removed to a Home, and her daughter told us we would have to get out because the Council was going to purchase the site. I don't know . . . the feeling that I'd gone through all this and got a place to live and then it was taken away . . . the feeling of utter tiredness – I've never felt so tired in my life as I did at that time. I'd telephoned my mother in a sort of triumph that we'd at last a roof over our heads, and she'd come up from Treworra to visit us and stayed at the Bedford Corner Hotel. Now, in despair, I telephoned her with this news, and she actually invited us to Treworra. I didn't want to go; I still hoped to find somewhere else for all of us, including Philippe. She asked could she speak to Louis. Louis said, 'Hullo, Gran! Mum's been crying!' I was annoyed about that, because I didn't want her to know! She was really worried about us. She said, 'If you can't find anywhere, you must come here.'

We got out of the house in Ferdinand Street just before the bulldozers moved in. I'd said to the landlady's daughter, 'How on earth can we get out?! We've absolutely nowhere to go! Nobody will take children!' She said, 'Have you tried the Salvation Army? The Salvation Army will take children sometimes.' So I tried the Salvation Army and the only hostel that would take children was their Hopetown Hostel in Whitechapel.

Philippe took us to the Hopetown Hostel in a taxi. I had the impression that the people who ran the place were absolute saints, and I had a bed to myself and the children slept together in another, but I could see that the place wasn't right for them, so I asked my mother would she be prepared to have them while I found work and earned enough money to pay key money for a flat. She said, 'Yes, of course!' and Phillippe gave me enough money to take them by coach down to Cornwall, where Tim and Birgitta, based at Owl's Gate, their Swedish house, were doing a little farming but mainly concentrating on running a Pony Camp, which was most successful. Surprise, surprise! My mother offered me a glass of sherry when I went into the drawing-room at Treworra. Before, perhaps because of my father, she would never have offered *me* a drink – in fact apart from a bottle of cooking sherry in the kitchen, she wouldn't have alcohol in the house. And yet here was drink in abundance, with home-made bottles of wine always going off with a bang in the airing cupboard. I felt at last I could somehow be friends again with my mother as long as my husband wasn't there, though I would never forget her phrase about not pulling my chestnuts out of the fire and I never, ever did ask her for direct financial help.

I left the children after a day or two – they were only too happy to be at Treworra – and returned to the Salvation Army for about a month, while I looked for a job and a new place to live. Writing had taken the place of dancing in my life, but I did make an attempt, a rather feeble attempt, to get back into dancing. It would have been impossible with the children and, anyhow, I'd have had to re-train for quite some time, but I happened to see Ronnie Curran's name on a poster in Shaftesbury Avenue – Ronnie Curran, the Scottish boy at the Art of Movement Studio in Manchester. He'd got into a revue. I thought, 'Oh, that's Ronnie!' and I went to see him. He'd lost his Scottish accent, he'd a sort of mid-Atlantic slick accent and he was covered in Max Factor and wore peculiar clothes. But he greeted me very kindly, he said, 'Well, it's the same old doll!'

I asked him my chances of getting back into dancing. He said, 'If you want to get back into dancing, you'll have to put yourself in shape a bit. I mean, did you know you'd lost a tooth?!' And I *had*, I'd lost a front tooth! He said, 'It's tough going, doll, and you can do it. But get yourself fixed up a bit first. Get that tooth put in and get your hair done and get yourself some clothes . . .' But he was thinking in terms of revue. I was concerned with getting back to ballet, which was absolutely impossible given the sort of life I was leading.

The Captain of the Hopetown Hostel was very nice, and there was no mention of religion at all, you didn't have to join in the services. Some of the inmates were very paranoiac, very bolshie. One of them said to me, 'I don't know what they've put me in this *hole* for! I wasn't supposed to come here at all!' I said, 'Well, you know, they do some pretty good work here.' She said, 'I don't want to be *concerned* with "pretty good work"! I want a home of my own!' There was one woman who used to take beer in and get drunk and sing. There was another on the gate who was always very snooty about granting you admittance. She couldn't keep you out, but she always pretended that she had the power. 'Well, I don't know, I don't know. I don't know anything about you. I don't know your name, and I'm not sure . . . You see this is a Home, a Home for respectable people. I don't know, I don't know. Your story *may* be quite true, but I don't know . . .' She would go on like this and eventually let you in!

That July I found a furnished room in Shepherd's Bush for me and Philippe. We had a gas ring on the landing and two single beds which we put together. It was a reasonably happy interlude. Philippe was changing, after the usual huffs, from factory to factory, but he was working on his play which he called *The Devil and Pink Bird*.

I took a job in a Lyons teashop in Shepherd's Bush – sometimes I was 'on steam', as they called serving tea, and sometimes I had to see that the cake-stands were replenished. While I was working at Joe's, I began a short story called 'Elizabeth Meets the Fairies'. For the first time, I was working with black people, and I got very friendly with them, I liked them. Nearly all the people who worked there were West Indian, except me, some London girls and Mrs Timmons, the manageress, who was also a Londoner. I made a friend of a West Indian woman from Barbados called Elizabeth. Elizabeth had one little girl, and her husband had died when they got over here. She was a little bit different from the other black people who worked at Joe's, because she was very curious about this new country that she'd come to. All she'd seen of it was London, and she wanted to know what happened in the country-side, what sort of houses people lived in, what did they eat, something about the life. So I wrote this story about Elizabeth and her little girl going into the country, and I made the little girl into Elizabeth, and Elizabeth met the fairies, which were the most English thing I could think of.

By this I don't mean that fairies in general are particularly English, but they seem to attach themselves to places. There's nothing in Ireland as Irish as the leprechaun. Welsh and Scottish fairies are more dignified, and usually life-size. Cross the Channel and you get something different again. Like my story 'The Voyage', 'Elizabeth Meets the Fairies' was centred on *A Midsummer Night's Dream*, and again it was a story about a child, but not quite a children's story. The fairies Elizabeth met were the four Shake-spearean fairies: Pease-Blossom, Cobweb, Moth and Mustard Seed.

All the people I worked with were warm and friendly, and the way they talked fascinated me. They used such terrific imagery. I couldn't understand a lot of it, but it would be something like: 'Oh, de day de ship went down! It was like de Day of Judgement. De wind blew like de Trumpet of Judgement. It was runnin' here and runnin' dere . . .' Or 'Where you come?' I said I'd come from the country on a farm. 'Farm?! Didn't know dey had farms in England! Farm. We lived on a farm. No good now! Tornado come. Den we think we come to England. Tornado, she blow like billy-be-damned and all de houses flutterin' down . . .'

There were two tables when we sat down for meals, and the white people sat at one and the black people at the other. After a while, I thought there was something wrong about this, and I went and sat at the black table. Mrs Timmons asked me to come back; she said I shouldn't eat with the blacks. I said, 'Why not?'

She couldn't answer really but, from then on, she and all the white girls were very stand-offish, and I somehow felt my days were numbered, I had an insecure feeling that I would be dismissed if Mrs Timmons could find somebody else. In fact, I wasn't dismissed; I left of my own accord because Philippe and I were moving from our room in Shepherd's Bush. And, whether by design or accident, *all* the black population of that Lyons teashop went as well. We all gave a week's notice at the same time.

Philippe and I moved from Shepherd's Bush because I had at last come to grips with the idea that we would never get a flat without paying key money. In November, I wrote to my brother, Tim, and asked him if he could possibly lend me about £300, and I could then get a flat and have the children back. It was about a fortnight before a reply came. He said he wasn't prepared to lend any more money unless Philippe went officially bankrupt; we already owed the £2,000 he'd lent for Parke and he'd written that off; he wasn't asking for the £2,000 back, but, for a further £300, those were his terms. (It so happens that everything *was* paid back in 1970 after my mother's death.) Well, nothing on earth would drag Philippe into an Official Receiver's Office. I said to him that he was in the *position* of a bankrupt and we wouldn't be any worse off, but he simply would not comply. I wrote to Tim and told him so. Then, in a very few days, I got another letter, this time from my sister-in-law, Birgitta, who was always a great friend of mine, saying that under a legal arrangement she owned at least half of the Treworra property, so she was enclosing a cheque from the Burgess Estate for £300; she also corroborated what I thought already, that having the boys for so long was too big a strain on my mother.

I could now go ahead. I went to the only place I knew which dealt with this key money racket – Central and Suburban Flats in Dean Street. At first the man quoted figures like £900 for what was called 'fixtures and fittings' to make the system more or less on the side of the law. I said, 'I'm very sorry, but I can't afford anything like that. I've only £300 to spend at the very most.' So he said, 'It just so happens I've a flat in Clapham which is only demanding two pounds five shillings a week rent and £300 for fixtures and fittings.' I asked for an 'order to view' and he came with me out to Clapham there and then to show me over the flat. It was on the ground floor of Bowyer House, a house in Voltaire

126

Road, with five floors and a basement, and attached to David Greig's, the grocers. There were side steps going up to the front door and, when you walked in, you walked straight into the kitchen sink in the little hallway. There was a small sitting-room at the front with a bay window, and a small shuttered bedroom at the back. In another *tiny* little room was a bathroom with a tin bath in it, a very antiquated gas geyser, a gas cooker and a lavatory – you had to cook in the same room as the lavatory.

The whole building looked terribly knocked about and an awful mess. It was an old house that had been turned, very unsuccessfully, into twelve flats. I said, 'I'll have to consult my husband,' and I brought Philippe over at the weekend to see the place – Flat 1 of this terrible Bowyer House, which seemed to have little in its favour except that Voltaire might have visited it when staying on Clapham Common with the Macaulays, who were friends of the Bowyers. Philippe said, 'Why not wait a bit and get something better? The children seem to be quite happy with your mother.' I couldn't stomach this; I realised that he was making the thing indefinite, and what he really wanted was the children to stay at Treworra so we could go on living an easy sort of life in Shepherd's Bush till Kingdom Come. I said, 'No. We've got to get the children back. They're always asking for us. Also, my mother shouldn't be burdened at her age with two growing boys. It's too much for her.' He said, 'All right. We'll take it,' and we did. The previous tenant had left curtains and carpets, and we bought a bed-settee for the shuttered bedroom and bunk beds for the children in the sitting-room – all on Hire Purchase – and gradually collected wardrobe, tables, chairs and so on from the junk shop over the road. My mother brought the children up in the car – whereupon, after welcoming *them*, Philippe disappeared into the shuttered room till she left – and I always think of that Christmas as a happy one because the family was together again. Then, in the New Year of '57, we got Bobby into Cresset Street Nursery School and Louis into Clapham Manor Infants, and I got a morning job as a clerk with Freeman's, a mail order firm in Stockwell. I could be home every afternoon in time to collect them.

Philippe and I, when we first went to live in this ancient seat of the Bowyers, went quite often to West End shows and we also joined two theatre *clubs* (the Hovenden and the New Watergate). I only went once with him to a theatre club (the Hovenden) – there was a terrific row afterwards because I talked to other people. But he went to the clubs often, and I think he may have had one or two girlfriends at this time. He used to talk a lot about girls that he met and, sometimes, he would stay away all night. He said that he was looking for girls to write about, and to act in his own play. When he went to theatres, I would go with him and we would leave the children in the charge of an old lady who lived in the flat directly above our own, a Mrs Tilling.

Philippe wrote under the name 'Louis de Jardin', and we would wait at Stage Doors so that he could hand a copy of *The Devil and Pink Bird*, which, candidly, I thought was awful but couldn't say so, to people he recognised. He gave a copy to Elizabeth Sellars, who was appearing in *Tea and Sympathy*. He wanted her to play his heroine, Yvonne. He also handed Anne Jellicoe, who had written *The Knack* for the Royal Court, a copy. She was very good to him. She *did* read the play and, although he was furious about it, gave some very constructive criticism. She said, in her letter, that the play *had* a certain power, but where it went wrong was to include too many ideas; better, she said, to give the audience a glass of orange juice from one orange that has been completely squeezed than to throw them a lot of oranges that have been only half squeezed.

So, meeting no success with this play, Philippe wrote a musical, and this, though it was derived from Frank Norman and was set in the East End and the cockney wasn't all that natural because he hardly knew the East End except to take me to the Hopetown Hostel and go there to bespeak a suit, was very funny – I remember laughing at it. At first it was called *East End Story*, then it became *Oranges and Lemons* and finally we settled on *Leap Year Story* because the hero was too shy to make love to his girl and she always had to take the initiative. Philippe wrote the 'book', and I wrote the lyrics and made up the music; I would sing the tunes to him and, if he liked them, go up a lot of stairs to a man in a little office in Denmark Street, Tin Pan Alley, who would tap them out on his piano and produce piano copies.

We went to see a very good musical called *Irma La Douce*. Shani Wallis followed Elizabeth Seal as the star of that, and she came out of the theatre arm in arm with a man who, wonder of wonders, happened to be her agent, and Philippe gave them *Leap Year Story* to look at. I happen to know she read it, because I had to go to her Park Lane apartment in the end to retrieve it, and it was lying torn and dog-eared on her bed. After *Leap Year Story*, we collaborated on another musical called *Bella Soho*, which was never completed. I still have some of the piano transcriptions and lyrics of each of these musicals – songs such as 'Harry' and 'Gruber Street Devil' and 'Hot Dog Salami'. (Philippe, though, destroyed the 'books', together with all his other writing, before committing suicide.) He was buying and reading a lot of literature now – for instance a new translation of *The Kama Sutra*, all the novels of Somerset Maugham, criticism by Mary McCarthy and Kenneth Tynan, Steegmuller's biography of Flaubert and Christopher Hassall's of Eddie Marsh, plays by Ibsen, Chekhov, Strindberg, Tennessee Williams, Eugene O'Neill . . . After he saw a play, he would always buy a copy of the text. I like doing this myself.

We came home one night, after an excursion to the theatre, and found the children in their bunk beds, all right and asleep, but they both looked very white and they'd large pads of cotton wool over their foreheads. Philippe, who was a chain smoker, had left an ashtray full of cigarette butts, and they'd found the matches I'd hidden, lit some butts and made themselves very sick. Mrs Tilling had put them to bed with these cotton wool pads, wrung out in cold water, over their foreheads. Louis has never smoked since, and Bobby just has a cigarette now and again, and never inhales.

After a term, Bobby was able to join Louis at Clapham Manor Infants School. They rather missed the country, especially all the animals. There was a little square of grass outside for them to play on, but what had been the driveway to Bowyer House was now an absolutely filthy lane where all the alcoholics and dossers of the district congregated because it was at the back of David Greig's supermarket and they could find food to eat in the dustbins . . . As I say, the children did miss animals and, for a long time, I thought, 'We can't have them. We haven't enough room for ourselves, let alone animals.' But one day, coming home from school, they found on the pavement a cardboard box in which there were two abandoned kittens, two very ordinary tabby kittens, and of course, they were frantic to keep them. In the end, I weakly told them they could. Philippe, when he came home, was very angry, saying we hadn't consulted him and the kittens would have to go. All I could think of was to take them to the RSPCA to be put down but, as the children were heartbroken at the idea, I secreted them in the corner by the gas stove in the kitchen, and I *think* Philippe sort

129

of forgot about them and then, later, used them as an example of how his opinion didn't count and nobody did what they were told.

Louis called his kitten Jacqueline after his sweetheart of the moment – I can never remember Louis, from Bowyer House onwards, being without a girlfriend; he was heartbroken when he had to go up from the Infants into the Juniors, because he was leaving Jacqueline behind. When I said to him, 'There are lots of girls up in the Juniors,' he replied, 'Yes, but none of them *love* me!' Bobby's kitten was called Tibby. Tibby was a bit of a nuisance because she would climb right up onto the roof. Bobby didn't seem to bother about this at all; he would stand on the lawn watching her and saying, 'Tib ain't arf a good climber! She ain't arf a good climber!' He was very cockney by this time. In fact, both the children were. They'd had very marked Welsh accents when we came up from Wales, but they very soon acquired tough cockney accents in self-defence because, at school, their Welsh accents were laughed at and disliked as something alien.

As regards the cockney accents, I had to take Bobby to the doctor for a diphtheria injection and she noticed a lisp he'd developed which I rather liked. She said, 'He must have speech therapy to get rid of this lisp. He's a good-*looking* child, a well *bred* child. This is going to be a great *handicap* to him later on.' When we got home I was telling Philippe that the doctor thought Bobby well bred, when there was a terrific commotion outside and we looked and saw Bobby standing on the wall, shouting at someone on the other side. 'Old big 'ead! Fat bonth! Old big 'ead! Fat bonth!' He lost his lisp soon afterwards when he got his second teeth.

The cats didn't last very long. They grew up but, one after the other, they got a kind of cancer which the vet said they caught from mice. They just started miaowing and miaowing and miaowing, and the miaowing became fainter and fainter, and I had to have them put to sleep. I don't think Philippe was sorry, because originally we'd preserved their lives against his wishes. But, as I've said elsewhere, animals with him were a very individual thing: any animal that he really did take a fancy to, he would do anything for. Before Tibby and Jacqueline were spayed, Jacqueline had a litter of kittens, all of which died except one, which had only two toes on one of its feet. Philippe made great friends with this kitten. He let him play with his fingers and called him Jiffy. Now, Jiffy he would do *anything* for. He used to buy special meat for him and cut it up. Unfortunately – of course it *would* have

130

to be the only cat he was fond of – Jiffy was stolen while foraging over at David Greig's. Philippe looked for him for days. Later, we took in another stray, a little white kitten who always looked somehow rather thin and disreputable: she never fattened up. We called her Mitzi after Mitzi Gaynor who, I believe, was murdered by the Mafia in broad daylight in Times Square, New York. I gave her name to the heroine, the persona, of a poem. Later she died having some kittens.

Doris Muldoon was one of the tenants at Bowyer House. The others were Mr and Mrs Tilling, several West Indian families, a prostitute called Jean, below us, and, right at the top, Raymond, an odd bod who seemed to live with a crowd of rather wild Australians professing to be actors and writers. There was an Irishman and his mother in another flat, and, behind us, an Irish couple with three children. The partitions between the flats were paper-thin, and the Irish couple were on the verge of a break-up. Their rows came through, word for word – 'And didn't it ever occur to you that *I* might want to go out?! . . . I didn't *want* the children! . . . If you were dead they'd never get you in the coffin because your John Thomas would still be sticking up! . . .' 'You'll get what's coming! You'll see! . . .' What *we* sounded like to *them*, heaven only knows! Mr and Mrs Tilling, every step they took we could hear. Philippe went up several times and accused them of tramping about on purpose – when he was writing, he couldn't stand noise.
 Doris lived in Flat 4. She was absolutely wonderful to me when Philippe died. She was an Irishwoman, in her fifties I suppose, but bright blonde. She was married to a half Irish, half West Indian sailor called Jack, who only did what they call 'off-shore trips'. He came home at intervals, and I always thought he looked like the typical sailor – a *huge* man with a great trunk on his shoulder. Doris was always nagging at him to leave the sea, because she didn't like being left alone at night, but the trouble was that he always *had* to go back to sea as they couldn't really stand each other for more than a fortnight; there were awful rows at the end of it. One time when he came home, he brought a parrot. I thought, 'Oh my goodness! He looks exactly like Long John Silver!' There was this great trunk on his shoulder and a parrot in a cage on his other side. Jack took opium and Doris couldn't stop him. My poem 'Parrot Song' is very much based on Doris and Jack and the parrot which used to walk about their flat. After my husband died, a

131

terrible stench filled Doris's flat; it absolutely reeked. Now, Doris was very superstitious, and Jack was away, so she came down to me and said, 'The death smell has entered my home, and it's your husband!' I went up the stairs with her, and there *was* this *terrible* stench in her flat. I pulled back the sofa, and what did I find lying there but this blinking parrot of Jack's, quite dead,

> For tragedy never is far away . . .
> Time ticks on to the judgement day,
> But the parrot turns all to a parodie,
> And a farce will intrude on a tragedie.

9

I've jumped too far ahead. At the end of 1956, we moved into this Bowyer House, loosely connected with Thomas Macaulay who, with Wilberforce, had been very much concerned with the emancipation of slaves, and where, by a kind of poetic justice, apart from the Irish, most of the tenants were their descendants. In 1957 and 1958, though Philippe was doing full-time metal work and I was working mornings at Freeman's adding up the figures on the weekly 'tickets' sent in by agents about the mail order stock they'd sold, we had caught the writing bug good and proper, and not only was I helping Philippe with songs and lyrics for his musicals, I was writing new poems and had embarked on a fourth short story called 'Dandy Davey', based on the gypsies I'd known in Dorset, one of whom I made to be a natural dancer who is discovered by a man very much like von Laban.

In the winter of '58, Philippe came home one evening and told me he'd give up metal work because the noise was making him ill and his hands were shaking; what he really wanted to do was to stay at home for the moment and write. His hands seemed steady to me, but there *was* something wrong with him. You see, his rages were definitely getting worse. I really was terrified now because sometimes he hardly knew what he was doing, and I daren't leave him alone with the children because I felt that they might upset something or do something mischievous and that he would get into one of his furies and perhaps hit them badly. It wasn't Bobby so much – I can't remember him ever hitting Bobby hard – but Louis. Apart from that incident at Parke, he really did black his eye once or twice. Also, there was one dreadful day when

I came home and Louis, with a lot of bruises on him, was standing in a corner, stark naked on a very cold day. Philippe was asleep – he'd just left him there and told him not to move. I told Louis to get dressed at once and get warm and, when I woke Philippe up, he flew into a rage with me and said that Louis had bruised himself on something, he'd never hit him and he'd never told him to stand there. It wasn't so, because a child doesn't tell lies in that way. Louis was too frightened to move from that corner.

Well, Philippe made another attempt to find a congenial job, and he worked for some engineers somewhere for about a fortnight. Then, when he came home one evening, he just collapsed on the bed, wouldn't eat, and wouldn't say anything except that I mustn't come into the room, I'd better sleep in the sitting-room that night. So I got cushions and a blanket, and slept on the floor of the sitting-room with the children that night. For a few days Philippe stayed in the bedroom. Even in the daytime he wouldn't open the heavy shutters on the window; he just stayed there in the dark, and I went to work and the children went to school. I left food, and I suppose he must have got up and made himself a meal and some tea or coffee while we were out, but he wouldn't see any of us.

Finally I said to him, 'Something is dreadfully wrong. We ought to have the doctor.' He consented, and Dr Kalra, an Indian, the son of an old man who treated the children for chicken pox when we first came and had now handed down his practice, came and saw Philippe, and said to me afterwards, 'There's nothing physically wrong at all, but I do think he should see a psychiatrist. I can recommend a good man, a Mr Bennett,' and Philippe, while drawing Sickness Benefit, started going for sessions on the National Health with Mr Bennett at the Maudsley Hospital almost every week for about two years.

I wonder if he told Mr Bennett how he abused the children. I wonder if he told him that, when I went to work in the mornings, he accused me, very explicitly, of going to sexual orgies, and that, if he saw me talking to a woman, he accused me of being a lesbian, and that, if he saw me talking to a man, he accused me of being a whore. Did he tell – and although he wasn't very big, he was a powerful man – did he tell that he would rush at me and spit on me and hit me with the full force of his hand across the face or on the head, and, if I wasn't absolutely on balance, I used to sometimes fall over till I learned, after taking the children to a circus on

134

Clapham Common, to pick up a chair like a lion tamer and hold it in front of me as a defence? Did he tell him that he resented me sitting up at night writing my own work, which was 'shit', when I ought to be cleaning the flat?

I stood against Philippe about poetry, and how I did so I don't really know because, when he found me writing it, he always flew into a rage. Poetry was something now I *had* to do, I don't know why, I really don't know why, in spite of the fact that it was making Philippe more angry than ever. Perhaps there was the feeling that he was being *unjust*, the feeling of 'Why *shouldn't* I do it!' When Bobby was eight and with Louis in the Juniors at Clapham Manor and better able to look after himself after school hours till I got home, I had taken a full-time job as a filing clerk with Hamblin's, the Queen's opticians in Wigmore Street. Surely, after a day's work at Hamblin's and in the flat, I was *entitled* to sit writing when the children were tucked up in bed?!

I began to think that some of my poems could be sent away for publication. Raymond, upstairs, was a self-styled poet. He asked us up to a party one night. I told him about my poems and that I wanted to try to publish some of them. He said, 'You ought to get *The Writers' and Artists' Year Book*. You can get addresses of publishers and magazines in there.' Only about five or six magazines in the list wanted poems, but the first of these I came across was *Adam International Review*. So, without knowing anything about *Adam* at all, I sent the editor three poems which I'd written recently.

One of these was 'The Dancing Vicar'. I'd never taken the children to church because Philippe didn't like that, but they wanted the social life of the local church, St John's, and they were members of the choir and the Wolf Cubs. St John's did a show every Christmas, and the vicar was a very good tap dancer.

> Jerk up the curtain
> The footlights flicker
> The spotlight lands on the dancing vicar
> Bundle of energy fervour and charm
> A shot of new blood in the half dead arm
> Only Mammon can mend the roof
> Beat it up vicar
> Cleave that hoof!

Why should a man
With the vaudeville feet
Choose to perform at the Sunday School treat?
Now worldly gain couldn't be the clue
For a dancing bishop would hardly do.
Can a soul be saved by the jazzman's beat?
I doubt it vicar
But – dig that heat!

The clerics cant-compromise
Bargain and bungle
The Ladies' Guild is the usual jungle
The inner music seems mute or drowned
In the supersonorganized Merry-go-round.
But the roof must be mended with hotcha-chas
Or the congregation might see the stars.

What is it sifts out of the deadpan pelf?
Why, the shining ascent of the vicar himself
In the midst of it all there's a hope grown faint
Yes, it might add up if it bred a saint.
The spotlight's lost him, the drums beat quicker
Go it you jazzmen
Come on vicar!

I *thought* my poems, on the bus, in the Underground, walking
along. It was then only a matter of scribbling them down and
constant revision. And holidays in Cornwall helped. Every summer
I went with the children to Treworra until they were old enough
to go by themselves – all through their childhood they spent their
summer holidays there.

Treworra was absolute heaven for Bobby and Louis. It was
freedom. They could play as they used to in Wales. They rode
every day. They fished. Tim had a boat, the *June*, a sailing boat
with a motor, at a little harbour called Boscastle; Bobby and Louis
and Tim's four children spent a lot of time sailing around on the
June. Then there were all the animals which they adored. And
Mother would take them around in the car, perhaps to go
swimming somewhere; 'Gran' was somehow the centrepiece of the
whole thing. At first I took them down by train to Treworra myself,
stayed for a few days, came back to London, then went back to
fetch them. Later, when I just took them to the station, they always

hoped I wouldn't go there to fetch them on return because Gran had always given them enough money to take a taxi. Needless to say, Mother had galvanised all the local people into acting, just the same as she'd done in Dorset. Very often there was something going on while I was there. I saw her in *Arsenic and Old Lace* in the theatre in Camelford when she was going on for seventy. She was very, very good. In fact she and Tim at one time had a Romany caravan which they used to take to various places in Cornwall to perform plays. They called their amateur company The Davidstow Players.

I sent the three poems to *Adam* during the winter of 1960, and I didn't hear anything of them for a long time; in fact, I'd forgotten I'd sent them. And then, one July evening the following year when I got back from Hamblin's, Jean, the prostitute in the basement, knocked on our door and said that, during the day while I was out at work, she had a phone call from a Mr Greene who asked whether there was a Miss Doubell in the same building. She said that she didn't know a Miss Doubell, so he asked was there anybody called Patricia. She said she did know a Patricia who lived in Flat 1. He said, 'Yes, that's right. That's the address – Flat 1, Bowyer House.' Anyway, this was a Mr Greene, and she had his telephone number which I was to ring as soon as possible. I duly rang Mr Greene, who wasn't Mr Greene but Mr Grindea – Jean had thought he said, 'Greene, dear,' He asked me to come to his flat the following Saturday morning at eleven o'clock. So, on a warm July morning in 1961, I first met Miron Grindea, editor of *Adam International Review*, and had coffee with him on the balcony of his house at Emperor's Gate in Kensington.

We had a very nice talk. He was a little man with grey, rather brushed-back hair and very sort of wide-open, grey eyes rather like a child's, and he was very nicely dressed in a nicely cut suit and waistcoat. He spoke with an accent. He was a Romanian who had come from Bucharest to London in 1939, running in front of the German troops as they marched in, and bringing with him this Romanian Jewish literary magazine *Adam*, of which he was the editor. No, he didn't found the magazine – he still has pictures of the founding members, and most of them were Jewish rabbis. But it was always a *liberal* magazine as its name indicates – 'Adam' simply meant Man or Humanity; the idea of Art, Drama, Architecture and Music was tacked on later. When he came to London and started an English version of the magazine, he didn't speak any English and he had to get people to translate. He spoke French but not English so a lot of the magazine was in French – it still is.

He asked me about the background to the poems I'd sent him. I've always felt completely daft explaining poems, but I did explain, and afterwards I said, 'I'm sorry. I've done it very badly. You must think I'm a very silly person.' He said, 'I think you're a very *frightened* person.' And I *was* frightened: I was frightened of a lot of things at that time. I was even frightened of visiting this house in Emperor's Gate. I was very frightened then really of meeting anybody, partly because of natural shyness, partly because I hadn't got any proper clothes, but mostly because of Philippe's violent reactions when I talked to other people. I knew it wasn't any good arguing with Philippe when he was in these moods, because they were absolutely irrational, so I used to keep quiet except for the occasional nervous laugh. I do *have* a nervous laugh and he would then say, 'What are you laughing at?! Why are you laughing at me?!' He would hit me if he thought I was laughing at him, unless I managed to get the chair to defend myself fast enough.

So Grindea was right about my being frightened – frightened of Philippe and frightened of the world in general. I was even having nightmares: an animal kept jumping at me and waking me up. Grindea was also right, and being very wise, when he said to me, 'The world is composed of two sets of people – those who are poets and those who are not. The poets may never write a line of poetry, but they have the poetic temperament, and you will find that you can talk to this type of person, whereas you're always slightly alien to the other.' He thought I should meet other poets. I said, 'They are on the page. I can read them in books.' He said, 'No. That is not the same. That's all right when you've arrived at a certain technique. You will develop by *meeting* other poets and comparing their work and their styles. It's obvious you've been writing very much alone. You have a talent and we must develop it. I have a friend, Howard Sergeant, who edits the magazine *Outposts*. He also runs regular Poetry Readings at the Crown and Greyhound pub in Dulwich.' He gave me the Dulwich Group's card. 'Tell him, when you go, that I am publishing your work and he will give you a reading. Yes, I would like to accept "The Dancing Vicar". It will be published in a most important edition of my magazine, the 300th edition for which there is going to be a celebration.' Meanwhile, he told me, I should submit poems not only to *Outposts* but also to the *Farmers' Weekly*, the *London Magazine* and *Encounter*, always mentioning his name.

I went home feeling absolutely on top of the world because I'd talked to this wonderful person. I really hadn't struck anything like it before. The nearest had been Kurt Jooss, and Lisa Ullman and Rudolf von Laban. I felt that, though I was a baby and very new at the game, I was being shown into a new world, and that he accepted me into this world. On one of his walls was a picture of a hawk. 'That's how Picasso sees me,' he said. He showed me some drawings that Miro had given him ... He was saying, to a certain extent, 'This is what you are now going to be part of,' and I found it very exciting. I told Philippe all about the visit. I shouldn't have done: I was *crazy* to do so. There was a terrific storm. He assumed that Grindea and I had been fornicating.

10

After about a year of sessions at the Maudsley, Philippe seemed to be so much better that Mr Bennett suggested he train as a Chartered Accountant. His paranoia, he said, was due to delayed-action shock from the worry of losing Parke, to his distaste for factory work – the noise, the people and the continuous need to keep a steady hand – and to his disappointments as a writer. He discovered he was very good at figures – Philippe *could* do anything with figures; he could work out problems very quickly – and he thought this gift ought to be put to some use; an accountancy job would be congenial and, incidentally, he would make a lot of money. So for two years, while receiving Sickness Benefit, Philippe went to an Adult Education Centre in Brixton, and was trained as an accountant. He qualified with flying colours and, as a fully-fledged Chartered Accountant, could command very well paid jobs, even without experience.

For his first job he was paid about £20 a week. This was really quite staggering, and the kind of money that we'd never heard of. The job lasted about three months. You see, he *was* very clever with figures, but he couldn't stand any sort of human error. When he got to this firm, its affairs, like the affairs of most firms as far as I can make out, were in a terrific mess. People had made mistakes; some had probably been fiddling. On his course, everything was smooth – it was just a matter of figures, and all the figures worked out. But when the human element came in, it drove Philippe quite mad. Of course, the usual thing happened. He said the whole system would have to be reorganised, it was completely hopeless, he couldn't work it as it was. This time he didn't get

140

in a temper and insult the boss. He just kept complaining and carping so much that, in the end, the boss said, 'If you feel like that, Mr Kass, you'd better go,' and he did.

Well, other jobs came very easily, though they kept blowing up in his face. The next one was Chief Accountant for a firm of meat purveyors, I remember, down in the City. But he just couldn't take the hassle at this firm either; he called his employers nasty names and swore at them and, of course, that was the end, they couldn't keep him or they'd lose face. In '66 after about six of these jobs over a period of two to three years, he had another of those attacks when he lay in darkness on our bed in the shuttered room, wouldn't let me in, except, this time, to take him food on a tray, and wouldn't see the children.

The children were at secondary school. Bobby was at Aristotle, a huge comprehensive. Whenever I went there, it seemed to me an absolute madhouse – there was always a terrific din, there were children throwing things, children running this way and that, teachers shouting. But Bobby seemed to thrive on it: he was very happy. Louis was at Henry Thornton Grammar. There was one terrible evening after he'd first gone there. Philippe bashed him across the face because he hadn't cleaned his shoes, and he disappeared. I waited till about ten o'clock and, by then, I was so worried that I went to the police. It was snowing and *very* cold. I said at the station, 'My son has run off after a row with his father. Can you help me find him?' They said, 'We can't do very much, but give us a description in case we see him.' In the small hours, he was picked up in Surbiton. He was trying to walk to Treworra. He'd had a fall on the icy road and was walking along, crying. It was getting light, about five o'clock, when the police brought him back. Immediately he got inside, he shouted, 'I'm not going to live with my Dad any more!' The policeman was very stern. He said, 'You *will* live with your Dad! We're not going chasing after you again! You stay at home, young man!' Philippe wasn't angry with him for running away, which relieved me very much. I think he was glad to have him back.

Now, back in '63, a West Indian family moved out of Bowyer House, and a Mr and Mrs Phelan, an Irish couple, took their place. Mr and Mrs Phelan had a daughter called Debbie, who would have then been about nine. I particularly noticed Debbie because she used to perform plays with her friends on the lawn and, though

141

they were older than she, Louis and Bobby joined her little drama club. A very earnest little boy called Joe Nolan wrote the plays, I remember. One was called 'The Prince's Bride'. He made a list of the cast which I've still got somewhere. Debbie Phelan was the prince's bride, Louis Kass was the prince, and Joe Crump was the wicked uncle. Who Bobby was, I do not know. Everybody danced the Twist at the end. It really was a very enjoyable entertainment.

In the spring of 1967, when Debbie Phelan was rising thirteen, Philippe must have felt better, because he opened the shutters of the bedroom, and what he saw was Debbie playing on the square of grass outside the house. In a completely different voice than he'd used for months, he quickly called me and said, 'Look at this! Look at this!' So I ran into the bedroom and it was unshuttered, letting the light in for a change, and, outside, Debbie was playing on the lawn. I said, 'Oh yes. That's Debbie Phelan,' and I told him the number of the flat the Phelans lived in. He then went into ecstasies about this girl: 'Oh, isn't she *lovely*?! Isn't she *beautiful*?! I've never seen anyone like her!' Well, she *was* a *pretty* girl. She had long black hair and very lovely blue eyes and a rather graceful way of moving about.

I was very grateful to Debbie – at first, at any rate – because Philippe came out of his room and he was completely different, quite good-tempered and happy again. He didn't go back to work, but spent most of his time watching for Debbie to come out and play on the lawn. This appeared to me quite innocent, and I think to some extent it was, because he would never have hurt this child in any way. He next took to sitting on a bench outside, and he would call Debbie over and ask her to draw things for him. He would rave about whatever Debbie drew – mostly flowers and leaves. He came in to me with one of these pictures one day and said, 'Isn't it beautiful? It's better than any professional artist could possibly do!' It was supposed to be a flower. I said, 'It looks like a Brown and Polson's jelly!' 'Oh yes!' he drooled. 'She *would* draw a flower like a Brown and Polson's jelly!'

So it went on. Philippe, at this time, was really very charming because he was happy. In a certain way, he was in love. The attachment was only complicated by the fact that Louis was a little in love with Debbie, too, and he was beginning to be rather annoyed that she showed a marked preference for Philippe. He said one day, 'Look at them out there!' Philippe was sitting on the bench with Debbie, and she was drawing for him again. 'It's got to

142

stop! He's making a fool of himself! Everybody knows about him and his little Debbie!' I said I didn't know what he was talking about and he shouldn't say such stupid things, which was very unjust of me. At this point, Louis disliked Philippe very much, not only because he was sweet on her himself, not only because this romantic attachment was being made public – Philippe would occasionally even put his arm around her – but because Philippe had begun to write a novel about her. There had been a period when Philippe had lectured Louis and Bob about literature, how they should write too. He had made them write a novel each in several exercise books. Louis' was a sort of Robinson Crusoe novel about going to an island, and Bobby's was about a farm. One day, after a session of training to be writers, Louis said to me, 'You know, Mum, we're not going to have *anything* to do with literature and the arts, Bobby and me!' And they really haven't! They've always been of a very practical turn of mind. Louis is a telephone engineer, and Bobby began as a journalist and is now doing Public Relations for the Highlands and Islands Development Board. So *something* of it did come out in Bobby. Of the two, Bobby had most to do with Philippe. Philippe was never so hard on him as he was on Louis, who took most of the bashings. He couldn't bear to see Bobby cry, and would do anything to comfort him.

Well, I think the fact that Philippe began to write a novel about Debbie was just about the last straw! The novel was called *Tasmin Farback*, and really was appallingly bad. He invited me to read the start of it. It was very sentimental about this goddess-like creature 'on a green dais', which was the lawn, 'with one knee peeping courageously from her skirt, and the frill around her neck flattering the whiteness of her throat'. I said, 'Really, I can't say that I like it.' He grew very angry and said that I was jealous of Debbie, but that he wasn't ashamed of the relationship, he wanted to exalt and idealise it. I said, 'Well, you're not going to idealise it by sticking frills on it!' When I said about the frills, he started by saying, 'You're always pulling me down! You think you can write and I can't!' and then, suddenly, he began to laugh, and I laughed too, so that didn't end too badly.

In fact, Philippe was so charming during this period, I was invited to return to the marital bed. And the Phelans never suspected anything wrong in his friendship with their daughter, who was their only daughter and *very* precious to them. The friendship went on until the Phelans decided to move. They didn't move very

143

far; they only moved to a more pleasant flat overlooking the Common. I went to see them once or twice with Philippe, and Philippe visited them very often on his own, again for the purpose of seeing Debbie. But I had again left the marital bed, this time of my own accord, because I discovered that, when we slept together now, Philippe was confusing me with Debbie Phelan, he sometimes even called me by her name. I was having to be her, so I moved out of the bedroom and never went back. This was something I couldn't stand. It was something that seemed to me obscene in the real sense of the word.

Then, as winter approached, Debbie found a boyfriend of her own age, and Philippe semi-retired to the little bedroom and again closed its shutters. For several weeks, either sitting up in bed and writing page after page of *Tasmin Farback* on a special board with a bulldog clip, or working at a desk he'd made from an old piano which Louis had acquired from St John's but no longer wished to play, he virtually excluded the family from his life as he'd done before. There were no rages; he just ignored us except when he wanted food. To the best of my knowledge he didn't go outside the house unless to draw the dole and to buy his cigarettes. I was now working for a higher wage in the Accounts Department of Austin Reed in Red Lion Square; I was earning enough to run the home and he never offered me any extra money. When I got in at night, he was always in the shuttered room and he didn't want to talk. I did learn that occasionally, when I was out, he went upstairs to see an Indian friend of Raymond's from Sri Lanka, something of a writer and a poet. His name was Vernon and he visited our flat once or twice. I sensed that it was another love affair without physical relations, like the one with Debbie Phelan. I don't know, but I *think* there was a latent homosexuality in Philippe, the thing which perhaps attracted him to Somerset Maugham. When Beverley Nichols wrote scathingly about him, Philippe remarked that whatever Beverley Nichols said about Maugham was very revealing about Beverley Nichols. In fact, in '59 he wrote under the name of Louis de Jardin to Maugham, who was staying at the Dorchester, to express his admiration, and Maugham sent a personal reply.

Suddenly, Philippe stopped writing the novel, contented himself with mounting some of Debbie's drawings on pink satin and framing them in wooden frames. He would even come out of the bedroom sometimes and talk to us in quite a friendly manner.

Then, after framing the Debbie drawings, he began to frame picture-cuttings he'd collected of Tolstoy, Flaubert, Dostoevsky, Chekhov, all the great writers he idolised. He made a very large frame for a picture of Somerset Maugham captioned 'An un-extinguished flame' and, with this, he put a newspaper cutting of Picasso's *Crowing Cock*, which he captioned 'To draw you must close your eyes and sing.' and also the letter from Maugham addressed to himself. Next he became frantically interested in the Football Pools. Every Pools company in the country was sending forms, and they kept pouring through the letter-box, and he would sit there in this dark little room, continually filling in little squares and making permutations, which frightened me because he seemed to be driving himself madder and madder: all day and every day he was putting little crosses in squares. Even on Christmas Day and Boxing Day he hardly emerged. On Christmas Day he had never been happy, but on Boxing Days he had sometimes been quite fun, he had wanted to make a meal with yesterday's leftovers, curry some of the turkey and have olives and salami and a bottle of wine with it; he had talked; he was suddenly out of the misery religious festivals caused him; it was like the sun coming out; it was like cheering up again after crying.

All through that winter of '68/'69, when *I* saw him, he was dishevelled and dirty and in an old dressing gown under which he wore a shirt and underpants. It was a long winter and it snowed and the cold went on and on, and the sky was a drab grey-black. I felt in my bones that it was the weather which was affecting Phi-lippe above all. Right till the end of April this dark, cold weather persisted. One evening in May, though the evenings were getting lighter, I had to battle my way home from Austin Reed through sleet and a terrific wind. But I saw a bonfire in the middle of the garden with Philippe stoking it and neighbours' children playing all around. I thought, 'Thank God! He's come out!' He wouldn't speak to me, and I went straight into the flat, intending to tidy up the bedroom while he was still outside. The room had been ran-sacked: every single piece of paper kept there – his manuscripts, marriage certificate, birth certificates, medical certificates, even his beloved *Life of Napoleon* – was gone, had been placed upon the bonfire. Some of my own personal papers were gone too, though fortunately I kept most of my manuscripts in the other room, and most of our books were there too. I ran out to him and said, 'What on *earth* is all this for?' He said, 'Oh, I'm tidying up. I'm not going

145

to be in there any more.' I thought, 'If it's that, thank goodness! I don't mind about the papers going.'

Well, that night, he *did* sleep in there as usual, and I still slept on the floor of the sitting-room. But, when I came home from work the following day, the door of the bedroom was open and he wasn't there. I thought, 'If he's come out, perhaps he's just gone for a walk. That's fine. It will do him all the good in the world.' The room was scrupulously tidy, as though no one used it; even the bed was stripped. Both the boys had left school by now. Louis, who was a pupil on a farm at Chalfont St Giles in Buckinghamshire, was away. Bobby was still at home, working as an apprentice builder for Claridge's, a building firm in Acre Lane, Brixton way, but he was out, rehearsing for a show at St John's. Anyway I was alone that evening and, when Bobby came in, he went to bed. Still Philippe wasn't back, but we knew he had his own key. In the morning, Philippe *still* wasn't back. I thought possibly he might have left altogether – he was unpredictable: you never knew what he would do. I looked through his clothes, but his pyjamas and dressing gown were there and he hadn't even taken a toothbrush. I thought, 'He must have got hung up somewhere. He'd have taken *something* with him if he was leaving.'

Then I found a scrawled note on the chest of drawers. Philippe usually had very neat writing, but this was written like a spider and I *could* not make head nor tail of it. I showed it to Bobby and *he* couldn't read it. He said, 'It's something about a box of tools.' I said, 'I'll try to decipher it some other time. I *have* to go to work now.' And I remember Bobby stopping me and saying, 'Where *is* he, Mum?! Where *did* he go last night?!' It was almost as if he was afraid for him, that he sensed something had happened. But, strangely, I didn't sense anything. Right through that awful time, I'd never thought that Philippe would contemplate suicide and I didn't think it now.

So I went to work that day, said nothing to anybody, came home, and still Philippe wasn't back. Bob came in, we had supper. We tried again to decipher Philippe's note, but without success. Then Bob went out. He was still very worried about what might have happened. He said, 'Dad hasn't been well for a long time, has he? Ought we to go to the police?' I said, 'He may come in tonight. If not, I *will* go to the police. They found Louis when he ran away. They may find *him*.' So I waited that evening. I had some writing to do. I'd been doing some research on Beatrice Hastings for *Adam*

146

in the British Museum and I was writing up my notes when there was a knock on the door at about ten o'clock. I thought, 'Perhaps it's Philippe. Perhaps he's lost his key.' I went to the door, and there were two policemen on the step. 'Are you Mrs Kass? May we come in?' They came into the sitting-room. 'When did you last see your husband?' I said, 'Oh, thank God! Have you found him?! I've been worried out of my mind. He's been away since yesterday evening and we don't know where he is!' They told me that a man was found last night on Hampstead Heath and they thought it might be my husband. I said, 'Is he ill?' 'He's dead.'

I didn't cry or make a fuss; it just didn't register for a minute. I said, 'What makes you think it's my husband?' They said there was nothing in his pockets to indicate who he was, but there was a tailor's label in the jacket of his suit, a fawn herring-bone tweed suit labelled 'Sam Adkin' of Whitechapel; they had been to the tailor and the tailor remembered that the suit was bought by Mr Kass and they had traced the name to here. I knew then for certain that it was Philippe's body they had found. They went on to tell me that it was a very bizarre death because he had been found lying on a mackintosh in thick undergrowth under an umbrella. His eyes were bandaged. At first they had assumed he had been murdered but on, examination, it was discovered he had eaten a large meal with wine and then taken a massive dose of pheno-barbitone. In the morning, I would have to go over to Hampstead Police Station, then on to the mortuary to identify the body. They had already been upstairs, as they'd tried to find me through the main door, and they'd asked Mrs Muldoon to come in and sit with me after they'd gone.

So, when they'd gone, Doris came down and talked to me in a very kind, uninhibited sort of way, and she eventually induced me to cry. I was in such floods of tears when Bobby came home that she decided to take him to her flat and tell him herself what had happened. She must have done it very well because he was quite calm when he returned. He said, 'I knew something like this had happened all along. I can't explain it, but I knew that Dad was dead.'

The next morning Bobby went to work, but I had to go to Hampstead to identify Philippe's body. Doris came with me. I was in a queer state of shock. I remember thinking in the Tube that I wouldn't be able to get out at Hampstead Station because, somehow, I wasn't noticing the stops and the train seemed to be

147

just going in one journey to the end of the line. I relied on Doris, who got me to the police station from where we were driven to the mortuary. I can't remember much of what the mortuary was like. I went down a long passage and, suddenly, there was a light switched on, and there was Philippe: it was dark, but then – it was like a stage set – a light was switched on, and I saw Philippe lying there behind a window. He was covered up except for the head and shoulders, and he was wearing a collar and tie. His eyes were closed and he looked as if he was asleep, and rather childlike. I didn't cry. I just turned to a policeman and said, 'There can't be a shadow of doubt. It is him.'

We were then taken back to the police station, and I was asked to go into a little room by myself where a policeman questioned me. I think he still had at the back of his mind that it might be murder. He wanted particularly to know about Philippe's connections. Did he have any connections on Hampstead Heath? Was there any reason why he should *come* to Hampstead Heath? Was he a homosexual? It was on the tip of my tongue to say I wasn't sure, but I said, 'No, he couldn't have been. Otherwise he wouldn't be married to me.' Oh, there were a lot of such questions. There were photos of the children in Philippe's wallet, and the policeman may have wondered if they were boyfriends or children that he was molesting. Finally he said that he was satisfied it was a case of suicide and not of murder. He added, 'I've never known so many suicides as recently. Early this morning a young boy hanged himself because his boyfriend went with another boy to the pictures.'

I was given Philippe's clothes in a parcel, and his spectacles and his wallet and about five shillings in change. I remember the superstitious feeling I had about this money. As soon as we got out of the police station, I said to Doris, 'I must find a church.' She said, 'Do you want to pray?' I said, 'No, it isn't that, but I *must* get rid of this money.' So we found a church and I put the money in the offertory box in the porch.

We went back to Bowyer House, and Doris rang Austin Reed and said that my husband had died suddenly and I wasn't coming in. I hadn't eaten and it was about three o'clock, so she invited me to her flat and she cooked some eggs and potatoes and we had a meal. Meanwhile, Louis had returned from Chalfont for the weekend and, when I got back from Doris's, I had to tell him what had happened. Louis, quite unlike Bobby, was completely shattered, although, of the two, he was the one Philippe had treated the worst. He cried and stamped round the room and shouted, no, bellowed like a baby. I went to Doris again. I said, 'Could you come in? Louis is very upset by this, and I don't really know what to do. He's stamping round the room and saying, "It's our fault! It's our fault!"' So she came in, and she had a way of calming him down, I think because she wasn't a member of the family. He said, 'Well, at least he's got his revenge! He's done it on us now!' He knew Philippe as an angry man, and he saw this suicide as part of his anger, a thing he'd done to punish us.

When Bobby was home, too, we examined the contents of Philippe's wallet. There were the photos of the boys. There was a notebook with, inside, 'The Waste Land' torn from a book. On the back of 'The Waste Land' he'd written 'A story reminiscent of Svengali and Trilby and/or Pygmalion taken from the known life of three characters known to us.' I'll never know if this was a note about his novel about Debbie or if he was referring to my relationship with Miron Grinde who, at *that* time, I regarded as something of a God. At the end of 'The Waste Land', at the bottom, he'd written:

Mignonne, allons voir si la rose;
Allons gai, bergères;
Que de passions et douleurs;
Je vois des glissantes eaux.

Now, it's very strange that he should write in French, because he didn't know much French and he certainly never *wrote* in French. But he knew that I read French and liked French poetry and that I particularly liked the line 'Mignonne, allons voir si la rose' from Ronsard. The rest of the words are by somebody else. Maybe they're his, maybe by Vernon, who did sometimes write in French, but it's all in his own handwriting. It *could* have been meant as a message for me. There was certainly a message for the boys on a separate piece of paper – a tidy version of the indecipherable note Bobby and I couldn't read. It said, 'To Louis and Bob, Bob and Louis, both as nice and just the same to me. For Louis the blue box of tools. For Bob my wireless set and pen. Bless you both and good luck. With love from Woolley' – Woolley was what Bob and Louis sometimes called him; it was derived from Bob's efforts to say 'Philippe' when he was a baby.

It was incredible how well he knew them, although he'd hardly spoken to them or even seen them since they'd left school, because Louis was going to be the one that worked with his hands and Bobby the one that would need a radio and a pen. Of course, he was always interested in their *education*, and was disappointed when Louis sent in blank O Level papers so he wouldn't have to do his A's, and when Bobby, although he was fairly bright, only passed O Level English and French. But he wouldn't buy them birthday presents or Christmas presents or anything like that – I would have to buy them and say they were from both of us. And *I* had to provide them with pocket money.

That night, the boys slept in their bunk beds, and I slept in the bedroom on the bed that Philippe used to have. There was a dreadful feeling that I'd failed him. I hated myself. I thought, 'I did nothing for him. At the end I wouldn't even sleep with him. I acted like a jailer, I only took him his food and then went out again. When he wouldn't allow me to stay to talk, I should have overridden him. If I'd been a stronger person, I might have been able to snap him out of it, I might have been able to say, "I'm *going* to stay! Now you *talk* to me!" but I wasn't strong enough to *do* that!' Also I hated myself for being afraid of him, because, by now, I should have been able to get over my fear. On the other hand, I realised that what he had been going through was a kind of suffering absolutely beyond my understanding, and I was glad that he was out of it. There was also the lifting of a heavy weight – there wouldn't be this dark and shuttered room in the background any more.

I didn't go in to Austin Reed for about a week because there were so many matters to attend to. For instance, I had to go to Brixton, to the Town Hall, for what they call a 'Death Grant', because I didn't have enough money for a funeral. I had an interview with an Indian who questioned me about finances. He said, 'Wasn't there a Will?' I said, 'No, there wasn't a Will. He had nothing to leave.' He said, 'Well, yes then. I think a Death Grant can be arranged. It'll be about £90 and you may have to pay it back later.' In the event, I *didn't* have to pay it back.

Of course, my mother and my brother were very anxious to help in any way they could. Tim asked did I need help with the funeral. I explained that the Borough was paying for that. When I mentioned there was going to be an inquest, he said, 'Ah . . . yes . . . Well, that will be bad. You must get Legal Aid.' I suddenly realised that he thought I'd killed Philippe! I had always thought Philippe would kill *me*, as it happens. I said, 'There's no reason for Legal Aid. It's only to go and answer a few questions.' And that was all it was: it wasn't an ordeal. A reporter came to see me, just after the inquest; he wanted to know if I could tell him anything about the murder. Everybody had made up their minds that Philippe had been murdered!

At Bowyer House, by this time, most of the West Indians had been replaced by Africans, who made a colourful sight in their long robes and little pillbox hats and beautifully embroidered tunics. One couple were making wedding cakes on the premises, and doing very well by it. According to Doris, there was a big sort of boarding school in Surrey where African children were sent, after babyhood, to be brought up on the tribal system . . . Anyway, Doris spread the news of Philippe's death around the house, and all these Africans came to see me in their beautiful African costumes: each family came to the door and I let them in. I wasn't prepared for this at all. The men made speeches of consolation and quoted little bits from the Bible, adding, 'He did not disgrace his house. He left his house to do this thing' – they seemed *enormously* grateful for that, and I've never found out whether they thought it was bad luck to have a suicide in the house or whether it would have meant trouble with the police. And, all the time the men were talking, the women kept up a sort of humming – uhuh*u*huh uhuh*u*huh, a kind of moaning and groaning – and swayed to and fro, and moved one hand in a circular way round their faces.

The Africans all said that they would come to the funeral at the St Pancras Cemetery, East Finchley, where Philippe was going to be buried in what I suppose would be called years ago a 'pauper's grave'. They loaded up their cars with flowers, and I picked a huge bunch of lillies of the valley which had come up absolutely in their hundreds in the front garden. There were several cars full of flowers and Africans and Doris and her husband Jack, and Bobby and Louis and me. Unfortunately we lost the way to the cemetery. We only got there when the parson or vicar, or whoever it was, was just finishing the service without anybody else at the grave at all. He said, 'Oh, you've come to the funeral! Well, I'm very sorry, I can't do it again as I've got to go on to another one.' He asked me, 'What is your relationship to the deceased?' I said, 'I *was* his wife.' To give him his due, he did offer to hold a memorial service

151

later, but I said I didn't want one. So, anyway, we put the flowers around the grave, which was then being filled in, and we very soon left. I was coming out of the trauma of it all by that time, and I did think, 'I'm sure Philippe has arranged we should be this late on purpose!' You see, the last thing he would have wanted was a religious funeral.

The boys recovered very soon. Bobby was the closest to Philippe, but I think, even for him, it was a weight lifted, because there had always been this thing in the background that might explode. Louis is like Philippe in many ways – he *looks* like Philippe and he has a paddy like Philippe, but I pray that it never will be manic. I was terrified that they might be scarred by the whole experience, but I don't think it did anything very terrible to them, and things were much better for them afterwards. As for me, I can't say that I loved Philippe at the time he died. Illness is a terrible thing, especially when it involves sickness of the mind, and I'd lost him, and he'd lost me, many years before.

Since Philippe died, I've never had a permanent sex relationship. I'm very much in sympathy with Stevie Smith, who said somewhere, 'I am not a marriage person, I'm a friendship person' – but then, I've never achieved a permanent platonic relationship either. I can't sleep with anybody I haven't a genuine affection for. Philippe knew this, and I think his jealousy and wild imaginings when I met and spoke to other people were caused by a fear that I might sleep, and *enjoy* sleeping with them. He just couldn't bear the *idea* even; he wouldn't *accept* the fact that I was faithful. When I was at Hamblin's and he wasn't working and we were very short of money, he tried to persuade me to become a prostitute so we could live better. You see, it would have been a completely impersonal thing, and he wouldn't have minded that. I suppose this is the psychology of the ponce – that, as long as the woman's heart is with *him*, it doesn't matter who she sleeps with. Frankly, I think that after his physical attraction to me wore off, he found me sexually rather dull; he would have liked me to be more like the prostitutes he had used as a seaman.

Everything connected with Miron Grindea, he resented bitterly. He knew that he stood for the life I had always wanted – civilisation as opposed to the kind of savagery I was being offered at home. When a year had passed since I'd met Grindea and he hadn't yet published 'The Dancing Vicar', and all the magazines he had re-

152

commended had rejected the poems I sent them, *although* I had mentioned his name, Philippe was certain I had fornicated with a crook! And Poetry Readings at the Crown and Greyhound, were, of course, a cover for sexual escapades and orgies!

11

I had followed up Grindea's suggestion in '61 about contacting Howard Sergeant of *Outposts*, and Moira Caldecott, the secretary of the Dulwich Group, told me that their readings, under his chairmanship, were always held on the last Wednesday of the month; the next reading would be given by Jon Silkin and the poets of *Stand*, a Northern magazine of the Left. So, very much against Philippe's wishes, I went to the reading, terrified and shy. I'd never been to anything like this before, and I can't say I enjoyed the evening. It was all very stiff and formal. Howard Sergeant listed all the poets' successes, and the poets sat there looking like something the cat brought in. Their poems mostly went over my head, and I didn't find any of them at all moving or charming. One of the poems by Jon Silkin was about the Jews of York who were massacred. It contained the rather odd idea that the respectability of York was a punishment for the massacre.

After the reading, I decided, for the first time in my life, to go to the bar and order a drink, as everybody else was drinking. I ordered a glass of red wine, sat down alone, and stayed alone, not talking to anybody. From what I could make out, the majority of the audience were sixth formers and masters from Dulwich College. Howard Sergeant is a very kindly man, and I got friendly with him later, but he has thick spectacles and a way of looking at you as if you are absolute dirt, as if you shouldn't be there and you've somehow gatecrashed. Anyway, I didn't introduce myself and mention Grindea. I daren't, I simple daren't, because of this awful way he has of looking at you; but I put my name and address in the Visitors Book, so I got notices of all the meetings thereafter, and I usually went to them, much to Philippe's disgust. 'You're going out again? Off for sex? Don't blame me if you're attacked. *I* won't be there to help you.' Actually, I *was* attacked one night coming home from Dulwich. The meeting ended as usual at about eleven, I caught the 37 bus back and, as soon as I turned into the lane to Bowyer House where the dossers and alcoholics hung around the dustbins of David Greig's, I felt a hand on my shoulder, and a man tried to pull me down. He said, 'You live in this house, don't you?! Everybody knows what sort of women live in *this* house!' He was very drunk, and I shouted and screamed and knocked him off balance and he ran for it.

I was always completely alone at the Crown and Greyhound meetings until December. At December meetings, it was the custom to have readings from the floor; at the others, the poets who read had already made a reputation. I remember going to this meeting in a thick fog. I got off the bus and crossed the road. You could hardly see a thing. I went round the corner that leads to Dulwich Village, and I literally bumped into the back of a boy who had stopped to light a cigarette. He said, 'Are you going to the poetry reading?' and we walked along together talking. He had recently left Dulwich College. I asked him did he like it there. He said, 'No. It was miserable. I wish my parents had been poor and then they couldn't have sent me.' This was Anthony Barnett, who published one or two poems afterwards and edited a magazine called *Nothing Doing in London* which appeared just now and again. He was the first person at Dulwich that I really contacted and was able to talk to.

That was a nice evening, because he brought some poems to read and I rather liked those. In fact, all the poems from the floor that evening *did* something to me – they were stimulating, they didn't go over my head, and I listened to them. I read 'Three Welshmen Sang' and, after I'd read that poem, I sort of became a member of the Dulwich Group. Howard Sergeant spoke to me afterwards and said he liked the poem very much and, though he didn't offer to publish it, he said, 'You must read for us sometime.' And he did give me a reading, no, readings, there eventually, once with Edwin Brock and the rest of the committee of poets responsible for the running of the Dulwich Group, and once with Ruth Fainlight, Allan Sillitoe's wife, and another poet whose name I can't remember. I wasn't paid. Nobody was paid in the Sixties. Even famous poets gave their services free. It was only in the

155

Seventies that the Poetry Secretariat was formed under the auspices of the Arts Council. If you were registered with that – it's a kind of Trade Union – you had to be paid £40.

At these earlier readings, I was *frantically* nervous. Luckily, the audience reactions were very good. I think it was to my advantage that I knew my poems by heart, though I always carried them with me in my wicker picnic box – sometimes your mind can go blank. Knowing the poems means that you can look the audience in the eye, you can compel attention far more than if you're reading. Many poets sell themselves very short because, as they are *reading*, the way the audience hears them is far less exciting than what is on the page. You can '*get*' an audience by reciting. But I do concede that, for the deepest and best poetry, it is sometimes good to read and drone because this gives the audience a chance to hear it in their own way. Many of my poems even come out in different voices which can either give an extra dimension or distract. Unfortunately, some poets you can't *hear*. Anna Madge is a case in point. Not only are her poems difficult to understand and, therefore, better on the printed page, she has a very soft voice.

There was a period in the middle Sixties – I'd been on the Dulwich Group's Committee for about two years – when Howard Sergeant suggested that members of the Committee sometimes arrange meetings and take the chair, as he wouldn't always be present. When my turn came, I consulted Miron Grindea about who to ask to read, and he advised me to invite Anna Madge and her mother, Kathleen Raine. They are both fine poets, and, though Kathleen Raine is a poet of great integrity, she had once played a nasty trick on Howard Sergeant when he invited her to read. As she was the star of the evening, he left her till last. When, after the interval, he announced her, she had quietly slipped away. He thought she would re-appear in a minute or two, but she never did. She's a *strange* woman. So, I was pretty sure that she wouldn't accept when *I* invited her. Relations between her and Howard Sergeant were strained, and I was not really a big enough fish to attract her. I wrote to her at her home in Paulton Square and, sure enough, she refused in an emphatic letter, saying she did not think it would be a good idea if she read with her daughter. I rang her to try to ask her to change her mind. I asked 'Is that Kathleen Raine?' A voice, which sounded very much like her own, said, 'Who is it?' I gave my name and business. Whoever it was said she would inquire whether Kathleen Raine was in, but she returned, after a pause, saying that Kathleen Raine had left the house and she didn't know when she'd be back.

In the event Kathleen Raine didn't read, but Grindea persuaded her to let him bring her in a taxi. She would not come *in* to the reading, but stood by the doorway of the room and listened to her daughter without meeting her. Anna Madge was hard enough to hear *inside* the room! The poets I had invited to read with her were Peter Robins, Anne Goossens, and Ivor Cutler. Nobody knew about Ivor Cutler in those days. He arrived wearing what looked like an African robe and an old-fashioned nightcap. He gave a very amusing reading. Grindea gave Kathleen Raine and me a lift home in a taxi afterwards. Neither of them seemed at all interested in Anna's reading: they only talked about Ivor Cutler.

Another tense occasion I remember from the days of Howard Sergeant was when a *breast-beating* poet was the main reader. He kept saying, 'Why don't you stop me?! Why do I write these things?!' When he said, 'Why doesn't somebody *throw* something at me, throw a *table*, throw a *chair*?', somebody *did* throw a chair. He shouldn't have said it: it was his own fault. Fortunately he ducked, and the chair whizzed over his head. The publican was very good about it: he didn't make us pay for the chair, which was in pieces . . .

Well, time went on and, as I say, I heard nothing from Grindea about the 300th edition of *Adam* and publication of 'The Dancing Vicar'. Philippe said, 'You realise that man's not going to publish the poem at all?! Or else he'll publish it as somebody else's!' I rang Grindea up. He said, 'I *shall* publish your poem in *Adam* 300 and it *will* be soon.' He invited me to come and see him again. I accepted, and Philippe insisted on coming too, to supervise the proceedings. So we both went over to Emperor's Gate, and Grindea gave us drinks and, when I mentioned that Philippe also wrote, he asked him about his writing. Philippe was very rude, answering in monosyllables, and wouldn't tell him anything. I broached the subject of 'The Dancing Vicar' again. I said we were both rather worried about it as I'd sent it nearly two years ago. He said, I'm now preparing *Adam* 300 in which your poem will appear. It contains some material from Cocteau, but I'll have to go to France to see him about it again – he's very ill in Antibes.' So we left. It was a very uncomfortable interview. I felt that Philippe was going to explode at any minute.

157

The following year, 1963 – I was still working as a filing clerk for Hamblin's in Wigmore Street – there was a message for me one evening to say that someone was waiting for me at the Staff Entrance. This was Miron Grindea. Would I join him in a café for a cup of coffee? He would like help with his editorial for *Adam* 300. Over coffee, he laid out the proofs for this editorial on the table, and asked me whether I could suggest how it could be put into more colloquial English. I read what he had written, and made one or two suggestions. I said I would like to take the editorial home, and think about it. He said there was no time. I had helped enough already. (With Grindea, though everything was published late, there was *never* any time!) He didn't, in the event, use my suggestions. I'm very glad. It would have been wrong to use my English – it wouldn't have been *him*.

Grindea had gone on to say that he would like me to help him with some research at the British Museum, we could work on the days when the BM was open after five. He would show me how to use cross-references and how to pick up information from books not directly on the subject. He outlined various projects he wanted me to work on, including work on the lives of Freud and Van Gogh. And had I heard of Natalie Barney, the model for the heroine of *The Well of Loneliness*? It so happened that I *had* heard of *The Well of Loneliness*, because Joan Randall, the maid at Four Winds, used to read me passages from Radclyffe Hall's book which was at that time a very forbidden, banned book and considered very wicked indeed, but I hadn't heard of Natalie Barney. At the end of the interview I agreed enthusiastically to help with his researches, though I knew this would be unpopular at home. The new worlds that Grindea had opened up were too enticing to refuse, especially as he also said he would like to publish *more* of my poetry. I worked for him at the BM I'm sure for five years, and, every now and then, he would come up to me and say, 'You've worked very hard. Please accept this,' and give me £5 or £3 or £2 in cash.

In 1964, *Adam* 300, with my poem in it, *did* appear, and I was asked to read it at the celebration held at the French Institute. The girl I worked with at Hamblin's was called Donna, and her parents had a stall in Petticoat Lane. I told her I was going to this party, but didn't have a good enough summer dress, so she got me one very cheaply from her parents' stall – pale-blue pleated nylon, with a white lacy top. For about ten minutes before going

158

onto the stage, I was shaking like a jelly. I'm the same to this day. Just before I go on I'm a quaking, shaking mess, and then, as soon as I go on, I don't feel nervous any more. I always rehearse what I'm going to do beforehand, but it always comes out a different way. Somehow the audience puts something into it. The front row of the auditorium was reserved for performers, and Anthony Barnett came and sat down next to me. As he wasn't a performer, someone who *was* moved him out, which I didn't like at all.

There was some music – someone sang and a violinist played. Mary Grew and Hugo Manning read some of their poetry. Grindea gave a talk about Cocteau, who was now dead. When I recited 'The Dancing Vicar', it came out as a rhythmic chant, almost a song. Mary Grew said afterwards, 'We've got an Edith Sitwell here,' but I don't know whether she meant it as a compliment or not . . . Grindea was introducing me to everyone as 'this great poet'. It was rather embarrassing. What he may have meant was, 'I have discovered something which has the *potential* of a great poet.' Of course, he's an eccentric, and you can't take everything he says seriously; he often speaks on a puff of wind; he name-drops and what he says is usually geared towards pushing his magazine. He is an enigma: I don't pretend to understand him. And he *still* calls me a great poet. He has met with great poets, he has mixed with great poets, and I want to believe that I *am* a great poet, and, in part, I *do* believe it. The fact that he says this echoes something in me: there is something in me which tells me that I am a poet. But being a *great* poet – this is not true. Not because I haven't the ability, I think, to *be* a great poet, but because I haven't the stature, I haven't published enough, I have talent which really isn't yet born.

At the *Adam* party – Philippe wouldn't come, of course, and Louis and Bobby were in Cornwall – I was introduced to a Professor Lavrin. I was a little drunk, having downed the burgundy on an empty stomach. He said that 'The Dancing Vicar' showed an affinity with the Slav poets! He would like me to translate some poems from the Slovene which he intended to publish in book form. Being slightly lightheaded, I said Yes, this would be most interesting. After he had gone off to talk to somebody else, I realised that I didn't actually know what Slovene was. However, he had given me his card and said that he would see me in the British Museum as he also worked there, and see me he did, and instructed me to translate five poems by five different nineteenth-century

159

Slovene poets. Translating was not so difficult as I imagined. Slovene is one of the many languages of Yugoslavia, and most of the poets used French as a second language. After studying a little Serbo-Croat, I translated from French versions laid beside the originals. Professor Lavrin's book was published eventually. He gave me a copy, and paid me £5. I similarly translated some Indian poems for Grindea's '71 edition of *Adam*, working from French versions and maintaining the rhythm of the Hindi, Gujarati, Oriya and other originals.

No, I wasn't paid specially for this work – it came within the cash hand-outs for general BM research. As did translating Picasso's ten poems entitled 'Trozo de Piel' ('A Scrap of Skin'), which appeared in the magazine in 1967. I worked on these with the help of a Spanish dictionary and a man and a girl who had lived in Spain and spoke fluent Spanish. They're beautiful poems, and I often had to fight these people because, although they understood the Spanish literally, they didn't understand the poetic sense. Everything is seen with the eye of a painter. People coming out of church are not just *like* upright radishes, they *are* upright radishes.

All these activities were a great source of grievance to Philippe. Through Grindeas, I was accepted by Edward Lucie-Smith into 'The Group', about twenty poets who met once a week on Fridays at his home in Sydney Street, South Kensington. Philippe, who was far from joking, said the meetings were orgies. Before I went one evening, he held me by the hair in front of the children and shouted, 'You see this woman?! She *looks* all right, well, she gives you your food, but actually she's evil, she's *evil*! Never forget that! She's *evil*!' Poetry meetings were all orgies, and not only was I sleeping with Grindea, I was sleeping with Raymond upstairs, even the vicar. I was confiding in Grindea now and once, at the BM, when I arrived with a black eye, he said, 'Why don't you divorce Philippe?' I said, 'You can't! He's helpless most of the time. You can't marry, then go away because it's not as nice as you expected!' I don't think I ever seriously considered divorce . . .

But these meetings at Edward Lucie-Smith's. The first thing you had to do when you joined 'The Group' was to send a batch of your poems, and he would keep these in a filing cabinet. Then an evening would come, devoted entirely to your work. You would read your own poems and the group would listen to you and then criticise, and they'd have your work before them on the page because Edward Lucie-Smith had made photo-copies of them in advance. George MacBeth was a member. Peter Porter, Alan Brownjohn. Powerful men in poetry, if you call it power in poetry. But they had pull, all of them. Alan Marshfield, who's becoming quite popular now, was a member, also Fleur Adcock and Jeff Nuttall. Gradually I began to put in my word: it was at 'The Group' that I learned to wait for a silence, a break in the conversation, and jump in. It always amazed me that people listened.

One evening, John Horder read his poems. Everybody but me thought that what he was writing was sheer pornography. I had a battle about this, because I felt that the poems went deeper than that. For instance, one poem was about a circus with a bear-woman in a cage and the ringmaster managing to get out of the cage before he was eaten. The ringmaster was always absent-mindedly twiddling the rings in the noses of the seals, not realising the pain that he was causing them. Bear was spelt b-e-a-r, but everybody said it meant b-a-r-e. Now, this poem was so well put together that it seemed to me it *couldn't* be pornography, so I said that, in Celtic mythology, seals have a connection with the souls of women, and this was what was meant by twiddling these rings in the noses of the seals, and the escape from the bear-woman was simply a matter of a man wanting to keep his liberty. I still think there is more to John Horder's poems than pornography. At that time we were just coming into the Permissive Age, and everybody thought it fun to be pornographic. Jeff Nuttall, I considered, really *did* write pornography. Subsequently he's written some quite good poetry and edited his own magazine.

Usually poems were torn to shreds, but my reading, as a critical evening, was a bit of a flop. I read 'Line, Circle and Spiral', which I've mentioned to you before. That was the one about which Alan Brownjohn said nothingness is a fourth shape. I read 'The Hanraghan Brothers', about the Irish lodgers in Crewe. I read 'The Dancing Vicar' . . . All the poems I read were received enthusiastically except one, though, after 'The Hanraghan Brothers', a woman said it wasn't long enough, she was just beginning to know them when they disappeared, and, after my poem called 'Abortion', Martin Bell said, 'There's a recurring mention of Oedipus. You're laying yourself open to comparison with the greats.' Edward Lucie-Smith argued with this. He said it was very rhythmic, it sounded as if there was a metronome behind the words, which was in keeping with the Greek idea; the poem also reminded him of some of the Elizabethan poets, especially the build-up to a rhyme at the end.

But there was one poem everybody *did* agree was rather trite and not very deeply felt, and *I* realised this, too. It was a very short poem called 'Romany Boy', which began:

> Call off your dogs, rai, and let me live, rai,
> Where the school bell's out of hearing,
> Where the wood-fire flames go flaring,
> Where the roadways wink the eye, rai,
> Where the roadways wink the eye.

I've used these lines recently as the refrain of a poem about teaching.

I think those meetings stopped just before the Seventies, when Edward Lucie-Smith had to travel. Though he was a rich man and we only drank cups of coffee, he paid for all the postage and photo-copying himself. I had been warned that he was a vain man who liked being flattered. The only Edward Lucie-Smith *I* knew was a very kindly, roly-poly teddy bear.

Another person at that time who was not what I expected was Michael Foot, the MP. In this case, he *looked* different. Grindea had introduced me to Elizabeth Thomas, the literary editor of *Tribune*, who ran the monthly Tribune Group readings at the Regent's Park Branch Library, Robert Street, NW1, which he chaired. He had the appearance and the speech of a very old man. It was a tragic thing. Not long before I met him, he had been in a terrible car accident which had this effect. Seeing him on television recently, he seemed to be younger than when he chaired the Tribune meetings. Elizabeth Thomas was Welsh and he had a Welsh constituency, and they both liked 'Three Welshmen Sang', which was published in *Tribune*. Another poem of mine they published, on November the 11th, 1966, for Armistice Day – it's called Remembrance Day now, isn't it? – was 'The Flying Dutchman':

> I seen her, mates, I seen her,
> She'd the Devil's shape and form,
> The God-Forsaken Dutchman
> Flying black before the storm,
> But I couldn't hardly tell you
> How it was, nor what it meant,

162

> She was how the workhouse looked
> The night me mother spent the rent . . .

The persona of the poem was an old-fashioned sailor, not a sailor of today. The Flying Dutchman was something very well known in Cornwall when I was a child.

I think Elizabeth Thomas paid me £5 for each of those poems. I liked her tremendously. She was very much a socialist, married, a happy woman, with a slight Welsh accent. I got drunk with her once or twice in the pub opposite, when we quite let our hair down. But she was always 'the literary editor of *Tribune*', and she never told me anything about herself and I never told her anything about me. It was a matter of poetry. One night, we began by quoting Shakespeare, and it went on to politics and how poetry shouldn't be used for politics – or so *I* thought, but she thought that it should. We then talked about South Africa and Apartheid. We argued and, of course, the argument got more and more fuzzy as we got more and more drunk.

The *Tribune* readings were on the same formula as the Crown and Greyhound to the extent that a famous poet read with, perhaps, another two. But they differed in that they were 'dry' – they weren't in a pub – and there was always a public discussion about the poems and poets afterwards. The discussions were always enjoyable, and I was now plucking up courage to say my piece. The star of the evening would usually be a political poet with very marked Leftist ideas. One was Jon Silkin, another Leonard Cohen, another Hugh MacDiarmid. *I* read one evening with Dennis Brutus and David Craig. *I* wasn't a Left poet – I think that Elizabeth Thomas just liked my poetry.

I'd now been published in *Adam* and *Tribune*, and, oh yes, again in '66, Howard Sergeant, who liked a poem he heard me read at the Crown and Greyhound called 'On a Symphony by a Modern Composer', wanted to put this into an anthology of English poets he was making for a special issue of *Poet International*, an Indian magazine published in Madras and edited by a man called Krishna S-r-i-n-i-v-a-s (I can't pronounce it). The poem begins with an incident at Parke when I broke my wrist retrieving a cow which Bess had herded into the river:

> Once, far away, half under anaesthetic,
> I felt the texture of pain from a broken wrist

163

And yet felt nothing, only the threads of my fingers —
Thin wires vibrating on chiming stalactites,
Leaving a taste of metal on the tongue . . .

I was supposed to get paid for this, but the money never came.
When the magazine came out, Krishna S-r-i-n-i-v-a-s wrote me a
very glowing letter: 'I was so grateful to you for your wonderful
poem which was published in *Poet International.* I cannot begin to
thank you for the wonder that this poem gave me. I shall shortly
be coming to London. I should be grateful if you would send me at
once by return of post eight pound notes which would greatly
facilitate my journey.' I've always felt very guilty about not sending
those eight pound notes.

In 1967, though, I was paid £10 by Norman Hidden and £10 by
the BBC. I'd begun to go to meetings run by Norman Hidden at
the Lamb and Flag in Rose Street. He was a poet at Oxford at the
time when Auden and Spender were there, and it's rumoured that
he was always trying to prove that he was as good as them, because they wouldn't have him in their group. But he made a great
splash with poetry readings. The Lamb and Flag was absolutely
packed out; *everybody* used to go there. He also ran a terrific Poetry
Marathon at the Mayflower Barn, Chalfont St Giles, not far from
Milton's house, with poets reading one after the other for about
two days. The Mayflower Barn is very old — Americans like to visit
it when they come here, because it's supposed to have been built
from the timbers of the *Mayflower* when she was broken up. It was
a beautiful place to read poetry.

   I can only remember one dose of this marathon, but the press
took a great interest in it, and said what a wonderful revival of
poetry this was, which it wasn't. I read 'The Runaway Heart', a
poem which I'd read at the *Tribune* reading with Dennis Brutus
and David Craig — in fact, I'd ended my reading with it. It was
sparked off by the shooting of President Kennedy. Everybody was
writing poems about President Kennedy's death at that time,
Auden included, and I thought that, as the Tribune Group was a
political group, I'd write up this poem that I'd had in mind for a
long time. It came out rather in the style of the old American
ballads, and with nothing whatever to *do* with President Kennedy,
though there was something of Robert Service in it. My mother
had a copy of *Rhymes of a Red Cross Man*, given to her by her

164

fiancé who was killed in the 1914 War. I seriously enjoyed the book as a child.

> Did you hear the story of Boss McGroo?
> He was awful sick and they said he was through,
> Then along came the men of the medical art
> And they fixed him up with a plastic heart
> Up and down up and down up and down . . .

Well, when I'd read 'The Runaway Heart' at this Poetry Marathon, Norman Hidden wanted to publish it in his magazine, *Workshop*, and he did. The magazine was a mouthpiece for the contributors at the Lamb and Flag. That meant pretty well the whole world, because the Lamb and Flag readings involved about a dozen readers who lined up and had a ten-minute spot each after a main reader had read for about half an hour. Norman Hidden also invited me to do a main reading at the Lamb and Flag, with a special request to include 'The Runaway Heart'. I read this after 'Three Welshmen Sang' and various other poems. I remember John Pudney read that evening, and also the blind poet I admire very much, John Heath Stubbs. The occasion was recorded for the BBC by George MacBeth, and subsequently broadcast in his programme, *Poetry Now*, on the Third Programme. My family in Cornwall tuned in and congregated round the radio, though they never listened to the Third Programme as a rule. I believe Auntie Nora said at the end, 'Why didn't Pat read?' She hadn't recognised my voice with its different accents.

I also recited 'The Runaway Heart' at a tea party given by Miron Grindea and Carola, his wife who is a very fine pianist. They doubled up with laughter when they heard the poem. They said I must read it at the French Institute in October, when there was to be another *Adam* celebration, this time to mark its new – and temporary, as it turned out – affiliation to the University of Rochester, New York, and to announce the result of the *Adam* £100 Novel Competition, judged by L. P. Hartley, J. W. Lambert and Michael Ratcliffe. There would be the usual entertainment of music and poetry, and I would be reading with Fernand Auberjonois and Ivor Cutler, and I must wear a nice dress. Well, I had one or two dresses that might fit this description, but they were in rather pale colours, very feminine-looking. I said, 'Can you see the voice of Boss McGroo coming out of a dress like that?' So Carola said, 'Oh, never mind. I've got a plain black skirt and a black blouse. That's neutral. You can read any poem you like in that.' So she lent me the black skirt and the black blouse and, on the night, I changed at Austin Reed and came straight from work.

But I got hung up. Oh, it was an absolute nightmare. I *couldn't* get a bus: all the buses were full. And, at first, I couldn't get a taxi for love or money. In the end, I *did* manage to get a taxi, but I was literally within seconds, and I had to pretty well *run* onto the stage to do my piece. Grindea was *furious*: '*Why* are you late?! You *knew* what time it was!' I was trying to explain all about being held up by the traffic, when I had to perform, and, by the time I'd finished, he was quite all right again. Well *then*, of course, Jack Lambert announced that you'd won the Novel Competition jointly with somebody called Zygmunt Frankel. And before you expanded yours, both winning novels were published *eventually* in the magazine. *And* you were both paid! *Adam* doesn't usually pay for contributions, but, I suppose, as this was something that was advertised . . .

I've never told you before, but *I* submitted a novel for the same competition. In the dim, distant past, I'd thought of publishing my four short stories – 'The Fisherman's Tale', 'The Voyage', 'Elizabeth Meets the Fairies' and 'Dandy Davey' – as a collection. But Grindea, at the time he was about to publish 'The Dancing Vicar' and I thought he was God, said, 'Short stories are no use. There's no market for short stories. Write a novel.' After that, I submitted the stories singly to magazines, and *Argosy*, to whom I submitted 'Dandy Davey' which is longer than the others, wrote to me and said they liked it, but it was much too long, it was really more like a short novel. I told Grindea about this criticism, and he said, 'Send it as a novella to Faber, and mention my name, tell them you've been published in *Adam*.' I did this, and Faber sent it back, saying it was too short, I should develop the theme – a gypsy girl who becomes a dancer – and turn it into a full novel.

Well, on buses and in the Tube and in cafés near the British Museum – I can't write prose, like poems, in the head and keep it there for writing down afterwards – I filled reporter's notebook after reporter's notebook, and blew up 'Dandy Davey' into a full-scale novel which I called *Sparks in the Leather*, which I thought a better title with its implication of the feeling in the skin that made the girl want to dance, and of the fact that her dancing shoes and boots were made of leather. The next problem was finding a typist, let alone scraping up the money to pay for one. The woman I was using in Gypsy Hill, West Norwood, drank a lot and made endless mistakes. For this full-scale novel, I found a man in Chalcott Place, off Sloane Square, who typed several copies of the book, one of which I sent off to Faber. Faber sent it back in due course, saying it made pleasant reading, but they felt there wouldn't be a public for it; they said – and I knew this was so at the bottom of things – it was a story about a child, but not really a children's story, and yet it was too naive to be interesting to grown-ups.

I then gave the book to Grindea. He said, 'Adam is having a Novel Competition. I'll read it and, if it's worth entering, I'll put it in.' Well, he *did* read it and he said that, though it was very publishable material, it wasn't right for *Adam* – and certainly it would not have been a match for your beautiful *Summer Overtures* or Zygmunt Frankel's *Octopus* which tied with it. However, he kept his copy, saying, 'I'll see what I can do.'

I didn't expect it, but Grindea placed *Sparks in the Leather* with London Authors, Herbert van Thal's literary agency in Upper Brook Street. Van Thal didn't read it, but his secretary, a very young girl just from school, was wildly enthusiastic. It was sent to Collins, who returned it with much the same criticism as Faber, except that Collins also said it had a timeless quality which was disturbing. After that, I believe the enthusiastic secretary left, and the manuscript stayed on van Thal's shelves for three years. I kept writing and telephoning for news. Shortly after Philippe's death I called at the office, and asked for it back. Herbert van Thal himself looked through a lot of manuscripts, found it in rather a dusty condition somewhere, and handed it back. Perhaps I was being too impatient. I probably had an attack of arrogance – I was feeling, then, that I was quite an important person. With the dozens of coffee-stained reporter's notebooks, filled with my inelegantly biro-written drafts, I only have one typed copy of *Sparks in the Leather* left. The others may have gone into Philippe's holocaust. If he happens to be listening to us now, I'm sure he's saying, 'Art?! Literature?! Bullshit!!'

12

The woman at the next adding machine to mine, in the Accounts Department of Austin Reed, was a Greek Cypriot who went to worship in a Greek Orthodox church every evening after work. We became quite friendly, and she used to give me clothes for poetry readings. She told me her daughter was living with a man outside the Greek community, an Englishman she greatly disapproved of. From her descriptions, I couldn't see that there was very much wrong with him, except that he wasn't Greek. She was crying quietly one morning while we were working, and she said, 'This man, he's now married her. I'm so lonely. I can't share her life. She's completely gone out of it. It's as if she's dead.' I said, 'Well, you go to church every evening. Does that help?' She said, 'I go to church every evening to pray that my daughter shall be hurt as I have been hurt.'

It seemed to me that nobody could hate like that, except a Greek. It was like all the old Greek tragedies. What I wanted to avoid most with Philippe was hating him, because I think hatred is a very corrosive thing. And I hadn't begun to hate him before he died, and I didn't hate him after he died. There was fear, of course, and I think fear has a lot to do with hatred – they're very mixed up together. But I'd never begun to hate him to the extent that I wanted to hurt him.

When he died, I was able to work harder than ever – on my poetry and on another novel, *The Banks of Vesuvius*, which went much deeper than *Sparks in the Leather*. I was also revising and correcting my first long poem, 'The Dream of Mitzi'. While delving in the British Museum for Grindea, I had come across *The Dream of*

168

Gerontius by Cardinal Newman. In one passage, an angel explains to Gerontius that, at the moment of death, it isn't immediately possible to transport a human soul from one sphere to another; to avoid disintegration and madness, there must be a time when the soul leans on the material things which are familiar to it through the senses, until it is able to recognise them as signs and symbols of the spiritual life. This inspired me to imagine what would happen to someone like Jean, the prostitute in the basement of Bowyer House, who was absolutely frank about what she was, when *she* died:

I used to think you went up when you snuffed it
Dunno why
Course I knew it'd be down for me,
Wouldn't be right else
But I had a feeling –
P'raps it was the Virgin Mary,
She went up,
But I knew a ponce once, read books.
And he said the world was round,
And if Australia happened to be on top
When she took off
She'd a gone down,
Which he shouldn't of said.
Because, as I said, you never know, I said
Who might *ear* you, I said,
And he said 'Christ! Who's buggin us now?'
And that wasn't all he said which he shouldn't,
So I said well, I said, if she did, I said,
She only did it with Joseph, I said,
And he laughed,
Which he shouldn't.

Then *I* had this dream –
It was when me time come,
There in the orspital,
With all the eavenly ost standing round in white coats
And me spread out on the ironing board,
And in this dream
There wasn't no floating up nor diving down neither,
I sits up,
Swings me legs over,

169

Lifts up my arse
And walks,
And when I looks back
They was all flappin about as if I done summink wrong . . .

I gave the name Mitzi, the name of our cat, to the persona of this poem, which Grindea eventually published in *Adam* in 1971. Before that, I recited it at the Lamb and Flag. George MacBeth, who was then in the Third Programme 'Talks Department', which included all poetry, used to go quite often to the Lamb and Flag. In those days, he was a black comedian, a very tough poet, laughing about things I think I might not *dare* to laugh about. Anyway, he heard 'The Dream of Mitzi', and was wildly enthusiastic. He said I must record the poem for broadcasting and, a few weeks later, I went to the BBC – my one and only visit – saw MacBeth over the proverbial *horrid* cup of BBC coffee, and we recorded it. Well, time went by, and 'Mitzi' wasn't broadcast and, in the end, I wrote to MacBeth, asking whether anything was ever coming of this recording. He wrote back and said he couldn't use it because he thought it should have been recorded as it had been at the Lamb and Flag, with an audience reaction; without the audience reaction, it didn't sound the same.

I was very depressed by MacBeth's rejection. I thought, 'That's the story of my life!' It had always been so, and it *has* always been so – people are wildly enthusiastic about my readings, but rarely publish the poems. I always enjoy the reading and I enjoy the applause and I enjoy the popularity afterwards and meeting people, but then I get an awful flat feeling: 'Well, what the hell! What possible good did *that* do you?!' Because reading *doesn't* do you any good: reading poetry does your stature as a poet, your reputation, no good at all. With me, at any rate, it has only led to the occasional publication of one, or a few, of my poems. The only thing that will help you, the only thing that will make you known as a poet, is publication.

Only twice have I been published in a *book* as a result of being heard. When *I* became Chairman of the Dulwich Group, I invited Howard Sergeant to give a reading. And, to my great surprise, he not only read 'The Runaway Heart' which he'd heard *me* read before – he read it in his own rather stilted Oxford accent and it sounded very strange to me – but he read it from the *Evans' Book of Children's Verse* which he had edited! I hadn't even been paid for

170

this! I didn't follow the matter up, though I believe he sent a cheque to Bowyer House, and it was lost because I'd moved.

The same poem had appeared, along with two others – 'The Song of the Mad Showman' and 'Gone Mad' – in *Doves for the Seventies*, an anthology of poems published in 1970 by Corgi and edited by Peter Robins. He had heard me reading for the Tribune Group and also at the Lamb and Flag, and he wrote to me asking would I contribute some poems connected with the idea of Peace. The anthology was launched by a reading at the Festival Hall. I'll always be grateful to Charles Causley. There was a great deal of free alcohol on a table in the room where the poets were waiting to go onto the stage – there were about ten of us, and we appeared one at a time. I was so petrified with stage-fright that I didn't see the bottles *or* the table, though everyone else was taking full advantage. Charles Causley must have seen this. He advanced on me with a large double brandy, saying, 'Come on, Pat! Tes all free!' This is an ancient Cornish joke and, after that, I relaxed, and things weren't nearly as bad. In fact, the reception I got was absolutely uproarious. Carola Grindea was there. She whispered to me afterwards a very wise thing: 'You stole the show. Be careful of that.' You see, there were an awful lot of influential people reading, and she thought I would offend them. And I think I *did* offend them: she was probably right. No commissions came to me as a result of my performance, but I got £10 for the poems and £10 for the reading . . .

Anyway, where are we? . . . Oh, yes. Austin Reed. Well, in August 1969, Austin Reed decided to move their Accounts Department up to Thirsk in Yorkshire. We were asked whether we would like to go with them, in which case they would house us, or whether we would like to leave, and, if we left, we would get redundancy money according to how long we'd been there. I opted to leave and, at the end of September, when the office closed, I was given £300 in hand as I'd been there about three years. We had a really nice time in that interim period, because there was nothing to do – we were paid for just sitting and talking.

One of the things we did was to play that silly game with a glass turned upside-down. You sit at a table, with the letters of the alphabet all round this upturned glass, and you all put a finger very lightly on the bottom of the glass, and the glass is supposed to move towards the letters and spell out messages. Well, one day, some of us decided to play this, and the glass wouldn't move. We were all saying things like, 'Of course it doesn't work!', 'It's always a fake!', when one of the typists, a dolly bird called Sylvia, and the last person in the world you'd associate with being psychic, came over from the opposite corner, and said, 'Oh yes, it *does* work! Never think of it as a fake, because it isn't!', and she put her finger on the glass, and said in much the same tone as one might use on the telephone, 'Can I have a spirit, please?', then walked away.

That glass began to vibrate immediately! It was absolutely uncanny. As soon as she touched that glass, it began to move! I had expected that, if it did anything, it would be a very slow process, but it absolutely *flew* across the table. First of all, it spelt out 'I am Jack', the name of the spirit. Then it spelt out 'Kathy', one of the girls' names, and that meant there was a message for Kathy. It then gave her an address, a number in a certain street, and it said 'Help' – she afterwards went to this address, and she found that it no longer existed, but there *had* been a place of that name which was bombed during the war. Then the glass gave a message for me. It spelt out 'Pat', and the message it spelt out was 'Book a success'. I'm quite sure none of us pushed that glass, but it did spell out that message, and I had a wishful think that it might apply to my new novel *The Banks of Vesuvius*.

The idea behind *The Banks of Vesuvius* was a story my mother told me of how she once went round with Aunt Susan trying to sell a Banks Bible, and a vicar they tried to plant it on told them to burn it because it was the fifteenth Bible he'd been offered that week. Aunt Susan was so shocked by this suggestion of the vicar that she had a row with him. Vesuvius was Aunt Susan's nickname when she was younger because she was volatile and always erupting, so *The Banks of Vesuvius* seemed to me an attractive title. The title also came from the fact that I was very much in love with the books of Rose Macaulay, and *The Towers of Trebizond* had an echo in *The Banks of Vesuvius*. The novel is highly autobiographical. The beginning has a Welsh setting, based on the village of Llanarth near Parke Farm. Dilys, the daughter of a parson, marries the local ne'er-do-well who deserts her and their baby son. She comes to London, the baby with her, intending to contact her Aunt Vesuvius, who has a flat in Red Lion Square. But she finds that her aunt is dead, and all that remains of her possession is a Banks Bible. She takes the Bible away, and it becomes a white elephant she can't get rid of throughout all her London misad-

172

ventures – even at the end of the novel, her small son is sitting on it, eating toast. Some of *The Banks of Vesuvius*, I wrote at weekends in the Tate Gallery – I do recommend the atmosphere of the place for writing purposes. I've *still* only typed out half of the first revision.

Though I owned a typewriter as far back as 1967, I didn't learn how to use it until I left Austin Reed. This is how I acquired it: In 1966, my mother wrote to me and said she was going to visit Felicity, my sister, who had emigrated to Australia. We've always called Felicity 'Duffy'. No, the name's nothing to do with plum duff, though she's now a very large lady indeed and she *was* a very sturdy child. As a baby, she couldn't pronounce 'stuffing' when she saw my mother stuffing a turkey. She called it 'duffing' and, from then on, would even call bits of mud she picked up 'duffing'. We shortened this to Duffy.

Duffy and Lionel, her husband, who she met while she was a student at Seal Haine Agricultural College when she was nineteen, have had a very chequered career. They married in '55, and Lionel kept going from job to job till they settled on market gardening in Frome in Somerset with the help of some government scheme. But they did badly on the market garden, and had to give it up, and went to live with my mother at Treworra, where they made plans to emigrate to Australia. They emigrated in about 1960. They had four toddlers, born within about a year of each other, and it was rather touching at the Air Terminal to see them all going together to this sort of unknown place, especially as I thought Lionel was unreliable. Actually, Lionel found his feet in Australia, and did very well. First he managed a huge chicken farm somewhere in the outback, and then, he found work as a long-distance lorry driver. Eventually, he started his own haulage contracting business in Liverpool, New South Wales, and it was at this point that Mother decided to visit them for Christmas, she missed them so dreadfully.

She went by boat, and I got some *ecstatic* letters, because she'd never been further than France and was revelling in this travelling. She was using watercolours – since my father died, she'd become a great amateur painter – and, somewhere near Aden, she'd come on deck to paint the sunrise, and seen an Arab sailor making his morning prayers. She thought she'd never seen anything so beautiful.

She only told me about the voyage back, in '67, *afterwards*. My mother was on very friendly terms with the captain and crew, and she knew that the captain had been warned not to go through the Suez Canal because a war was brewing between Egypt and Israel. He ignored this warning, thinking that, even if this *were* the case, the Canal would be safe as Israel was so far away. But the war, when it did start, was like a wild fire, it swept down to the Canal in no time. The ship was well and truly caught in the cross-fire – fishermen on both banks were scrambling for safety, and getting killed. The captain, seeing his mistake, sailed, with other ships, into a backwater of the Canal called the Bitter Lakes, and Mother was sort of marooned there for almost a month. She said food ran short, everything ran short except whisky, and there were parties every night.

During this month my mother did a great deal of painting, and what she painted mostly were the crew. The sailors fascinated her because, although it was such an uncertain time, they were always completely cheerful and, by keeping to the strict discipline of the ship and performing their set jobs at their regular hours, they maintained their own and everybody else's sanity. When, at last, the French Embassy in Cairo provided a helicopter to lift the passengers off the ship, a party was in progress, and my mother was well and truly pickled. She said to the sailors in farewell, 'Oh, goodbye, goodbye to all of you! I *shall* miss your beautiful torsos!' 'Mrs *Burgess*!' said the captain. 'That's the last time I ever give you whisky!' She was allowed to take a suitcase, so she only recovered two of her paintings as the others were in her trunk. In the suitcase were cameras for Louis and Bobby and, for me – oh frabjous day! Caloo! Callay! – a typewriter, my Hermes Baby, the portable typewriter I've used ever since learning to type while working for the Performing Rights Society after leaving Austin Reed. . . .

I *loathed* the Performing Rights, and I only stayed there for about sixteen months. Song titles came out of a computer, and you had to write each one down and put it on a card. You were continually correcting mistakes. If you thought a title was obviously wrong – for instance, if it had 'leer' instead of 'love' – you had to look it up and see what the right title was. The only good things I can say about the Performing Rights are that, while I was there, I had my first holiday in Paris and I learned how to touch-type – we were in Berners Street and Pitman's school wasn't far away. My mother's present of a Hermes Baby has by now saved me a fortune.

*

174

I owe my first holiday in Paris to my mother, too. She felt that, because of Philippe's death and as the boys had their own interests – girls, mostly! – I should go alone to Paris, where I'd never been and which she knew I'd love. Would I visit, on her behalf, two distant relatives in Neuilly, if she were to pay? Of course, I went. That was June 1970, and I don't think a year since then has passed when I haven't been back.

Needless to say, Miron Grindea was very interested to hear that I was going to Paris, and gave me the address of the hotel he always used – the Hôtel Trocadéro in the Rue St Didier. I've stayed there often since. It's a very small, cheap but nice hotel, where a lot of travelling salesmen stay; a Madame Matthieu keeps it, and the same servants have been with her for a long time. Grindea also asked me to visit the widow of Paul Celan, the poet, in the Rue de Longchamp, and Natalie Barney at the Hôtel Meurice in the Rue de Rivoli. I went to see Paul Celan's widow one morning. She was a textile designer, and very elegant: we hadn't very much in common. We were having lemon tea, I remember, and I said I liked French poetry and Grindea had shown me some of her husband's work. She told me, rather sourly, that her husband didn't write in French, he wrote in German. I rather piped down after that. But Natalie Barney was a *warm* person, who stroked my arm as we spoke! She received me in a wheelchair, and asked her companion to provide coffee after putting out a hand to welcome me.

Though she was ninety, Natalie was still very pretty and had a lovely skin. I think most of her hair had fallen out, which must have grieved her very much, so she was wearing a most beautiful white lace shawl around her head. She was a very rich woman, with estates in America still. She'd had to come from the Deep South as a girl of seventeen or so because of her lesbian tendencies. Back home she was thought of as a kind of horror story but, in Paris, people were much less strict about this thing, and, at her house in the Rue Jacob in the Latin Quarter, she evolved a salon where lesbians were sheltered, and their love *affaires* treated with respect. Otherwise it was like any other literary or artistic salon, except that no strong drink was offered, not even wine, only lemonade. I asked her about Proust, who I knew was a visitor there. She said, 'Oh yes, it was always rather an ordeal. You see, he was a great man and I was quite a young woman, and the salon wasn't very important. Somehow he always made me very

175

tired. He didn't talk very much himself, and I wanted desperately to talk to *him*, so I got into the habit of sleeping for at least two hours before he came.' She told me how much she had enjoyed her life in Paris, though sadness, for some reason, had always crept into her work – her poems and her novel, *The One Who Is Legion*.

Our interview took place in the drawing-room of her hotel suite. She hated the hotel, though it was the best in Paris, bar the Ritz. She said the waiters were tyrants and she didn't like being in a strange place and she wanted to go home to the Rue Jacob. But I knew she could never go back. She'd been told that she was only to be at the Meurice while her house was being renovated, but she was really there because she could be better looked after, and she would be dead in a very short time. It was afternoon, and girls, the tail-end of her salon, kept drifting in. They were all very pretty, all very elegant, and some of them quite young. I felt an absolute haybag among them. She introduced me as 'a lady who has come from Miron Grindea, and works for *Adam*'. This gave me some status, as they all knew that Natty, as they called her, had been celebrated twice, and was to be celebrated again, in this famous English magazine.

The two relatives my mother asked me to visit were elderly sisters – a strong and spry one, Tante Julie, and an ailing one, Tante Elie, always on a sofa. I'm afraid I rather played truant. What I wanted to do was explore the City, sit in the cafés, go out to Versailles. I said on that first visit and thereafter, 'I've only got one day,' and then, in 1973, Tante Julie, the strong and spry one, died, and Tante Elie went to the South to be looked after in a Home.

Though they're not nice people if you get on the wrong side of them, I like the policemen of Paris – there was one who showed me round the dark little street market and the arcades of the Bastille. My favourite haunt of all is the Palais Royal district, where I usually buy at least one article of clothing on the Rue St Honoré. I've bought a silk dress – a Cardin marked down to the equivalent of £30. It was something that couldn't be sold in the *maison de haute couture* because there wasn't enough material under the arms. I always now buy my underclothes in Paris – they're so much better made in France, and they last much longer . . .

A lot of the reason I go back to Paris is because it's very exhilarating to have a language which is partly yours through your grandmother, and having it come back to you. I go to the Comédie Française every night if the programme changes. I've seen Racine, Molière, Marivaux . . . I went to a Marivaux play once. It went on and on. I went to sleep. I woke up again, and the talking was *still* going on. I went to sleep again and I woke up again. There were two intervals, and the play lasted till twelve o'clock, and nobody seemed to think this peculiar. *Cyrano de Bergerac* is my favourite I think de Gaulle was right, you know. When he saw it, he said, 'This is the very spirit and blood of France!' And it is – all France is in that play.

When I first started going to Paris, it was considered very infra dig for a woman to sit in a café alone. The waiters automatically assumed you were a tart, and very often either wouldn't serve you at all or took a long time doing so. I thought this very silly, and used to sit in the Café de la Comédie and in the cafés on the Avenue Kléber on purpose. One warm summer's day in 1975, I went to a café on the Kléber, thinking, 'The waiter probably won't come.' But all this attitude had changed: suddenly everything was all right, and I was served at once. This was because the prostitutes were all on strike – they'd locked themselves up in the churches; the Madeleine was full of them. The waiters knew that I couldn't be a prostitute, I was just an innocent tourist – otherwise, I'd be locked up in the Madeleine! . . .

But, in 1970, I had, of course, to return, after this lovely present of Paris from my mother, to the dreaded song titles at the Performing Rights. A short while afterwards, maybe a month, she wrote to me saying she was coming up to Brighton to stay with an old school friend, Margaret Reid; could I join them for a day? When I telephoned to say Yes, she was absolutely overjoyed: 'Oh, I'm *so* glad! I was afraid you wouldn't be able to make it!' – her reaction seemed somehow exaggerated. We had a very pleasant day, visiting the Planetarium and Prinnie's Chinese Pavilion and, after lunch at Margaret Reid's, walking along the esplanade, and out as far as Hove and Palmeira Square, by that beautiful Regency crescent, where Grindea now lives at No. 1.

This was the last time I saw her before her final illness. It never struck me that there was anything wrong, but I, think she must have known then that she was going to die soon.

I didn't, then, hear anything very much of her until the winter, when Birgitta, my sister-in-law, wrote and said that she had developed stomach trouble and a very bad cough, which might be

177

due to the change of climate after Australia. I went down to Treworra to see her. The doctor had ordered her to stop smoking, but she was still drinking home-made wine, and I thought she was improving. Then I got another letter from Birgitta, saying she was much worse and smoking like a chimney; the doctor was making no trouble about this smoking, which she thought was a bad sign. When I went down for Christmas – by myself, as the boys were staying with their girlfriends – I knew that she was very ill indeed, but I still wrapped her Christmas present, a nightdress that I'd bought in Paris with a little embroidered *lisette* to go with it. I'd intended to wear them myself, but didn't, as I thought they would be nice for Mother as she was ill. It didn't occur to me that I'd never be able to give them to her.

I arrived the day before Christmas Eve to be told that she'd been in Plymouth General Hospital for a week, and was dying of leukemia. Tim drove me to see her at once. She was being kept unconscious by drugs to relieve the pain. I took her hand, and she opened her eyes for a moment and said, 'Pat!', then sank back into unconsciousness. She was still unconscious when, late on Christmas Eve, a doctor advised Tim and me to leave her. Tim came into my room early on Christmas morning in floods of tears. He had just had a message to say that Mother was dead. I stayed at Treworra till her funeral. She was buried in the same plot as my father in the graveyard of Davidstow village church. Louis and Bob who had loved her, attended. There were many tears. Birgitta, trying to comfort me, said, 'It's such a peaceful place to be buried and, if she looks from here, she can see Treworra.' In a burst of anger – and it's something I'll always regret because I was so fond of Birgitta – I blurted back, 'She can't *see* anything! She's *dead*!'

13

I left the Performing Rights Society the following May, not because of the £1,000 or so I was to receive under Mother's Will after paying back the £2,300 I owed the Burgess Estate, but because they were only keeping their fastest workers for using a new computer, and I was *sacked* – with no holiday money and with only a month's salary in compensation. I was sick of offices – Freeman's, Hamblin's, Austin Reed, the Performing Rights ... Vowing I'd never work in one again, I studied cards in newsagents' windows and ads in the *Evening News*, and took down telephone numbers, and rang for odd jobs as furniture polisher, baby-minder, *anything*. What the Will *did* influence was my decision, the previous February, to leave Bowyer House. In the knowledge that there was money coming to me, and with the £300 redundancy payment from Austin Reed I'd safely put aside, and a legacy of £500 from Auntie Nora who had died a year before Mother, it was possible to consider moving with the boys to somewhere more spacious and less haunted by memories of Philippe, to somewhere without the lavatory in the same place as the gas stove.

Though a law had been passed putting an end to the 'key money' racket, I couldn't, at first, find accommodation at a *rent* I could afford. Then Doris Muldoon told me about the Ideal Homes Furniture Company down by the Angel, Islington. The company employed an army of very good-looking young men to go round knocking on doors and persuading people, mostly widows, to let rooms to anyone who would buy furniture from Ideal Homes. This, of course, was another racket, because accommodation was what customers wanted, and they would pay exorbitant sums for the

179

furniture, which wasn't very good. To obtain a flat, I put down £300 for a three-piece suite and a room divider and two carpets, so they found me something, at a rent of only £5 a week, at 17, Rosendale Road, West Dulwich, on the border of West Norwood. The tenant of the house, a Mrs Wallis, a courageous old Scotswoman, lived on the ground floor with an hotel lavatory attendant called Frank Utting, but said she felt less nervous with tenants upstairs, and offered us the first floor and the attic above. Though the place had been built in 1872 and neglected, it would seem, ever since, the first floor consisted of a large kitchen, a large sitting-room with a bay window, a large bedroom and a bathroom and lavatory, and the attic had two rooms where the boys could live when the windows were mended and the ceilings sealed against damp with waterproof paper. You reached them by a little twisting stairway, which I seldom climbed once they had settled in. For our £5, we also had the use of the garden! It was an incredible bargain and, in the ten years that I was there, the rent only went up once – to £6 – because of an increase in the rates.

Another great advantage of living at Rosendale Road was the fact it was only a twenty-minute walk from the Crown and Greyhound. Howard Sergeant had handed over the chairmanship of the Dulwich Group at Christmas 1969, to Alasdair Aston, a master at Alleyn's, a school near Dulwich College. Alasdair was an attractive man, and I could talk to him. He was a scholar and could quote poetry till kingdom come (being a Scotsman, he knew all the Scottish Ballads). After readings, we would always be the last out of the pub, where the landlord would come and join us for the final drink.

Alasdair arranged all readings which involved the Poetry Secretariat, whose listed poets had to be paid £40. Ted Hughes came once; so did Seamus Heaney and Brian Patten, and there was an uncomfortable evening when Stevie Smith condescended to grace the 'Dog' with her presence. Howard Sergeant had invited her, but she demanded too large a fee, plus dinner and taxi fares and accommodation for the night. As he wasn't frantic about her poetry anyway, his attitude had been 'It wouldn't be worth it.' But Alasdair decided that it would. He invited her through Michael Hamburger, the translator, who lived in Dulwich and was a friend of hers and volunteered to transport her back and forth and to ask her to dinner and to stay the night.

Alasdair usually began his evening with an unknown poet,

180

saving his star performer till after the interval, but this wouldn't do for La Smith, who insisted on giving her reading *before* the interval. She brought a large following, so the audience was good, but the reading was perfunctory and she sang some of her poems in, what seemed to me, a very unmelodious croak. As soon as her reading was finished, she left, refusing to talk to anyone, and without so much as a smile. Most of her audience went with her, so the readings which followed were given to a great many empty chairs. Stevie Smith's poetry is famous for its compassion, but this evidently didn't extend to us. Alasdair asked me to chair the second half. Afterwards, he was waiting for me in the bar with my usual glass of red wine. He told me that Stevie Smith had been in such a hurry to get away that she had slipped on the icy road and broken her ankle. True, she was an old lady, perhaps ill, perhaps in pain and therefore crabbed, but, to my shame, I could not feel sympathetic: I thought, 'Poetic justice! Serves her right!'

I, not Alasdair, arranged readings by 'lesser knowns' such as Nolan Walsh and Raggy Farmer, which means I arranged *most* of the readings. Nolan Walsh, Michael Fitzgerald, Ferenz, and Frank Bangay were part of a little nucleus of avant-garde poets who read in the basement of The Troubadour café in Old Brompton Road. I read there myself quite often. It was a free-for-all. A boy on the door would ask you if you wanted to read, and he called out the names in the order you'd come. It was always very hard work at the Troubadour. The footsteps overhead sounded like thunder and you had to *shout* to make yourself heard.

Nolan Walsh was an enthusiastic and dedicated poet, rather immature, but Michael Fitzgerald, though undisciplined, was a natural poet, very lyrical . . . Ferenz was a boy, of Hungarian extraction, with an unusual style of reading: he read his poems at such a speed that only a line here and there stood out clearly, a method which was strangely effective. Frank Bangay was from Hackney, and he ran a group called The Fighting Pigeons with Dave Sheen, the editor of the magazine *Inklings*. Raggy Farmer, a Marxist who wrote songs rather than poems, I originally met as Ivan St Clair at the Trafalgar Arts Centre in Adelaide Street, just behind St Martin's. Eventually he ran a club, which he called 'Grannie's', over the Helvetia pub in Old Compton Street, where he sang songs and read poetry under the name of Raggy Farmer. Though he was really very smart and dressed in the latest fashion, for *poetry* he liked to look a cross between a drug addict and a

181

tramp, with dark glasses and baggy ploughman's trousers held up with string braces . . . I found other poets at the Three Horseshoes in Hampstead, where Leonie Scott-Matthews ran a poetry group called 'Pentameters' – also at the Orangery in Holland Park, where Eileen Warren ran hers.

The Lamb and Flag was no longer a place where I could look for poets – early in the Seventies Norman Hidden stopped the meetings there, partly because he was moving out of London, and partly because of hassle with a rowdy element of Marxists and pornographers. Where I *did* make a discovery was at a house in Grangecliff Gardens, Upper Norwood. This was Brian Dann, and 'discovery' is the wrong word, because, with two other poets, Michael Rowes and an alcoholic called Frank Alcock, he was running the Poetry in Croydon Group at the Dog and Gun, and issuing the poetry magazine, *Pick*, as well as *Pick Broadsheets* devoted to individual poets. Brian Dann was so enthusiastic about poetry that he seemed to *live* it. He was enthusiastic *and* prolific. He still *is* enthusiastic and prolific. He's a great experimenter with tape-recordings and electronic music and word processors, using cutting techniques and making insertions to get special effects. He works extremely hard as a poet. As he's also a Local Government Officer, I don't know where he finds the time . . . The house where I first met him was his own. Here, as part of the Crystal Palace Triangle Association, he held poetry readings once a month.

The Association, though it was right on my doorstep, was something I heard about through Miron Grindea. It began as an environmental pressure group to save the Crystal Palace Triangle, the oldest part of Crystal Palace, and, by dint of enthusiasts knocking on doors in the neighbourhood, went on to include a Madrigal Society, a Play Reading Group, a Chess Group and a loose-knit brotherhood of poets, musicians, painters and writers.

The poetry meetings at Brian Dann's house were quite different to those I'd been used to, in that most of the poets were amateurs. To begin with, I felt that the thing wasn't serious enough, but there was always an old lady present who attracted me very much. This was Amy Gemm. Because of Amy, I went back again and again. Amy was a supreme Disrupter of Poetry Readings. She might stop a poet in the middle of a poem by saying, '*I* can't see any sense in that! Well, it's . . . it's *rubbish*! What do you *mean*?!' Then she'd let him go on a bit but, before he could get to the end of his poem, she'd talk to the person next to her: 'Oh, did you hear

182

of that terrible accident last night down by the King's Arms? Well, I waited till the crowd had gone and then I talked to the police, but they didn't tell me much, only that a man got killed . . .' Then somebody else would read, and Amy might say, 'We could do without *her*, couldn't we?!' Yet she was a very affectionate old lady. She always kissed everybody when she came in. Joyce, Brian's wife, was perfectly charming to her, because Joyce is charming to everybody.

At Christmas, we didn't read our own poetry, we read Christmas poems by other poets. I remember once I read T. S. Eliot's 'Journey of the Magi'. Amy sat through this, completely bewildered and dumbfounded. Then, after about ten minutes and in the middle of somebody else's reading, a very serious one, she suddenly shouted at the top of her voice, *'It's "We three kings of Orient"!!'* That was how Amy was. *I* thought she was wonderful, but – I can quite understand – Brian in the end pretended he wasn't running the meetings any more, and that meant that, because Amy took the Crystal Palace Newsletter in which he advertised, he had to send out personal invitations. Amy cried bitterly on what she thought was the last night of these meetings. She said, 'Why isn't Brian going on?! Oh, I've heard such beautiful poetry here, and Joyce has always got such beautiful things to eat!' She was really very sad, and also very complimentary.

Meanwhile, of course, Brian was running Poetry in Croydon and *Pick*, with Jerry Orpwood, best known for his autobiographical poem, 'The Round Wood', more in the foreground to replace Michael Rowes, who had gone blind. The readings were now at the Blacksmith's Arms, where it cost less to hire a room. Frank Alcock was drinking so heavily, and was becoming so unreliable that Brian and Jerry manoeuvred him off the committee. Frank was very aggrieved as he had *started* Poetry in Croydon!

In fact, Poetry in Croydon didn't last very long after that. I remember in the summer of '77 it did readings for a week in conjunction with performances by the London Symphony Orchestra at the Fairfield Hall. Brian Dann read. Jerry Orpwood read. I read. Carol Rumens, who was then unknown but has since made quite a splash writing poems about Women's Liberation, she read, too. The idealistic object of the exercise was that the orchestra would perform its repertoire and we, in the interval, would read poetry in the Crush Bar in keeping with the music. Of course it didn't work out, because nobody could hear us through the noise at the bar counter. And because of the fees demanded by members of the Poetry Secretariat and various other troubles, Poetry in Croydon had folded by the end of the Seventies, and *Pick* with it . . .

To get back to the Crystal Palace Triangle Association and Amy Gemm. Brian had undertaken to organise twice-yearly 'Kaleido- scope' evenings in the home of the late Oliver Stallybrass and his Norwegian wife, Gunvor, at the top of Westwood Hill – Oliver was the great scholar and intellectual who wrote *The Encyclopedia of Modern Thought*. These were occasions when the artistic threads of the Association were drawn together. Poets read poems, musicians played their instruments, singers sang, painters exhibited their work, and actors acted sketches written by writers. Amy was not only a member of the audience – 'She's got a husband, you know, yet she goes round to the baker's when it's early closing day. I've seen them . . .' – she sometimes read a poem of her own. There was no keeping her away from Kaleidoscopes at the Stallybrasses, as they were advertised, and there was no keeping her away from play readings at the Stallybrasses, either, as these were advertised, too.

Always featured in the Newsletter was a monthly play reading, directed by Oliver. There used to be supper provided, and I think you paid ten pence to go in. The drawing-room was two rooms that had been knocked into one, and one half would be lighted so that it gave the impression of a stage, and the other half could be made dark, even on summer evenings, like an auditorium. Oliver cast the plays himself, and paid meticulous attention to the details of costume worn, to suggest character, even if it was just a hat. I belonged to the group, and sometimes we acted, moving about with a book in the hand, and sometimes we sat on chairs and read, depending on the play. Shakespeare is very difficult to do sitting still, although we did *Hamlet* in that way – I was Ophelia. I was also Maria in *Twelfth Night* and a moronic, silly American woman in an Albee play. I also played Lady Caroline in Wilde's *A Woman of No Importance*. I know I was a very masterful wife and, at one point, when I said, 'Oh, no no! I must go and look after John!', Amy shouted, 'That's right! You look after him!'

The play readings still go on, despite Oliver's suicide – I've been to one or two. But they're not so regular, and they never seem to me to have the force that they had when Oliver was there. There's no eager beaver, no central pivot. And Brian Dann still does

184

Kaleidoscope evenings, though only once a year. Amy's not as lively as she was. I think she's feeling her age very much. Somebody has to fetch her . . .

When we first went to 17, Rosendale Road, the boys rather thought they were out in the sticks, till they and their girlfriends began to appreciate their privacy and independence in the attic. Louis always had a girl in tow. So had Bobby, but he used to suffer dreadfully because the parents of his girls always wanted him to get married, mothers used to show him what their daughters were saving for their bottom drawer; in the end, he would have to cut and run. I was sort of sandwiched between sets of lovers – the boys with their girlfriends above me, and Wally and Frank, both in their seventies, below.

I doubt if Frank approved of Louis and Bobby. He assumed that anybody under the age of thirty was a hoodlum. He'd been an army man, and spoke in a peculiar clipped manner. He was known by the young people of the district as 'the colonel'. When he passed them he'd say, 'Yee-obbos! Yee-obbos! Good-for-nothing yee-obbos! What are their mothers doing?!' He was usually on his way with Wally to the Rosendale pub or to the Brick in Romany Road. Wally had only one leg, and used a crutch in the house but, to go out to the pub with Frank, she put on an artificial leg. Their place downstairs was so dark, they had to have electric lights on all the time. And, before they could have any hot water, they had to stoke an old-fashioned range – we depended on them stoking that range for a weekly bath, until I installed an immersion heater. Wally was quick-tempered, and Frank was often in a state of angry picklement, so they were constantly banging doors and shouting. 'You were with that woman again, Frank! . . . You *were*! . . . Just because she's got diamonds in her hair!' 'Wally, you're telling lies! You're *always* telling lies! Anyway, what about you, Wally?! What about you?! You never do anything but pull me down! You're always sniggering, sniggering, sniggering!' – lovers' tiffs, you see; all about nothing, and absolute rubbish.

Soon after we moved in, when the boys were doing up the attic for themselves, I took a few days' holiday with Tim and Birgitta in Cornwall. I returned to find Wally and Frank rather hostile and forbidding, and Sheila Purbrick, a next-door neighbour who had welcomed me with tea on arrival, looked like a dog with bristles raised. The boys, in my absence, had given a house-warming on

185

the grand scale. There was a kind of powder everywhere, but I suspected nothing. Then, when I went to pay the rent on Saturday, Wally said, 'Oh, there's been terrible things happening while you've been away! I'm sure it was nothing to do with you, Pat. I'm sure that you are most respectable.'

I asked the boys what on earth had been going on, and they told me the story. The amplifier of their record-player had been blaring, full blast, out of a window, and not only the people they'd invited came to the party, but every drop-out for miles around dropped in as well. The trouble started when no more could be *got* in. People were literally packed one against the other in the flat, and the disgruntled ones left out in the garden, after shouting abuse, managed to get onto the roof and started climbing in by the windows. Sheila Purbrick from next door came out to complain over the back fence about the general behaviour and, when she did so, someone on the roof tried to pee on her head. In fact Louis and Bob had lost control of the situation and were very frightened.

They were even more frightened when there was a drunken cry of 'Murder!' because someone was found in an attic room, lying on the floor as if dead. People crowded into the room to see the body, and, finding it was only Kim Tremaine, a friend of the boys from Bowyer House days, who had passed out, mixed up a bucket of cement which Bobby was using for building work, and plastered his hand to the floor. The idea was that he would be trapped there, and I'm only glad that he woke up before it completely hardened. But he did wake up and, in revenge, he went about sticking cement on people and throwing balls of it at them, which, when they missed, stuck to the furniture and walls ... Anyway, Louis and Bob made a terrific effort afterwards to clear up the mess. Wally said they'd spent two days at it, and had really worked very hard. They had apologised to Wally, but they hadn't apologised to Sheila Purbrick because she'd not only complained unfairly during the party, she'd complained again the next day. I myself couldn't be too angry with them, but I did tell them that it mustn't happen again – I think they were very determined that it *shouldn't* happen again. I was going to apologise to Sheila on their behalf but, in the end, I didn't because she kept throwing out remarks about parents who couldn't bring up their children. We were on bad terms for several years. Sheila simply adored babies – not children, but babies – and her second husband couldn't give her any more. When, eventually, the Borough Council gave her permission to run a foster home simply for small babies, she forgot all about her quarrel with me. It was really wonderful to see the change in her. She was frantically busy, but she told me, 'I love nappies and bottles and babies crying in the night and getting up to see to them.' And she *did*!

I think it was in 1973 that Louis acquired a permanent girlfriend called Lynn. He took her from Bobby, and I expected a terrific row over it, but Bobby was in one of his usual situations where marriage had been mentioned by the girl's parents so, when Louis took her over, he was really very relieved. Louis and Lynn, when they were coming home one night, heard scratching and yowling from inside a dustbin. They took the lid off, and found a very tiny black kitten which hadn't yet opened its eyes. We decided to call it Lulu after Louis. So that's my Lulu.

Lynn was a very nice girl, plump with a little round face. She was only two years younger than Louis, who was about twenty-three, but she looked fifteen. Her father worked for the Post Office as a telephone engineer. Louis liked him very much – Louis always took a great interest in each of his girlfriends' fathers because I think he was looking for his own. After his initial try at farming, he had done all sorts of jobs. But Lynn's father persuaded him to knuckle down at night school and get some O and A levels to become a telephone engineer like himself. He hadn't thought of using his brain before – neither of the boys had, until after Philippe died and we moved house, when Bobby decided to go to night school, too.

So Louis qualified as a telephone engineer, and worked with Lynn's father, and decided to marry Lynn, whose parents, Londoners to the core, wanted a large church marriage. But the arrangements for this marriage got so complicated and there was so much etiquette to be studied, that Louis, never one to bow to convention, chickened out, and Lynn chickened out after him. Instead, in '75, they arranged a marriage of their own – a very small affair at a Registry Office, followed by a reception at the Crown and Greyhound. Bobby's current girlfriend came, a very silent young lady by the name of Jackie. That was a relationship I could never understand. Bobby seemed to find her silence very attractive. It was a very *strange* relationship, and I'm glad it petered out. They may have been unconsciously taking the advice given to new Samaritans: 'Never be afraid of silence.'

187

For a time, Louis and Lynn, who was a radiologist at St Thomas's, lived in Louis' room in the attic at Rosendale Road. Then they moved to a flat of their own in Lewisham, though Louis was hankering after somewhere in the country. Both he *and* Bobby longed to be somewhere in the country. They looked on their time in Wales – the bits of it they could remember – as time spent in the Garden of Eden; and the same for their holidays in Cornwall with my mother. A friend of Lynn's, a doctor at St Thomas's, invited them both, and Bobby, to his wedding in the Highlands of Scotland. Louis and Bobby wanted to live in Scotland right away. In '77 Louis exchanged with an engineer in the Perth GPO, and rented a cottage, East Cottage, one of three joined cottages on Easter Rhynd Farm, owned by Mr Hay, the curling champion for Scotland, four miles from Bridge of Earn and seven miles from Perth. This was also handy for Lynn, who got work as a radiologist in the hospital at Bridge of Earn, while he went around in his van, mending telephones.

Now, *I* thought they were living together at Easter Rhynd very happily. But Lynn developed dizziness and tiredness, and her hair began to fall out and she began to put on weight, until it was discovered she had a small growth on the pituitary gland, which had to be removed by an operation. Louis was left alone a lot during this illness, and they were both too young to cope with such a difficult situation. In '79, when Lynn came out of hospital, she returned to her parents in London, and Louis divorced her. Very soon afterwards, Louis told me he was living with a Scottish girl, a telephone operator at Bridge of Earn Hospital, who he intended to marry. He invited me to East Cottage to meet her. Her name was Wilma, and I went up to meet her with very mixed feelings – I thought of her as 'the other woman', as someone who had muscled in when Lynn was only just over her operation, as someone who had caused my son's divorce. But, when I arrived, it was impossible to dislike Wilma. She was a very simple, very young and very unspoilt Scottish girl, and her father and mother were two of the nicest people I had ever met – he's a lorry driver, and she's the Cleaning Superintendent at Bridge of Earn Hospital, and they live in a most beautiful cottage at Strawberry Hill, one of the loveliest spots I know. In 1980, I went with Bobby and his fiancée, to the wedding at Perth Registry Office. Louis and Wilma were ecstatically happy. Bobby and Olivia were happy. I was happy that everybody else was happy.

188

Bobby, having got through his apprenticeship in the building trade and qualified, found it wasn't enough for him so after studying at night school and achieving three A Levels, he alighted on the editor of the *Streatham News* (or it may have been the *Norwood News* – he eventually worked for both; they belonged to the same group) and asked him did he think there was any chance of a job as a junior reporter. The editor said, 'Get me three news stories, send them in to me, and I'll see what your writing's like. If they're all right, you've got the job.'

Bobby talked to me about this. He couldn't think *what* he was going to do for these stories. So I told him we were having Adrian Henri for a reading at the Crown and Greyhound. Adrian Henri was a Liverpool poet who was quite famous, though *I* didn't think much of his poetry, so Bobby came to the Dog on the night and did a little write-up. For the next story, he decided to get an interview with Kit Pedlar, who had written the television series 'Doomwatch' and several books of science fiction. He lived in Dulwich, and Bobby was friendly with his son, Mark. He was very kind and gave Bobby a long interview. For his third story, he wrote about how some local yobbos had amused themselves by driving cars of a local second-hand car dealer into one another and smashing them. He got the job he wanted, and was soon put onto the *Brixton News*. In fact, for some time, because it was new, Bobby *was* the *Brixton News* as he was the only reporter on it.

Bobby and Olivia were married in 1980, shortly after Louis' marriage to Wilma. Bobby, as I've already told you, is now a Public Relations Officer for the Highlands and Islands Development Board and Olivia runs the Women's Page of the *Highlands News*. They live in Lochardil, a suburb of Inverness, where I visited them last year.

14

Good heavens, the boys can't *support* me! – it's as much as they can do to support themselves and their wives, and Louis now has Ben, a baby son! When they lived with me at Rosendale Road, they each contributed £2 a week towards household expenses. Because of the low rent, and my savings, and the dribs and drabs coming in from the Burgess Estate after Mother's death, and a £90 a year income from my one third share of the water meadows at Treworra inherited from Daddy, things weren't so pressing as at Bowyer House. That's why I could risk freelance jobs instead of regular office work. Also, after Philippe's death, I had a Widow's Pension, though I've always thought it a bit cockeyed you should get a pension just because your husband dies, when a husband doesn't get one if his wife dies. And, in those early Seventies, I was earning at least a *little* money from poetry readings – Leonie Scott-Matthews of 'Pentameters' didn't pay me, but I got £10 from Eileen Warren at the Orangery in Holland Park, Raggy Farmer paid me £10 at Grannie's, and I got £2 and £3 for spots at The Troubadour, £10 from a girls' secondary school in Streatham, and £40 plus fares and dinner and a night's accommodation from Alan Bates of the Leicester Poetry Society.

My freelance jobs included polishing antique furniture with antique wax for an antiques shop in James Street, off Wigmore Street. That didn't last long because, strangely enough, I saw an advertisement in the *Evening News* for somebody to polish antique furniture in a private flat. I felt I was quite good at this now, and they were offering more money, so I went instead to this very luxurious flat, full of very beautiful antique furniture, in Knights-

190

bridge. The flat belonged to a couple called Borges. The lady was the Australian Ambassador's daughter, and her husband was a captain of industry, and they had a small, very lovely baby. I worked for them from nine to twelve, Mondays to Fridays, for £2.50 a week, sorry, £2 10s a week – this was 1971/72, and the United Kingdom hadn't yet joined the Common Market. While they were away at their mill house in Sussex, I kept their furniture polished, and, when they were in London, I cleaned.

I didn't get on very well with Mrs Borges. She was rather unpredictable and temperamental. I think she'd been accustomed to having a lot of servants, probably aborigines, in Australia. She complained when I didn't wipe the greasy rings off the bath. She didn't like me cuddling the baby. One morning when I arrived, the flat had been broken into. I rang Mrs Borges at the mill. She got into a terrific flap – 'Call the police! Get a locksmith!' and so on and so forth. I did everything she asked, and she came up from the mill with the baby, in an awful stew. It was afternoon by that time, and I had to go to a job elsewhere. She said, 'What do you mean "You've got to go"? You haven't polished the furniture yet!'

Another job was spring cleaning for an old lady, well over eighty, at Nell Gwynn House, Sloane Avenue. I was to be paid a pound a morning. The first morning, she asked me to put all her winter clothes into store. The trouble was that she'd been a lady's maid, and she knew exactly how to do this and I didn't. At the end of the morning, she *did* not want to part with a pound note! She said, 'Of course, you know that I shall have to go without food to pay you this?! I'm paying you for packing, when you don't know how to pack. My old charlady was very good, and *she* didn't charge a pound. I mean, I daren't tell her that I'm paying you a pound, because I paid her very much less, and she would be very hurt indeed.' She held the pound note in her hand and, every time she was going to give it to me, she pulled it back again. But I stood there, and eventually I did get it. I went back every day till the end of the week, but her continual haggling wore me down and, on the last day, I didn't ask for my pound.

In 1972, I had an afternoon job, which was to fetch Charlotte Adams, a little girl of six, from Paray House School in the Sydney Hall, Pond Place, South Kensington, and take her home to Markham Street, off the King's Road, and stay with her until her mother arrived. Sometimes Mrs Adams went out in the evenings, so then I would stay overnight or, if it wasn't too late, she would take me home to Rosendale Road in her car. She was a very friendly woman and I liked her. She had been divorced from her husband in Africa, and had come back to England with Charlotte, who had two bigger sisters at boarding school. Charlotte was a very intelligent, very pretty little girl, blonde. The only thing with Charlotte was that I *could* not make her eat properly. She only liked cucumber, so I continually had to make her cucumber sandwiches.

At Paray House I used to occasionally meet the headmistress, Miss Lahee-Williams, a small, slim, very spry fifty-year-old, stylishly dressed and with fair hair and glasses. The girls always curtsied and the boys bowed to her, before they were let go – a very good system, because a child couldn't leave without her knowing. One day, when I arrived, Charlotte was having a dancing lesson. The class was doing a Breton fishermen's dance, a very charming character dance indeed. I commented on this when Miss Williams came out to say goodbye, telling her that I had been through a dance training. She said she had a great opinion of Charlotte as a potential dancer and had just entered her for a Sunshine Competition – I had sometimes entered these competitions myself, when I was a young girl; they're in aid of blind children. In due course she asked me for some advice. We arranged something together, and she invited me to accompany them to the competition, make sure that Charlotte was ready to go on. Charlotte didn't win, though I thought she was quite the best dancer there.

After that, Miss Williams and I talked quite often. She told me that she had been trained as a classical ballet dancer, but had always been a teacher. After teaching in three private schools in England, she was converted to Catholicism and entered an enclosed order of nuns in Paris, from where she was sent to a convent in the village of Paray. Here, if you wanted to speak outside certain times, there was a bell in the middle of the Great Hall which you could ring, but only in dire emergency. Well, how Miss Williams ever managed to sustain periods of silence at all, I don't know, because, when I knew her, she kept up a continuous flow of talk. She said to me, 'You know, dear, when I went to Paray, I was always ringing the bell. The Reverend Mother wasn't at all pleased. Before I arrived, that bell had only been rung once in two hundred years. And she didn't like it, either, when I told her I'd come into a convent to worship God, and not because of Jesus. I told her I wasn't particularly *interested* in Jesus. I said to her, "Why *did* he

192

come?! We've had nothing but trouble since he was here. And look at the people he went and talked to! Why couldn't he talk to *decent* people?!" Do you know, dear, she *couldn't* see it?!'

She had then come out of the convent with her health ruined and with a thyroid complaint that had to be treated. Stranded, with no job, and with a family that couldn't help her, a former ballet friend told her that the Sydney Hall could be rented from the Jehovah's Witnesses at a very small rent, and she lent her enough money to start Paray House, as a private day school offering a ballet education. There are several of these little schools around London. They call them 'ballet schools' and, traditionally, they're always cheaper than ordinary schools. Paray House was then, in '72, £300 a term – it's now £650. It had about sixteen pupils, but the number usually varied between twenty and thirty. Boys were taken from the age of four to eight, girls from four to eleven or twelve, when they took Common Entrance and went on to boarding school, except for stage children who might go on to the Corona or Italia Conti schools.

At the start of the summer term, Miss Williams was having to cook the school lunches herself because the cook had left her in the cart. She asked me if I could possibly cook them instead. She was very exact – I was only to take an hour and a quarter, and I was only to be paid for an hour and a quarter of an hour at 7/6d an hour. I agreed to do it. I now had a full schedule. I worked for Mrs Borges first, then went down to Paray House and cooked the lunches, then waited around to take Charlotte home at half past three; sometimes, during the waiting around period, I read a story to the kindergarten babies or listened to the bigger girls reading, and asked them questions to see if they understood – also at 7/6d an hour. Well, the cooking arrangements were *appalling*! It was a church-hall-sort-of-building, with one big hall and a kindergarten, which was also the kitchen, behind. The kitchen was bare boards and a great big deal table and an old-fashioned stone sink and two gas rings, screened off from the kindergarten. At lunchtime, the children in the big hall pushed their desks to the side, and spread out tables. I'm quite sure that no Inspector would have passed the cooking arrangements, *or* the loos and the washrooms.

Miss Williams said that there had been an Inspection when she first came. At first, she said, the Inspector had been rather chary, 'but when he saw what the children were learning, dear, he said, "Certainly, Miss Williams. I can see no difficulty over your being

193

here whatever." ' Lunch was very simple – it *had* to be very simple with no oven and only the two gas burners. I made stew with potatoes, and sometimes we had fish fingers, sometimes sausages. Some of the children didn't like what I gave them, but I thought it a lot better than what I was offered at St Christopher's in Blandford. I never made a pudding as such. The children had either tinned fruit or little jellies which I poured into little bowls early so that they would be set in time. The children didn't have water *with* their lunch, they could have glasses of water afterwards.

Next, when her ballet mistress left, Miss Williams asked me whether I would take her place, so I gave some stock ballet classes – *barre* work with *pliés* and *grands battements* and *battements tendus*, and polka steps and gallops. Lisa Ullman and Laban had always said that I had no talent for teaching at all, and that I was a performer, and yet here I was teaching, at the age of nearly fifty, and enjoying it! I wasn't sure whether I was proficient, but Miss Williams *was* sure, and she offered me a full-time job. From January 1973, I was to be employed to teach at Paray House as well as to cook. I would be paid 10/– an hour (soon to become 50p) and I would take a junior ballet class and be responsible for the kindergarten babies. Ten shillings an hour at the school amounted to more than I was earning as a freelance and, now that Charlotte had disappeared down to Surrey, with her mother who had re-married, I agreed to the proposal.

I shall always be grateful to Miss Williams. When I came to Paray House on a permanent basis, she left me absolutely alone with the kindergarten to make my own mistakes and to fight a way through. I think if she hadn't done that, if she'd kept criticising, I might have left. I was very unsure of myself to start with but, as I made contact with the children, I began to gain more confidence. One member of the kindergarten was Charles Meynell, a little boy of about six. His mother, Vilma Meynell, was very ambitious for Charles, though he was a slow reader and writer. Charles and I got on well, and Vilma asked me if I would look after him sometimes at her flat in Sloane Street for 5/– an hour, which I did. It was a matter of putting him to bed, staying overnight and going back with him to Paray House in the morning (I wasn't paid for staying overnight). Charles could be rather an exhausting child. We played cricket in the hall of the flat, and we wrestled sometimes. He wasn't much of a one for books, but he liked to be read a story.

That summer, Vilma told me that she had been buying and

selling houses in the New Forest, but there was an even better opening for this in Northern France; as I spoke French, would I spend the summer holiday, about two months, at her cottage in Normandy, looking after Charles while she went off prospecting for houses and buying and selling? I was to get £4 a week. At the same time I could give him lessons in reading and writing. I was thrilled to go, as I didn't, of course, know Normandy at all.

Vilma was already in Normandy, but Mr Meynell came and picked us up and took us to Weymouth, where he parked the car and boarded the ferry with us to Cherbourg. I half expected the crossing would be like my Dover to Dunkirk crossings to Paris, which are very short, but this was a *long* crossing, it took all night. And there were those *awful* seats you get on Cross Channel ferries, with a sort of piece coming forward at the top so you can't sleep or even sit comfortably. Why they should instal such instruments of torture, I do not know. Mr Meynell disappeared to a cabin he'd booked for himself, and I was left to toss and turn with Charles on my knee. I'd never before spent such an awful night, and the process had to be repeated on the return journey and for the next three years.

But Normandy, when we got there and Vilma met us with her little Ford banger, was a revelation, a joy. Seen in the early morning with the sun getting up, Normandy is very beautiful indeed. The Normans were absolute wizards in stone, and their flair for building lives on. Cottages, and little churches even, were in the old Norman style, which I recognised from Salisbury, always my favourite cathedral. At Port-Bail, about a kilometre from Village le Havre, the hamlet where Vilma had her cottage, I *gasped*. Not only was there a church there actually built by William of Normandy before he came over as the Conqueror to England, but next to it was an ancient causeway stretching over a wide estuary, covered in a kind of cross between seaweed and heather which, with its purple blooms, looked like heather-covered moorland.

Vilma's cottage was a very ordinary stone cottage, two up and two down. But it wasn't quite Parke style – it had light and a fridge and a Calor gas stove and an Ascot for heating water, though you couldn't have a bath and the outside lavatory had to be emptied and there was no heating unless you lit a fire with the logs Vilma had stacked up against one wall. On this occasion, Mr Meynell stayed at the cottage for the weekend and then went back. Usually, when he was there, he stayed with Vilma in an hotel in

Port-Bail. She herself would be away most of the time, looking for properties, leaving me with Charles. We had to walk into Port-Bail pretty well every day to forage. I had to lure him along with promises of ice-creams and swimming.

Sometimes the sea came right in over the estuary, and lapped at your door. At other times you could walk about on the estuary. This 'moorland' was a great delight to Charles because, when the sea went out, it left little shallow streams and pools with crabs and shrimps, and he could fish. The Norman children fished too. Their method was very, very old, something that their grandfathers and great grandfathers must have done before them. They had a stick or a net and they made a great noise by shouting, and banged on the water, and the shrimps would come flying out onto the ground at the side of the pools and rivulets, where they picked them up.

I found that the war was enormously alive still in Normandy: people spoke about it as if it were yesterday, especially the men. Some had been in the Resistance – they were very glad to hear that you were English, because the British were something they had 'looked out' for. An electrician told me about seeing the landing craft coming in for the Invasion and how he used to signal from the cliffs at night. He was very interested when I said that I'd worked at the other end at Portsmouth and Southampton, and had seen the ships go out. He wouldn't say much about the Occupation, just that it was 'a terrible time, a terrible time'. I expected this, because hardly anybody who has been under the German Occupation will ever talk about it – probably, in order to survive, you had to collaborate to a certain extent.

Anyway, for three summers, I took Charles to Port-Bail almost every day when we both swam there at the little beach on the edge of the sand dunes, and I had to buy him expensive French ice-creams. Charles was a bit like Louis in that he *always* found a girlfriend to play with. He just said the magic words, 'Voulez-vous jouer avec moi?', and off they went, leaving me to sunbathe or to get on with *The Banks of Vesuvius* or to write down the occasional poem – actually, it was easier to write indoors when he was in bed. I remember that, when we got back to London in '75, and term had only been going for a couple of weeks, I was baby-sitting at the flat when Vilma came in, absolutely over the moon with excitement, because Charles had been accepted by Hill House – you know, the prep school Prince Charles – the other Charles! – went to, where they wear those lovely rust-coloured corduroy

196

knickerbockers. I went with the Meynells to Normandy for one more summer after Charles was yanked out of Paray House, and, whether it was a reward for my success in teaching him, or because Vilma had sold her Estate Agent business, I was taken on excursions in the car, and we often ate in restaurants. Carteret has the most beautiful beach and a lot of antique shops, where Vilma could pursue one of her side-lines, which was selling to the French the china she bought in Leamington Spa. She showed me her last purchase as an Estate Agent – a very beautiful *manoir*. She intended to sell it but, being a romantic and a great reader of historical novels, she said, 'Oh, *can't* you just imagine it?! I could trail around here in a Laura Ashley dress, and pretend I was back in the Middle Ages!'

French was useful at Paray House. Miss Williams asked me to use it in the kindergarten, because she herself only had time to do this with the bigger ones. The other members of staff were Mrs Whitehead, Lady Perowne and Miss A'Court (and an elderly pianist who accompanied Miss Williams' ballet classes). None of them taught French. Miss A'Court came in, almost every day, to read *to* the children – usually Fairy Tales (The Brothers Grimm and Hans Andersen). She wouldn't explain the vocabulary, and got very angry and went on strike if the children didn't listen. She left after I'd been teaching for a term. Lady Perowne came once a week to teach music – recorders for the older girls and percussion for the kindergarten. She was a kind and charming Welsh aristocrat, but with a distant manner which made the children mischievous, because they thought she wasn't interested in them.

Mrs Whitehead, whose speciality was Maths, was quite the best teacher, and had no problems with discipline. A bonnie ex-nursing sister, she still had the brisk calm that goes with nurses, and was outspoken in a way that made the children laugh – 'Oh, get on with it! You're not dying yet!' if someone complained of a cold; 'This looks as though you've polished the floor with it!' about some badly presented work. She could be outspoken with adults, too – 'Mrs Kass, go and do your hair and get a new pair of stockings! You look as though you've been pulled through a hedge and thrown to the uncircumcised!' Miss Williams, when she taught, was extremely patient, and could explain things step by step from first principles. The children responded to her eccentricities. Sometimes, after lunch, she gave them a little talk. I remember one on good manners: 'There's *nothing* so important as good manners,

197

and I *have* noticed, I *have* noticed in this school that we are becoming very lax about manners. Now, no doubt you've heard
about those miners who are on strike. Well, people may tell you
all sorts of things about that, but it's all due to *bad manners* . . .'
She *would* not buy books. I had to buy them for the kindergarten
at jumble sales.

The bigger girls were not allowed to use biros: they had to use
fountain pens. Boys, as well as girls, had to do ballet, no excuses,
though some of the fathers created murder. One of my abiding
visions is of Miss Williams having a row with an irate father, this
time about his *daughter*. At the summer Open Day, when the
children demonstrated their attainments in singing, music, dance
and drama, he complained at the top of his voice, in front of the
whole audience, that she had never had an acting rôle since she'd
been at Paray House. Miss Williams stalked down the aisle, stopped,
and fixed him with a gaze, and said, 'I can see *why* your wife left
you!'

It was because of my contributions to my first Open Day in the
summer of '73 – the kindergarten acted recitations of 'Clair de
Lune' and 'Il Pleut, Bergère', along with some English nursery
rhymes – that Miss Williams asked me to take some senior French.
So, the following year, I wrote and produced a play in French
called *Le Voyage*. The play began with a French family coming to
the seaside. Sophie Thynne, rather a ragamuffin of a girl, and a
lazy little thing, though very talented, was the awful baby of the
family, a part which she loved. Sophie was slightly under a cloud
at this time. She had waved from a lavatory window at some
workmen who were mending a roof on the other side of the road.
One of the workmen waved back with his hammer. Sophie, not to
be outdone, waved the lavatory brush. Unfortunately, she was seen
by Miss Williams, who was just coming into the school, and
severely lectured on her *bad manners*.

For the kindergarten, also in '73, I wrote *St George and the Dragon*,
using some of the words from an old mummers' play. José, a little
red-headed South American boy, was *very* good as the dragon –
he cartwheeled, and used his hands like claws. George was played
by an Italian boy called Milo. I kept having to spur him on to look
as if he was energetic enough to kill anything. Miss Williams never
allowed money or *time* for making sets and costumes, but I bought
remnants and old evening dresses at jumble sales. In fact, though

198

ballet was always taught at Paray House, not much drama production took place until I went there.

My next summer production was *Dick Whittington*. I was doing some more research for Miron Grindea at the British Museum, and I decided to find out as much as I could about the *real* Dick Whittington, and the play that resulted was a mixture of pantomime and the facts. In '76, I did *Hiawatha's Childhood*. The next year, I revived *Le Voyage* on a grander scale, incorporating a scene with the kindergarten walking round the stage, carrying towels and bathing costumes, and singing 'Je suis un petit garçon', something I'd seen children doing at Carteret when I was there with Vilma Meynell and Charles.

In '78, due to the turmoil involved in moving Paray House to St John's Church complex in World's End, I only did dramatisations of two French folk songs – 'Auprès de ma blonde' and 'En passant par La Lorraine'. I have a memory of three *minute* Arab boys, Nima, Ahmed and Sam, shouting 'O ho ho! Avec mes sabots!' with great gusto, because they knew it meant 'You're telling lies'!

We moved to World's End on the last day of term. Miss Williams had been looking for somewhere new for quite some time. She was being 'persecuted', she said, by the Jehovah's Witnesses. Firstly, they wanted more rent, which she didn't think they ought to have because, when the ceiling in the kindergarten started falling down, they wouldn't fix it, so she had to send for her brother who was a builder. Secondly, they were leaving texts around for Miss Williams to look at – texts such as 'THE WAGES OF SIN IS DEATH' and 'WHAT SHALL IT PROFIT A MAN IF HE GAIN THE WHOLE WORLD BUT LOSE HIS OWN SOUL'. These they displayed on the walls and left on the dais where we had our lunch. Thirdly, they suddenly announced that they were going to renovate the building, and so the place was full of dust, and bits of plaster were crashing down upon our heads.

Mrs Whitehead and I wanted to complain of harassment, but Miss Williams wouldn't *hear* of this. Perhaps she'd been given notice to quit. I don't know. Anyway, she found this St John's Church, at World's End Place at the end of the King's Road, which was built with a Community Centre which was hardly used except in the evenings for Youth Clubs, Alcoholics Anonymous and, oh, various activities of the church. Miss Williams and Mrs Whitehead went ahead with a furniture van and heavy items, and Mrs Job and I stayed behind to clear up and sweep, before following on afterwards by Public Transport with some boxes of books and toys. Mrs Job, a slight, grey-haired lady, a Methodist minister's widow and a friend of Mrs Whitehead, had joined us to teach Scripture and General Subjects during that summer term. She had a very strange mental make-up. She *said* she was no longer a Methodist but, to me, she seemed still like a Methodist through and through. She thought it a sin to speak sharply to the children, so they ran roughshod over her. Her moral viewpoint was that of a Methodist sermon. The poor were good because they were poor. Mothers who dressed stylishly must be bad mothers and flighty. You see, she *said* that she'd moved away from Methodism, but she hadn't. We once had a conversation about Benjamin Britten's music, when she mentioned that she'd heard something terrible about him and Peter Pears – 'This is happening more and more. It was the same in Greece, and it was the same in Rome, and look where it's got *us* now!' . . . I remember that as we were clearing the Sydney Hall, with express instructions from Miss Williams not to be too particular because of the Jehovah's Witnesses' behaviour, Mrs Job said to me, 'Not to leave things tidy for them would be wrong. That's the sort of thing that causes wars.'

St John's was a palace compared to the Sydney Hall. The kindergarten room was carpeted and light and clean. The only disadvantage of the place was that everything had to be put away in the evening. We had to pretend we hadn't been there. I had decided to make Tuesday painting day for the kindergarten. After lunch they used to come up to me and say, '*Painting! Painting!*', and I knew I was for it. At the Sydney Hall I'd only let them use crayons. They really liked using the powder paints I mixed for them to daub on large white sheets of paper. The room was awash after 'Painting!' The cleaning up and putting away afterwards took nearly as long as the lesson. Most of the artists had to be scrubbed before they could be sent home.

The Inspector who visited us approved of my 'method of teaching Art', but everything else I was doing seemed to horrify her. She said, 'There's nothing here! You must have clothes so that they can dress up! You must have water and sand! You must have animals!' I was quite unused to this. I was teaching the children as I had been taught myself, and our classroom was completely bare at St Christopher's. I got rather drunk at a poetry reading at the Crown and Greyhound, and I came home muttering 'Bring on the mess! Bring on the mess!' Water and sand were quite impractical, and we couldn't have animals, but I did buy more books at jumble sales, as well as old hats and clothes. The Inspector was German. She happened to walk in when the kindergarten were singing some French nursery rhymes. She was very scathing about this. She said Juniors, let alone Infants, shouldn't be taught French. If it had been German, she would probably have said it was all right.

She left saying she would return, but she didn't do this for three years. When she did come, she ransacked my cupboard and saw that we now had the dressing-up clothes, and scales and games and various odds and ends for making things, and she must have been satisfied, because this time she concentrated more on the children's education. I gather she was very hard on poor Mrs Job. She'd caught her giving a History lesson and telling the story of Alfred and the Cakes. She said, 'It shouldn't be like this. You must explain that History does not always tell the truth, that History is always written by the winners. You should give the children a chance to *argue* with History.' She watched me give a ballet lesson, and I purposely played Beethoven records to dance to. She went into ecstasies. She thought the children were *so* beautiful.

I don't know what it was about the St John's building but, as soon as we got there, Miss Williams was always ill. She would ring up in the morning to say, 'My knees have swollen up like footballs' or that she had flu. Also, she was slow about giving us the forms on which to write our termly reports. At the end of term she would invite us out to an Italian restaurant, produce the forms when we were all quite squiffy, and ask us to write the reports there and then.

Suddenly, in the summer of '79, the year after we'd moved, Miss Williams stopped coming in at all, and wrote to the parents to say that the school was closing. The first we heard of this was when parents crowded round us, asking what they were to do with their children next term. Mrs Whitehead, Mrs Job and I had a confab, and Mrs Whitehead put forward the idea that, if Miss Williams could be persuaded to retire, we could carry on the school as a co-operative. We approached Miss Williams and to our surprise, she jumped at the idea. We couldn't pay her anything for the goodwill of the school – I, for one, was still only earning 50p an hour – but we made her a sleeping partner, with the profits being divided into five, because Mrs Whitehead's husband would have to come in to look after the business side. We were each to be paid £90 gross a month, with £10 a month for travelling expenses, and to share profits at the end of every term (a sum which, it turned out, could be between £200 and £1,000). For her Open Day swan song, Miss Williams produced a play in blank verse called *Persephone*. After the performance, she was presented with a silver salver and a bouquet. She wasn't in the mood for making speeches.

My own productions at St John's? You want to hear about those, too? ... Are you *sure?!* ... Well, in '78, for our first Christmas just before Miss Williams retired, I wrote a Nativity play which I called *Writing it Down*. It was performed *in* the church. We did it again the following Christmas and, at the request of the vicar, John Smith, we did another performance at St Andrew's nearby, which was his church too. I based the play on T. S. Eliot's 'Journey of the Magi'. I didn't use Eliot's words, because they're not suitable for children, but I used the images and the story. As always, I incorporated ideas from the children. It was always *their* play.

The summer Miss Williams retired, I wrote and produced *two* plays – *The Prince Who Couldn't Shiver*, based on the Grimms' fairy tale 'The Man Who Couldn't Shudder', and *Le Trésor*, a play in French, based on the song 'Auprès de ma blonde'. In *The Prince Who Couldn't Shiver*, Aki, an Iranian boy, was the Prince, and Milo was the Gardener's Boy. A short time before the performance, they took it into their heads to play truant, and were found by the police halfway to Brighton. Miss Williams beat them with a coathanger and threatened to expel them. It seemed as if there would be no play, but she relented after pleadings from Mrs Whitehead and myself. In this play there was a Danse Macabre. I especially remember José and a Danish boy called Eric being ghosts with great gusto. What made the Prince finally shiver was a bucket of water drawn from the moat and poured over him by the Princess. To avoid making an awful mess, we filled a bucket with tinsel streamers and gold-foil fish.

The next year, I did a version of Eliot's *Old Possum's Book of Practical Cats* called *Practical Cats* – partly poetry, partly song and partly dance. I must have been clairvoyant, because the musical *Cats*, based on the same book, was staged at the New London theatre in 1981.

I had always wanted to try Shakespeare and, one year, at the old Paray House, I had planned to do some Shakespearean songs like 'Where the Bee Sucks' and 'When Icicles Hang by the Wall', but Miss Williams forbade this – she said children didn't *understand*

Shakespeare, to which I replied that this was because most *teachers* didn't understand him. But she was gone now, so in '81 I decided to do something about *Macbeth*. Needless to say, we couldn't do the whole play, but I took the witches' scenes and made them into a little play that could stand by itself. We called it *The Three Witches*. Alexandra Riley, Michelle Aylett and Tara Foot, a very strong combination, were the witches. Theresa Vaughan played Macbeth. Theresa was the eldest of a large, aristocratic English family. She was an all-round scholar, serious, but very nervous. But her voice, once she mastered her nerves, had a lovely tone, and she was always sure of her words. Kelly Griffin was all the spectres in the witches' cauldron – she insisted on wearing a horror mask from a joke shop. We had a box of stones for thunder, and the little boys were delighted at being allowed to flash the lights on and off for lightning. I also let them rattle a steel partition which was used to shut off noises from the church. When folded back, it made a very thundery noise if you rattled it. We went to a lot of trouble making the ingredients for the cauldron. For the fillet of a fenny snake, I baked the skeleton of a fish, and the children came up with various horrible entrails and glittering eyes that they'd made. Fortunately, I had a very lifelike papier-mâché toad – they wanted a live one. The two most gruesome ingredients, 'liver of blaspheming Jew' and 'finger of birth-strangled babe', they never knew about, as I censored them.

I *must* mention Catherine Bell, who was Hecate, the Queen of the Witches, and very regal and wrathful. She was a quiet girl, more academic than theatrical, and she played the part rather like an irate and dignified school-mistress. Last year, I had her play the Queen Mother in *The Girl Who Went to War*, a play I wrote, based on a Spanish legend, and she did this in much the same way.

15

I found all my work at Paray House very satisfying, but it was exhausting, especially as I had to combine it with poetry elsewhere. I had told Miss Williams that I was a poet at the outset. People used to ring me up at the Sydney Hall and at St John's about the poetry readings which I was either organising or giving myself. Very soon after being taken on full-time, I *had* to tell Mrs Whitehead what was happening, because Alasdair Aston kept ringing and she got into the habit of saying, 'It's your fella again!' – she was getting the wrong impression. I explained that he was a poet, that he was Chairman of the Dulwich Group, and that I was a member of his Committee and was helping him to arrange events at the Crown and Greyhound. In fact, in May '73, during my second term at Paray House as a regular teacher, Alasdair asked me to do an evening by myself there. I was now on the Poetry Secretariat's list so, officially, I received £40 for this – £20 from the Poetry Secretariat, added to £20 from the Group, but, as the Group couldn't afford this, I waived its contribution. I read 'The Dancing Vicar', 'The Double-Back Switch-Back', 'The Weir' and 'The Runaway Heart'. Then, after the drink interval – drink intervals were always very long under Alasdair – there was only time for 'The Dream of Mitzi'. At the end of the evening, Alasdair was in tears. He said, 'It's Bill come back again!' He meant Shakespeare!

I had never performed 'The Weir' before. You may remember, it's about a drowning man going back over his life. I wrote the original version at Bowyer House, *before* Philippe's suicide, because I'd been interested in a little paragraph in a newspaper about a student at Oxford who killed himself by lying down in a punt on the Thames and letting himself go over a weir. It's connected with the old idea that, when you drown, the whole of your past life rushes up in front of you, though, in my poem, it doesn't rush,

> The flotsam and jetsam float up from the weir
> Quietly,
> Each like a flower unfolding . . .

When I looked at the poem again at 17, Rosendale Road, it did look very much as if it was a premonition of Philippe's death and I made adjustments in the light of it; indeed, some parts of the new version struck me as so personal that I cut them out. I thought, 'I can't do this!' But the original poem wasn't a premonition. I was interested in suicide generally, and not in any relation to Philippe. Philippe may have influenced my choice of subject matter, my consideration of depression and the sorts of *character* that commit suicide, but, as I've told you, it never consciously occurred to me that *he* was suicidal. Before he died, I was writing about all sorts of things; I don't think any significance can be attached to the fact I wrote 'The Weir', or, indeed, any other poems about suicide, before he died.

'Tuesday', which I read at Edward Lucie-Smith's, made George MacBeth feel like committing suicide! – or so he said. That's one of my short poems:

> Upon reflection, I should think it's Tuesday.
> Come in, then, Tuesday. Let me see your face.
> How grey it is, how stony grey and cold,
> Like a dead face there in the windy tree.
> You swallowed Monday? – Well, then, rest in peace.

But I can assure you that this had no conscious bearing on my own state of mind, let alone Philippe's. It was just a general insight. Nor had the final stanza of my 'Litany of the Animals', *Homo Sapiens:*

> May the mind that has planted a Beethoven in our bellies,
> And a whisper of pain among the symphonies –
> 'My Carl, he shot himself, and I loved him so' –,
> And could yet find means to misdirect the bullet,
> Look after us all.

I wrote this stanza after moving to Rosendale Road, when I found a book about Beethoven, my favourite composer, at a jumble sale.

I'd already written three stanzas – *Squirrel*, *Giraffe* and *Frog* – about the idiot/sane mind which seems to govern the natural evolution of the animal kingdom, and I knew, even before Philippe died, that I wanted something, for *homo sapiens*, to do with the suicidal tendencies of the world in general as I saw it then, but couldn't get a strong enough image – or not until I read this book, in which a passage about Beethoven's son, Carl, seemed to be relevant.

I completed the poem, and first read it at the Orangery. When I looked at the audience afterwards, they were sitting in absolute silence with blank faces, and this rather scared me, because I felt that they hadn't understood. Carl, you see, was Beethoven's adopted son. He led Beethoven an awful dance. He kept getting into trouble with women and into debt, because Beethoven had spoiled him. In the end, Carl tried to shoot himself, but only succeeded in giving himself a flesh wound, and later joined the army.

Some of the local poets, like myself, Stella Stocker, Peter Meares, Michael Gerrard, Pat Bradley and Katherine Stenger, had got into the habit of going home for coffee and further talk, either with Alasdair, or with me at Rosendale Road. A young poet stayed with me at Rosendale Road one night after the others had gone. He said it would be nice if we could live together, given that he was about to be thrown out of his digs and I had quite a lot of space. He was very good-looking, bolshie, and attending a Therapy Group at the Maudsley Hospital. When he kissed me suddenly, I realised that he was the same sort of person as Philippe, that he was trouble. I said, 'I'm not at all sure . . . I shall have to think about it . . . No, we *can't* live together.' Later the next day, he turned up on the doorstep with a suitcase, saying it wasn't right that I should live alone, I needed company. Well, I wasn't quite alone, because Bobby wasn't married yet, and was back and forth. I said I didn't need company, and I sent him away, and I've not seen him since.

In the autumn of '75, Alasdair Aston disappeared. People were turning up at the Crown and Greyhound for readings, and there weren't any readings there. Alasdair had always been saying in a very loud voice how horrible his wife was and how he hated Aberdeen and everything in Aberdeen because she was from it. He would say this quite publicly and, because he made it all so public, and for so many years, nobody expected him actually to leave her.

206

But this was what had finally happened – he had left her, and gone to live in Chiswick. Right through '76 there were no Dulwich Group meetings at the Crown and Greyhound.

There seemed to be a coldness in everything once the poets had gone. Meetings had taken place at the 'Dog' since before the war, and it seemed to me an awful pity that they should stop, as the Group was one of the last bastions of poetry. In '77, I thought, 'I wonder if I could start them again.' I thought this as a result of a chance meeting during the summer with Alan Palmer in Norwood High Street. Alan had been Treasurer for the Dulwich Group since Howard Sergeant's time, and he was worried about what to do with the little money that was left in the kitty: a £90 grant from the Southwark Council applied for by Alasdair for 1976 had been paid, but there were no readings. I asked him then and there whether, if I managed to get the Group going again, he would handle the money side. He said, No, he hadn't the time and he would soon be moving. I realised that I would be on my own, but I went to see the landlord of the Crown and Greyhound and asked him would he agree to poetry once a month again. He agreed, subject to a rent of £10 a reading, which I was willing to pay, though he had never charged Alasdair – Alasdair was such a good customer and brought so many of his friends to the Dog that he didn't have to pay for the room (the banqueting room) at all.

I then visited Alan Palmer to collect the financial papers and the mail which had accumulated since Alasdair's departure. Among the pile was a letter from one William Radice, asking whether he could read to the Dulwich Group, and enclosing a sample poem. The poem seemed quite good, so I invited him as my first reader. I made posters and distributed them on a round I was to come to know only too well – the Poetry Society, the National Book League, the Arts Council Poetry Library, the Arts Council Bookshop, the Arts Centre in Adelaide Street, off Trafalgar Square, the Battersea Arts Centre, the Norwood Library, the Crown and Greyhound itself . . . I also sent notices to as many of the Group as I had names and addresses for. I charged a 25p entrance fee, and the arrangement was that guest poets would in future be paid what money was collected after the landlord had been paid his £10. I decided that the first half of every programme would be devoted to one guest, and the second half to readings from the floor – 'Has anybody got a poem?' and they would pop up; 'Has anybody else got a poem?' and somebody else would pop up. Guest poets would stay for the second half, during which there would also be discussion – their chairs and mine would be moved to the front of the table, and the audience, when possible, gather closer.

Well, in September '77, William Radice gave his first reading under my management, and I've never forgotten it. Quite apart from the large retinue he brought with him the meeting was well attended, but *I* found his manner of reading very affected. I've heard him talked of, since, with a measure of respect, and as someone who has rejected the fleshpots of the world to follow the grail. I asked him, as a courtesy, would he care to come to future meetings. In all seriousness, he said that he couldn't – the train journey would involve a long wait on Selhurst Station and he might catch cold; it would be a terrible thing if he died before he had written his best poems.

After Radice, which means 'radish', I think, in Italian, the readers included Hubert Nazareth, a talented Indian poet who has since become quite well known as H. O. Nazareth; John Greatrex, who ran the Crystal Palace Sports Centre and had a talent for light verse; Joe Winter, a serious poet, rather opaque but with a gentle style; the Troubadour Poets; Michael Gerrard, a small, rather unnoticeable man who worked as a librarian in Deptford, a very fine poet who should be better known, though I'm not sure that he would want to be (two of his poems stick in my mind – one about Pallas Athene, and the other about a snooker game); Peter Meares, whose best poems concern a wild Irish seaman by the name of O'Meara; Pat Bradley, who I think wrote poetry as an antidote for her hard and horrific tasks as a social worker, running a hostel for alcoholics in Camberwell; Alan Gillott, a young poetry enthusiast; Molly Moorehead, a Yorkshire woman who had been secretary for the Arvon Foundation, and whose poetry had an authentic North Country flavour though it was inclined to be cosy; Patrick Cunnane, a talented poet who had organised his own group of poetry performers called 'Worthless Words', who were highly amusing and original, and recited surrealistic and concrete poetry while moving around with queerly shaped bits of wood and plastic . . .

Oh, yes, there was also Frank Alcock of Poetry in Croydon. Though he was rather a dull performer when sober, I considered some of his poetry very fine. Once, at the time of Alasdair Aston, we had a mass walk-out of the Irish – Frank Alcock, sober, was too much for them. We had quite a lot of Irish labourers at the

Crown and Greyhound, who would come into the pub for a drink, and then come upstairs to listen to the poetry. The Irish are like the Poles – they allow that poetry exists, which most English people don't. This mass walk-out in the middle of Frank's reading was very depressing. I was sitting there listening to Frank's droning, and I'd lost the thread, and I suddenly saw all the Irish get up and leave. I thought, 'He's bored them to death.'

But, anyway, I invited him to read again at this period when I was Chairman. The thing was getting him to the Crown and Greyhound safely. He was married to Josie, his social worker, who drove us in her car. Frank had somehow managed to get well pickled beforehand, and kept embracing Josie, and completely hiding the road. At one point, somewhere near the Crown and Greyhound, he asked her to stop. She said, 'Frank, I'm *not* going to stop! You're *not* going into a pub! You're not going to drink any more before the poetry reading!' With that, Frank threw himself at her, and she fortunately had enough presence of mind to apply the brakes. She said, 'Frank, will you *sit* down!' But he was out of the car, and off like a lamplighter. I got out and chased him along the road, but he'd disappeared, and we had to go to the Crown and Greyhound without him. I allowed readings from the floor until the interval, when he arrived completely plastered. He gave his reading, mostly about unhappy people he met in pubs, and then he disappeared again. The last I saw was Josie searching for him through Dulwich. He now lives in Dorset, and he's been dried out. Enclosed with one letter to me was a poem, the best, I think, that he's ever written. It is about a frosty day, and begins: 'It's hard here, hard.' I could just feel, in the very fibre of the poem, the struggle he must have gone through, but, nonetheless, I'm almost sure that this story about him will have a happy ending.

I hadn't received grants from Southwark Council for '77 and '78 (you'd to apply formally in the spring of a preceding year), so in '78, to get one for '79, I formed a Committee with Alan Gillott as Treasurer, Michael Gerrard, Secretary, Patrick Cunnane, Publicity, and Pat Bradley, Joe Winter, Peter Meares, Molly Moorehead and John Greatrex. As a result, we received £70 in both '79 and '80, but nothing for '81 as we hadn't earned enough money at the door. I did most of the work. Everyone except Alan Gillott and John Greatrex held their positions only in name. Alan Gillott took the job of Treasurer seriously from the first, and tried to make the

Group financially viable. John Greatrex, until he left the district, helped me with the drawing and distributing of posters, as Patrick Cunnane was usually too busy with 'Worthless Words'.

For the April '79 meeting I wanted to invite Howard Sergeant to the Dog, as I knew he would attract a large audience. But Howard replied that he wouldn't come unless he was paid through the Poetry Secretariat (probably for prestige reasons). This meant paying him £40. I rang Olwyn Ellis of the Secretariat to ask for help. I did so with mixed feelings. Firstly, I felt that this £40 demanded by well-known names was destroying Poetry Groups; secondly, I had memories of an uncomfortable experience in the time of Alasdair Aston. We were in very low water, and, when Christopher Logue came to give a reading, we said, 'Would you mind reading for Olwyn Ellis's £20 and waiving the other £20 because we simply haven't got it?' He said Yes, he would read for £20 and waive the other £20 but, as we were only paying him half his fee, he would only do half a reading. And he did just that! He read his poems very quickly, bent double and in a very low voice and giving no little talks in between, and left immediately afterwards. The balance of the evening had to be filled up with readings from the floor! . . .

Anyway, when I rang Olwyn Ellis about Howard Sergeant, she said there would be no trouble about obtaining a contribution towards his, or anyone else's, fee, as the Crown and Greyhound was still on her books, Alasdair Aston had never officially stopped the readings. So, with her support, I was able to have Howard and, subsequently, some very well-known names. I think it was when delivering posters at the Arts Council Bookshop and Poetry Library for this reading of Howard's that I stayed to listen to a reading by the Russian poet, Yevgeny Yevtushenko. At the end, he was subjected to a barrage of questions, rather loaded questions really because, although he'd started off almost as a dissident in the Soviet Union, he was now very much in favour of the system and he was pooh-poohing all the ideas that there were arrests in the night, and that things were any worse for writers in the Soviet Union than they are here (about which he was probably correct!). All of a sudden, he moved out of the group surrounding him and came over and kissed me. This was something I didn't expect at all. He said, 'What is your profession?' I said, 'I have to live, so I teach at a school, but I'm a poet.' He said, 'Yes. I knew it at once,' and he gave me a copy of his book, signed 'Elia'.

210

In May, we had Peter King, a long-haired Irish poet who, at his best, had wit, and whose poetry I already knew fairly well. In a poem called 'Boards' he has likened himself, and his contemporaries, to boards in the all-the-world's-a-stage set-up, walked upon by the actors. He himself is quietly and patiently wiggling at a nail so that he can eventually prise himself loose and trip the buggers up. Alan Brownjohn came next – a gentle, charming man who writes not very exciting poetry, but is highly respected and much publicised. Then we had Sidney Carter, a practising Quaker whose poems were much concerned with God. The following year, when I was snowed under with paperwork for the Group, I asked him if he would take over as Chairman. He refused, as did William Cookson, the editor of *Agenda*. Nobody wanted the job for which I hadn't time enough and for which I hardly, any longer, had the strength.

On Hallowe'en, very appropriately – yes, this was still '79 – we had Frank Bangay's Fighting Pigeons group, including Dave Sheen, who was now very much 'into' astrology and witchcraft. As well as reciting, they sang and played guitars. Frank Bangay is an uneducated poet, but very good. He woke up in an orphanage at the age of eleven, with no recollection of anything that had taken place before that, and nobody has ever told him how he got there. In November, Michael Ffinch, a poet much concerned with landscape, came down to us from Newbiggin-on-Lune in Cumbria. The meeting was a disaster because so few people came. You see, even names on the Poetry Secretariat list, who you thought would draw a crowd, very often didn't. And the population of Dulwich had changed: the sort of people who were interested in poetry seemed to have moved out. Dulwich had become a very, very expensive area, and the only people who could afford to live there were the stockbroker type. For the Christmas meeting, two boys, Paul Bonel and John Hayes, played the clarinet and sang in a semi-classical style that was very pleasant on the ear. Both words and music were their own work, but their performance was so short that most of the evening was taken up with readings from the floor.

We started 1980 with Steve Griffiths, a Welsh poet from Anglesey, whose relaxed, easy manner somehow makes you feel part of the poetry. He was followed, in February, by Gavin Ewart, a charming man but, to me, rather a flippant poet, not prepared to take himself seriously. In March, in a different vein, we had the blind poet, John Heath-Stubbs. Because of his fame, there was quite

211

a large audience. When he had read with me at the Lamb and Flag, I had thought that he was too much of a scholar, that everything came out of books. But at the Crown and Greyhound he gave a most beautiful reading. His poems were mostly on Greek and Roman themes, and none the less interesting for that. I arranged for Michael Gerrard to fetch him in his car – he'd asked for a taxi, but I thought Michael would be more reliable. I think they reached fairly good terms, and, by the time he got to the reading, he was relaxed and happy. At any rate he appeared to be much happier than at the Lamb and Flag. We had a long talk that night, and I admire him very much.

In April, the then Poet in Residence for Southwark, Leo Aylen, read from a book of his, which had just been published, called *Sunflower*. In May, we had Eddie Linden. Eddie Linden is a wild, redheaded, leftwing poet from Scotland. Sooner or later, in every gathering of poets in London that I have known, you came across Eddie Linden, usually at the centre of some violent argument. Though he himself is unlettered, his magazine *Aquarius* is one of the best poetry reviews. Between his poems, and other people's which he read from *Aquarius*, he asked me to read passages from *Who is Eddie Linden?*, his biography by Sebastian Barker. It was a very successful evening. Afterwards, he gave me a signed copy of *Who is Eddie Linden?* with, for some reason, a sunflower pressed inside it. What, exactly, *is* the significance of sunflowers? . . . Peter Porter read at our next meeting. He was not very exciting, but he had improved a lot since I first heard him at Edward Lucie-Smith's. It's strange, but very often, when I've asked a young poet what poets he admires, he will list the 'greats' such as Yeats, Eliot and Auden, and then he will say, as a kind of afterthought, 'I like Peter Porter.'

After the summer break, we invited Patricia Beer. She reads with a pleasant West Country accent. Her face, even, says 'The West Country', and there's something about her that tastes of butter. She seemed to have come far enough away from her Plymouth Brethren background to be able to look at it almost with affection. Though she is from Devon, there's a little of the Dorsetshire poet Barnes about her, but only atmospheric, not voice or rhythm, and there's no hint of dialect. Carol Rumens, the feminist, who was next, is a shy, fragile-looking lady, and she's *not* a good reader – at Brian Dann's house, she was often told off by Amy Gemm. On the printed page, though, she is much stronger. The title of her second book, *Strange Girl in Bright Colours*, seems to me magic. Nolan Walsh, who read in December, was as enthusiastic as ever – he later went to live in a commune in Hampstead, and, recently, he was organising an energetic campaign for the Labour Party.

In December I couldn't find anyone to read, so, as we'd no money, I did a reading myself. I started with 'The Weir', which someone had asked me to include. Next I did 'Please May I Be Excused?', based on 'Romany Boy' – its first performance. Then came 'The Finding of the Nail', also new, and it was based on the old nursery rhyme, 'The Horseshoe Nail':

> Did you hear how the horseshoe nail was found
> In a fallen tree, far under the ground?
> Beaten hard by the ponderous weight of dust,
> It was found without blemish or sign of rust . . .

I finished with a cowboy poem, another new one, called 'The Degradation of Jehoshaphat Snudge':

> My friends, listen well to this tale I shall tell,
> And it's better to pity than judge
> How an unspotted cowboy to ruin was lured,
> Then weep for Jehoshaphat Snudge.
>
> Now Jehosh never gambled, nor spat on the floor,
> And no girl did he take to his bed,
> And, iffen his horse took a shine to a mare,
> He would hit the poor thing on the head . . .

I should have said I *intended* to finish with 'Jehoshaphat Snudge'. I'd then to do several poems by popular demand – 'The Hanraghan Brothers', 'Three Welshmen Sang' and 'The Runaway Heart'.

Our financial difficulties were bad enough, but yet another landlord was hinting at putting up the rent to £20. And, as the Banqueting Room was being renovated, we were now only able to use the smaller room beside it. That was where I performed at Christmas, as did Jerry Orpwood in January '81, when he read his lovely autobiographical poem, 'The Round Wood', about a boy meeting a gypsy at Epsom. Then, when *that* wasn't available, we were asked to use a storeroom behind the bar on the ground floor. Brian Dann read there in February. He's best at comic poems – 'Dedicated to Teacher', about a child with a loose tooth, is very funny indeed. Allan Sillitoe also read in this storeroom in March. He's a better novelist than a poet, but I liked *him* very much. He really listened to the poems from the floor and, in the discussion afterwards, had a quiet way of getting down to the nitty-gritty.

In May, Danny Abse, a Welsh/Jewish poet, a GP and the brother of Leo Abse, the politician, was shocked by the venue – the storeroom was large, rather bare, with junk furniture stacked on one side; we usually sat on barrels but, because his reading was to be televised by BBC Schools, the landlord provided chairs for a change. I explained that we couldn't have the Banqueting Room as a Rotary Dinner was being held there, and the room beside it was being used as a private bar. The TV crew were delighted with the room and said it had just the right atmosphere for poetry. When the audience of about twenty began to trickle in from the bar, Abse asked me whether we usually had such small numbers. I said that it was becoming more and more difficult to attract audiences for poetry; other groups were having the same problem. This, he said, was incorrect: there was a large demand for poetry; we should work harder at publicity and invite more popular poets. I replied, in a raised voice, that I was a writer and not the right person to put bottoms on seats. He shrugged his shoulders, and I walked away with a niggling sense of guilt that what he said was true. Just the same, I didn't feel like telling myself to promote poets I didn't like – the ones I *did* like were either too expensive or too little known. Perhaps because of this exchange, I was unreceptive to his poems. I had always thought he was much overrated, but was able to say what I usually said by way of introduction: 'At the Crown and Greyhound, we don't go in for blurb, because we believe it kills poetry. I will now let the poet speak for himself.' Actually, there was one poem he read which I liked – the poem 'Song for Dov Shamir'. Afterwards, as a kind of penance for my uncharitableness, I bought a copy of his *Collected Poems*, which he signed.

On Midsummer Day, the 24th of June, 1981, Tom Pickard, a very good poet from Liverpool who has nothing to do with the Liverpool Poets, was scheduled to read in the storeroom, but the landlord had locked it, and nobody could find the key. In desperation, I invited Tom Pickard and members of the Committee, and anyone else who wished, to come back with me to 17, Rosendale Road, to have the meeting there. It was a wonderful meeting, and Tom Pickard's poems were excellent – Left, angry and funny, but with substance. He read as if from the floor, with other poets

214

coming in between, and there was talk, and conversation about the poems, with drinks and a supper of cheese sandwiches and salami sandwiches which the Committee helped me to make.

Before Michael Gerrard took Tom Pickard back to his hotel, we held an informal Committee Meeting, and made up our minds that there would be no more Dulwich Readings at the Dog. At a formal meeting to wind up the Group, about a fortnight later, I discovered that the Committee wanted the readings to go on, *and* at the Dog! I said I wasn't prepared to run them, and nobody else was prepared to take my place, so we decided, instead, to have informal readings once a month at Rosendale Road or at the homes of other committee members, sending out invitations to regular attenders whose names we could get from the Visitors Book. There was no money to distribute: I'd even been paying the landlord his £10 rent out of my own pocket.

16

Lambeth Borough Council had by now declared 17, Rosendale Road unfit for human habitation. Mr O'Toole, the landlord, was more interested in the antique lavatories in the house than seeing to the rotting windows, the leaks in the roof and the falling ceilings. He said, 'I'll give you new lavatories,' which we didn't need at all; I presume he wanted to sell the old ones. All he did was take out the lavatories and put in new ones which were far less efficient.

So I was in my sitting-room one night, and there was a crackling noise – probably the noise people say they hear before a coconut falls off a palm tree. I thought something had happened on the stairs and I went to investigate and, just as I got out of the door, there was a *terrific* crash and half the sitting-room ceiling crashed down all over the furniture. It was an old-fashioned ceiling, very thick, like thick concrete, and moulded all around. Really, I think I could have been killed if it had fallen on me. I complained at once to Mr O'Toole through Wally, Mrs Wallis, the old lady downstairs whose tenant I was. She was very nice about it. She and her boyfriend, Frank Utting, the old 'colonel', were sitting in their kitchen in their usual state of Saturday picklement, and she immediately said, 'You look as white as a sheet. Have a nip of central heating!' This was whisky, and I was very glad of it. The landlord *did* come and put a makeshift ceiling up and paint over it, but subsequent falls of ceiling he wouldn't do anything about at all – the ceiling in the lavatory, part of the ceiling in my bedroom. Eventually, when the ceiling in the bedroom was hanging by a thread, I bought a second-hand four-poster. I saw it advertised in *Exchange and Mart* and, by scraping and scrimping, I managed to

216

buy this thing, and what I did was put a piece of hardboard over the top. I felt safer after that: I didn't run the risk of being knocked out and smothered in the middle of the night.

Wally was the first to go. That was in '78. The ceiling in *her* sitting-room had fallen down. Sheila Purbrick next door thought she should be rescued not only from her awful living conditions but from Frank. Wally and Frank's rows were getting worse; also, Wally was having to ask Sheila for help to get Frank home when he fell in the street. Sheila, being a Scotswoman like Wally, was able to pull some strings and get her into sheltered accommodation belonging to a Scottish foundation near Golders Green. St Ninian's Court is beautiful and very peaceful, and I really think it gave Wally a new lease of life. I visited her quite often after she went, in this little dolls' house she'd been given. Frank visited her, too. He had an old age pensioner's travel ticket, and he went over twice a week.

Next to go was my lodger, a singer called Mike Shirn I'd put in the attic when the boys had gone. I was still having to plaster the attic with waterproof paper, and he *had* to be rehoused. As soon as he went, the ceilings up *there* started to come down! Mr O'Toole had died and Mrs Constantinades, his daughter who inherited the place, all she wanted to do was sell it. Mike was offered a *very* nice flat on a housing estate in Knight's Hill. So when Mrs Constantinades sold the house to a Nigerian in 1980, only Frank and I were there. All this landlord wanted to do was to get us out, and he served us notices to quit, which at least meant that we didn't have to pay any rent. Some time before, my bag had been stolen, and I'd had the locks to the house changed, so this new landlord was never able to get in. He would come and shout at us: 'I'm only allowing you to stay here by the goodness of mah heart! You get *out* of here! You *not* making no effort to get out! I'm the landlord here and I should have a key! You get a key made for me so I can come in, send my workmen!' I told him, 'There are no locks on any of the doors *inside* this house. If you have a key, you can walk straight into my bedroom.' He said, 'I don't *want* to walk into your bedroom!' This shouting landlord was on the doorstep every two or three days, trying to panic us, but neither of us *were* panicked, because we knew that he couldn't get us out. In fact, I think Frank rather enjoyed it. Sometimes this awful shouting happened quite late at night. I couldn't summon the energy, but Frank shouted back things like 'Temper, temper! I don't like that

217

sort of language! It's all recorded! You swore at me! If it ever comes up in court . . .!' I would just stand at the doorway, with Frank at the back of me if he was in, and let the shouting finish, then say Goodnight, and shut the door. The Council had made Frank several offers of alternative flats, but he wouldn't go because they weren't near enough to Wally; he always advanced the theory that he must have somewhere near in case she should call for him when she was on her deathbed.

In '81, during the school's summer holidays, I got a letter from the Lambeth Housing Office to say that a flat had been found for me at 19, St Faith's Road, Tulse Hill, the flat where I'm talking to you now. I collected the keys next day from the Council offices in Clapham Common, and found St Faith's Road with the help of an A–Z. I expected to find a flat at the top of a tower block, but it was the ground floor of an ordinary bow-fronted house, gabled, semi-detached, painted white and with a little garden in front and a big one behind, in a very quiet road. At the front was this nice light room we're sitting in, leading from a large kitchen and hallway, off which there's a bathroom and a loo and a fair-sized bedroom at the back. The rent was £17 a week, and there was a hole in the kitchen window, the loo didn't work, the bedroom window was rotten and an overflow pipe at the back was gushing away, making a green streak down the outside wall. Nevertheless, I fell in love with the place at once; compared with 17, Rosendale Road, it was sheer luxury. Curtains in the first-floor windows and people sitting on the low wall between the houses indicated I wouldn't lack neighbours, and there was a back garden where my cat, Lulu, could enjoy herself. I didn't notice the cracks in the wall that would widen day by day, and I didn't know that the gas fire I'd get from the Council would let out such a smell.

About a fortnight later, in September, I moved in with the help of Sheila, after frantic measuring up and packing and laying of carpets. I was rather worried about leaving Frank by himself, as he was over eighty. It did seem to me that this very tough landlord might try Rachman tactics if he couldn't get his own way. But, the following summer, he got a flat in Whetstone, not too far from Wally – it was a family flat, far too large for Frank, with several bedrooms but, as he insisted on being in Whetstone and there was nothing else in the area on offer, they put him there in the end. That winter, there was a bout of very, very icy weather. He was sitting in his flat one night, when a huge water tank burst over his head. The water came down and flooded the room literally to the ceiling. Frank was nearly drowned: here he was, poor old soul, part freezing, part drowning, with all his things ruined. He got out somehow. Water was running down the stairs; tenants were running this way and that. And, on this absolutely icy, freezing night, with a blizzard blowing, Frank set off for Wally's, down the road.

At three o'clock in the morning, Wally says she heard a tap-tap-tapping on her window. She was too frightened at first to go to see who it was but, in the end, she did, and there was Frank, not only drenched through, but with the water actually freezing on him. She took him in at once and probably saved his life by getting his clothes off and putting him straight into a hot bath – he was practically unconscious. Then she put him in her own bed and she slept in the sitting-room, or so she told me. You'd think the sheer shock of having all this happen in the middle of the night would do something to an old man, but Frank didn't suffer from any after-effects at all. Well, yes, there has been one after-effect: he hasn't been drinking so much – I don't know whether *that* is the result of shock. And now he has a bed-sitter even nearer to Wally. He's really much better off there, because it's a size more suited to somebody who won't clean. He doesn't cook either, but there's a Luncheon Club nearby, and he often goes to see Wally, who feeds him.

Here a Nigerian family lives upstairs at the front. They're rather noisy and athletic – the lampshades in here rattle precariously – but I don't mind this, as the lady at the back, over my bedroom, is quiet. They've now got rid of a large Alsatian which they rarely exercised and which barked and cried, and scratched the floor. Soon after I moved in, the Nigerian lady paid me a visit. She had unexpected guests and wanted to borrow some money to buy beer. I'm superstitious about lending money, and said that I'd no money, but could give her six cans of beer. She accepted these, and hugged me, and went away chewing a carrot which she took from my vegetable rack. Her name is Tota, and she is very beautiful, as all her family are. The beer was replaced, but I'd have preferred her to treat them as a gift. The woman upstairs at the back is Austrian, a retired nanny, now working as a cook in an office canteen in Knightsbridge. She's a small, stout woman who looks like Queen Victoria, and she sings in an amateur choir.

Next door is a commune for people who have been in Mental

219

Homes and are trying to learn to cope with life outside. Most of them have grown up with slow speech and children's minds. Many people I know shake their heads when they see them, but they're far less dangerous than most ordinary neighbours, who can gossip and interfere.

One of the reasons the Council took so long rehousing me was that I insisted on bringing Lulu. I said she'd been a good friend to me and I thought it would be very despicable to have her killed just because I was going to move. So, although it is in the regulations quite plainly that you're not allowed to have animals, when they provided me with this ground floor flat and no more was said about Lulu, I realised that the regulation was one made to be broken. Just before she came here, she had an operation to have a growth on her tummy removed; it had to be done, literally, when I was moving. I went and fetched her, and she woke up in this strange place, and, if I was a cat, I would have thought that I'd died and gone to heaven. At Rosendale Road, because we lived on the first floor, she never spent much time outside. But suddenly, here, she could go out when she liked. She walked around very gingerly at first near to the house, and then went further and further down the garden, smelling it and chasing birds. I got a handyman to put a cat-flap in the back door. I'm sure she's been a much happier cat since we've been here.

I'm inclined, though, to miss the huge Norwood Cemetery, which was at the end of our back garden at Rosendale Road. This place fascinated me. It was shut during the night and, in its way, was a sanctuary for all sorts of animals. Foxes lived in there; I saw a stoat once running across a path; there was a badgers' sett; you would often see hedgehogs coming out, even running down the road. Shortly before moving here, I'd to catch the last bus from Brixton and when it dropped me at the corner of Norwood High Street and Robson Road, I heard what was unmistakably a nightingale, singing inside the cemetery. It was just so lovely, so wonderful . . .

What I want to say now is rather important because I may have given you the impression that, from the time I adjusted 'The Weir' in the light of Philippe's death, I was able to move forward and away from thoughts of him. It's true that, when I settled in at Rosendale Road, I led a much happier life. I was more comfortable than at Bowyer House. The children were growing up and had their own little rooms in the attic, and they were more or less secure and off my hands. I was attending various literary events, meeting new people. Because Miron Grindea had given me confidence, I was having conversations in the sort of atmosphere I hadn't experienced since the Art of Movement Studio in Manchester after the war. But this happiness, this kind of peace, brought with it a complication because, somehow, the fact that I was all right, the fact that I sometimes felt like somebody's very spoilt and pampered mistress, though I didn't know whose, accentuated the guilt feeling about my husband's death. Now that I was distanced from it, I wondered more and more if I could, perhaps, have talked to him or made some contact instead of getting out of his bed and keeping away from him; perhaps I should have opposed him more often and not put him in a situation where he was so shut up inside himself. So many years of constant and violent accusation made me think there might have been something in what he said. It began with me not being experienced in housework and cooking, and, especially at Parke, which was a hard and primitive life anyway, I knew I *was* at first at fault. But, though I wasn't the 'dirty whore' he kept calling me, was there something of a dirty whore in me which *he* saw and *I* wasn't altogether conscious of? Also in his worst rages, this accusing me of laughing at him . . . I thought, 'Well, I did do that from sheer nervousness.' Grindea had said once or twice, 'You're laughing at me!', when I hadn't been consciously doing so.

You see, I was arguing with myself. Part of me kept saying, 'No, you were not at fault. He was sick in the mind. It was nothing to do with you.' But the other part niggled and said, 'They weren't *complete* aberrations.' For instance, though I wasn't sleeping with Grindea in the British Museum, *was* I a little in love with him? A feeling that I had failed Philippe persisted and really got the upper hand. I blamed myself for being like Aunt Susan, who I remembered from long ago expecting Uncle Will to be rational when he couldn't be rational, and not treating Philippe like a sick person, always treating him as the man who had married me and being shocked by the things he said and did. When I got back between eleven and midnight from a poetry reading, he was often asleep. But, if he was awake, he'd get out of bed and make a terrific row – I had always told him where I was going in advance, and he could see that I had my little basket with the poems in it, but at his worst, he wouldn't acknowledge what I said, otherwise he would just grunt or shrug or say, 'Why don't you get paid for it? Why are we living like this?' He wouldn't have anything to do with my poems – he wouldn't read them and he wouldn't listen to them. The only time he did anything like that was early on when I was writing the lyrics and making up the tunes for his musical. Then, he'd tell me the situation he wanted a song for, I would sing the song to him and he would edit it. That had been, comparatively, quite a *happy* time. He may, later, have been jealous of my relative success. Even with the best of people it sometimes creates a barrier if you are accepted and they aren't. I used literally to *pray* that he would have *some* little success. This might have saved his reason. Even each job that folded through his own fault was another rejection.

Well, as I say, I had this guilt feeling at the back of my mind. I had never wished Philippe dead, but I had sometimes wished that he would go away and never come back, and, of course, I remembered this, and thought, 'Now he *has* gone away, and he's never coming back, and I wished it.' It seemed, as I say, that it wasn't right to be so peaceful, to have such a happy spoilt existence. When, in '76 – the year there was that lull at the Crown and Greyhound because Alasdair Aston had disappeared – I saw a television programme about the Samaritans, appealing for volunteers, I thought, 'I don't know, but perhaps Philippe, by turning the violence that was in him against himself, gave me and the boys another chance in life, a chance to *have* this happier existence. Perhaps, though I failed so badly with him, I might succeed in helping somebody else, or, at least, learn why I failed before.' Then I thought, 'No. I daren't take this on without some spiritual backing. I might say or do the wrong thing and push somebody else into suicide rather than take them away from it. If I failed to stop Philippe, I must have it *in* me to do this.' In other words, I thought that I might do more harm than good and that I wasn't strong enough or intelligent enough to help anybody very much. I decided that, before offering myself as a volunteer, I ought to get back to some sort of religion. It sounds stupid, but that's how it was, and I went to some services at St Luke's Church in Norwood and the Methodist church in Chancellor Grove, just round the corner from Rosendale Road.

It didn't work! I did *try* to get back to the Church, but I felt that a lot of things were being said *for* me, things which I didn't altogether believe. I mean, the Creed says about believing in the

222

Catholic Church, the communion of saints, the forgiveness of sins, the resurrection of the body and the life everlasting. Well, I was never *sure* about these things, and I wasn't made any the more sure now. Especially the resurrection of the body – I didn't see how *that* could happen! It was the same with a lot of the prayers. I don't know whether I am producing truth when I produce poetry, but it seems like truth compared with what I was saying parrot-fashion and what was being said for me in church, which didn't seem to ring true at all.

The only positive belief I have is that we are born completely bad, that, in order to survive, we have to condone all the sins of our ancestors; all we can do is try to be better. I also vaguely believe – and it's a paradox – that there is a part of God in us, what is called the human soul, and that this is completely pure and good and does eventually go back to wherever it came from, having had to get its hands dirty here for a reason no one knows; we are here, flawed nature, in the awful devilishness of the world to try to get better through learning to love truth, and, if we fall foul of truth by our actions, however well-intentioned, the soul hasn't benefited in any way from coming into this sin. Hitler was like Philippe in many ways – he could only think in terms of figures: he believed that he was doing the best for his country and that if the numbers were right everything else would be right. You don't know what's going on underneath the madness. We are judged in 'the council chambers of the soul'. It began to be borne slowly in on me that I wanted something other than these church services, though I didn't know what it was. All I knew was that, if I applied to the Samaritans, I must have some sort of cast-iron thing to support me, as I was floundering.

I decided in the early summer of '77 to go to a Quakers' Meeting. I came across the Quakers in a purely random way – I was looking for a number in the telephone directory and I saw, under S, the Society of Friends. I've always had a great regard for friendship, so I thought I would try it. I went along to the Friends' Meeting House at Streatham one Sunday and, at ten o'clock, I joined in their Meeting. It was a very ordinary little room with a table with a bunch of flowers on it in the middle, and you all sat round and just did nothing – or so it appeared. I must have fallen into the group spirit from the first, because people came up to me afterwards – there's always talk after a Quakers' Meeting, a general chat – and they said that they thought I was a Quaker who had come

223

from another group of Friends; they said that people who come without previous knowledge usually look very strange, as if they don't know how to sit or what to do. And I *did* fit into that Meeting at once. I just sat, completely silent, with my hands in my lap from ten until eleven o'clock, trying to shut out the world. I tried this in the Anglican manner Mr Drury had instituted in me as a child before I got into bed at night and went to sleep – saying first a made-up prayer of Praise, Thanksgiving, Confession, Petition and Intercession, followed by the Lord's Prayer. But I wasn't then able to push out everything and get a blank space, meditate, which was our purpose.

Nevertheless, after one or two Meetings, I realised that I liked the kind of people who were there, liked talking to them after the Meeting, over a biscuit and a cup of tea made by two of the elders. I felt that I was in a completely friendly atmosphere. You see, for one thing – and it's probably very bad for you – no Quaker will really say that there's anything wrong with you: you feel that they would support you in anything you did. There's a Quaker saying, 'Walk cheerfully over the world, responding to that which is of God in all people,' and you were *aware* that they started out with the idea that you were 'all right'. Anyhow, I became a regular attender, and it was the Quakers who gave me the moral support to write to the Samaritans later in the year. Not that it didn't take me some while to learn how to make my mind a blank during the hour's silences. But I learned this eventually from a radio talk on meditation, given by a Quaker. He said, 'Nobody needs to pay to learn how to meditate.' He was talking about the Maharishi, who had made a great deal of money teaching people this. 'All you need to say is, "Mary had a little lamb" and repeat that and repeat that, until gradually it gets smaller, it'll get to "Mary had a", "Mary", "Mary", "Mary". Then "Mary", which is completely useless and meaningless, will disappear, you'll find that your mind *will* be a blank and that you will be able to meditate, to listen instead of say.' And this is possible: I've done it, though you can never really tell who is talking to you or whether it's you talking to yourself:

?

Yes, I do listen,
And sometimes I hear.
I cannot live without You now, but still

A doubting ripple stirs on the mystic river –
Your voice or mine?

At Quakers' Meetings you speak when the spirit moves you, but there's never very *much* talk: it's an *event* when somebody has something to say, because they daren't say it unless they really feel that they're forced to by something inside them. I've spoken myself – I tremble all over, as I do before a poetry reading – and I've heard other people speaking but, strangely enough, it doesn't break the meditation, it sort of comes into it as part of the listening. Because you're all doing the same thing at a Meeting, you're somehow not on your own; there's a sort of telepathy that happens: you begin to get what we used to call at the Art of Movement Studio 'a group movement', a thing where you're aware of what the person next to you is doing, although you're concentrating on what you're doing yourself.

The poetry and the Quakers, they were two different worlds, and I liked the sensation: when I was a poet I was not a Quaker and when I was a Quaker I was not a poet. It was some time before I let anybody among the Quakers know that I *did* write; I've never let the Samaritans know. Poetry seeks truth, and the Quakers also seek truth, but in a different way, not so much at the Meetings, rather through discussions and Bible Study. It was at the discussions that I realised I could never really be a Quaker, I could only be an attender. The Peace Testimony and the doctrine of 'take upon ourselves the hazards of peace' seemed to be absolutely synonymous with the Quaker Movement. I decided that I *couldn't*, I couldn't really always believe in peace at any price. The Falklands incident finally finished me on that, because I was one hundred per cent behind Maggie. I felt that, if I tried to persuade my government to disarm, I might be risking a lot of other people's lives; I didn't want to submit to just anything.

And there was something else. The roots of the Quaker Movement are based on Puritanism, and a lot of people come to it by way of the various Nonconformist groups. There was always this sort of evangelical thing coming out, which I find ugly. On the other hand, they laughed at some of the remarks I made, and *that* I found unexpected from a Puritan group like this, who obviously took themselves very seriously and weren't very much in the habit of laughing at anything. They laughed during a discussion about 'Christianity and Its Roots' when I pointed out that the Christians,

225

having established bathing in their minds as a very wicked and pagan Roman custom, went to the other extreme and wouldn't take any baths at all, and this is how the phrase 'the odour of sanctity' came into being.

I much preferred Bible Study: I found that *very* interesting. When I joined, they were doing the Book of Isaiah, which I didn't then know much about, and I learned to be very fond of Isaiah, most of which is sheer poetry. It became apparent that he probably wasn't one person, but a very small, beleaguered group of poets, thinking, against the mainstream, that the Gentiles should be brought into the worship of Jehovah.

I can't tell you too much about the Samaritans, because we have a code of secrecy, but I wrote to them in September '77, saying I was fifty-four, a widow, and I taught at a small school, and I would like to join. I wrote to them at their Croydon address, which was the nearest Samaritan branch to where I lived. After three or four weeks, they offered to interview me, and I was interviewed by somebody I knew afterwards as Cyril, the Chief Director, a Methodist minister, the man that the Methodists chose to represent them when the Pope came to Britain. I told him in a sketchy way about Philippe and that, having failed him, I would like to learn why, and then, perhaps, I could help someone else. I had wanted to die twice in my life or, rather, I didn't care if I lived or died – once as a child when, after scarlet fever, an ear complication led to horrible abscesses which discharged right inside the middle ear, causing pain which went on for ten weeks; and once when having my first baby – but I explained that *suicide* was completely alien to me, and I couldn't really begin to imagine the state of mind of someone contemplating it. I think this stood in my favour, because Samaritans keep telling you not to cry over things, not to get involved. Anyway, after the interview, Cyril said, 'You'll have to do the training, but I know you'll be accepted.'

Every Samaritan branch has a different training centre. To train for the Croydon branch you go to a church hall at Purley once a week for about two months. I discovered that, in Croydon, there's a twenty-four-hour telephone answering service for people who are suicidal, and they sometimes provide someone for them to meet and talk to regularly, who is called a 'befriender'. The Movement was started by an Anglican vicar called Chad Varah. A young girl committed suicide, and he felt very strongly that she could have

226

been saved if she'd not been left alone and could have been persuaded to talk – and being with the Samaritans has taught me that this is, literally, the only way that you have any chance of stopping a suicide: beyond physical force and taking the tablets and whatnot away, the only possible solution is to get the person to talk. Various experienced Samaritans lectured us, and there were sessions where one person would pretend to be a client and another would be the Samaritan. The lecturer would then criticise the way the Samaritan had handled the problem. Sometimes two lecturers would play these little scenes between themselves, showing a right way and a wrong way. We were told not to give advice, which led to some debate as everybody on the telephone has their own ideas of how people should be treated. And it was strictly forbidden to put over any religious views, or to say anything about ourselves, as the service is anonymous.

When I was accepted at the end of the training, I said that I could only do evening or night duties or weekends because I was a teacher. This suited them very well at the time – *now*, because so many people are unemployed, they're demanding much more availability. But it was one of the rules laid down by Chad Varah that being a Samaritan will not interfere with your personal life or your profession. They gave me a Friday, which I always think was very kind of them – one Friday evening, which is from seven till half past ten, then the next Friday night, when you start at ten thirty and go on till half past seven in the morning. Friday was a good night, because there was no school on Saturday. But I've often had to stand in for other people for night and evening duties on other days, and, in term time, this was a worry. I had to be at school on the dot to let the children in – being late caused an awful kerfuffle and you got complaints from parents. You see, your relief can be late; also, if you get a call at the last minute, it's not really Samaritan etiquette to hand it over to somebody else.

Actually I've had quite a *lot* of extra night duties. Sometimes you're falling asleep between calls. But usually you can get a couple of hours' proper sleep between two and six. They have beds there, and you take your sheet with you. I always get into a nightdress, and lie down. I find that I can then feel rested whether I sleep or not: if I only lie down and then get up and clean my teeth and wash and do my hair, I'm ready for the next day's work. But it catches up with me the following evening at about eight o'clock and I *have* to have an early night. I only know the Croydon branch of the Samaritans but, there, a telephone is going almost all the time. Three of us do duty – a Samaritan Leader, and two ordinary volunteers like myself. At night, the Leader does an on-call duty at home, and you get him or her out if there's something untoward that can't be dealt with simply by talking. I mustn't say much about it but, with inflation, telephone calls have got so expensive that we've been asked to cut down. Some people phone us, and they are not . . . well, I don't like to say this . . . I suppose they *are* in need really, but they're often people who can't sleep or, when you come down to it, people who want to make a funny phone call – they're not in desperate need of the service. When we heard pips going from a public call box, we used always to say, 'Give me your number in case you get cut off, and I'll ring you back,' but now we only do this if we believe the call is genuine.

Croydon is one of the branches – it's rather an old-fashioned branch – that will not deal with sex calls. Many branches had what is called a Brenda Service, to which sex callers could be referred, but there were so many complications that in most of them it's been stopped. But, when a sex caller needs this service, he has to wait, he can't just ring up and masturbate at once, which is what he usually wants to do. He's told Brenda, who is all sorts of different people, will be available at a certain time, when he can ring her. We *get* sex calls at Croydon; it's just that we don't deal with them. Women Samaritans get most of the sex calls – a sex caller, if he hears a man's voice, will usually put down his receiver immediately. *Very* occasionally, a woman sex caller will ask for a man, or she'll latch onto a man, but these calls are not so obscene, she'll just sort of make love to him by telephone. I've never put down the phone on one of them, but what I say is, 'I think you really do need help. I will refer you to a male colleague of mine. It would be much better if you spoke to a man about this.' And then, of course, he rings off immediately! It's touch and go, because I've done this when there hasn't been a man on duty with me but, so far, my bluff hasn't been called. Some now ring up and say in advance, 'Is there a man on duty?' and I always say Yes, whether there is or not. Many are very subtle. They don't just start with heavy breathing, they start with a problem, which you have to listen to. They'll say they have a problem and they don't know how to discuss it, are you prepared to listen? Well, you say that you are, and they'll tell you, for instance, that they're having sexual relations with their mother, and it gradually gets more and

228

more obscene until you realise what's happening and you tell them they'd better discuss it with a man and they ring off.

One great danger with the Samaritans is that, after a few sex calls or hoax calls, especially late at night or early in the morning, you're inclined to be less sympathetic. Probably the next call will be completely genuine and you may not treat it as such from the start. Another danger is that you begin to develop a hard skin. This is what you have to guard against very much. Otherwise, you begin to treat everyone as a clinical case. There *are* Samaritans who do this: the whole thing becomes too pat. Freud in the end got to ascribing pat names for what were, in fact, *individual* conditions – the schizophrenia of one person will be quite different to the schizophrenia of another. There are aspects you can recognise, but you have to take into account the complete individual. This danger of becoming pat takes strange forms in the Samaritans. It might be saying, 'Oh, she's OD,' instead of 'She's taken an overdose of tablets.' She's just 'a patient', you see, and it's partly to do with this not getting involved. But I don't know ... For instance, a trained nurse or a trained doctor is perhaps more *use*. What good are tears of sympathy if you can't give practical help?

Yet another danger is becoming *bored* by a caller. I've known a man who rang once or twice a week and you got to thinking, 'Oh, it's him again! It'll be the same story. I wonder how his dog is *this* week!' After ringing us for several years, that man committed suicide. And there's one type of caller I find it difficult even to imagine. He, or she, will ring you, and you'll hear them breathing or coughing, you'll know they're still there, but they won't say a word. All you can do is keep saying, 'I'm still here. Can you talk to me?' But you can't go on for ever. At what point do you put the receiver down?

As I say, your main job is to encourage the people you believe to be on the verge of suicide to *talk*. Then you listen; you listen, and speak every now and then to show you're there. The sane clients have their own solution somewhere, and it's usually to do with letting go of something they're hanging on to. But they must bring it out themselves: if *you* say it, it hardly ever works. Practical matters are the only things you can really advise on, like 'Go to the drop-in in West Croydon to find somebody to talk to.' 'Drop-ins' are clubs, mostly for teenagers, where someone can get advice, say, on how to get off drugs; some eager beaver manages to find a

229

room and a few chairs, and starts a drop-in; I think they do a lot of good but, unfortunately, there aren't many of them around. Or you can say, 'Use the soup run at the Town Hall Gardens', or 'Go to the Marriage Guidance' or 'Go to the police' or 'The Citizens' Advice Bureau will soon sort you out on that.' But it's better not to say any of these things until you've listened to them for a little while. I mean, say someone rings up and says, 'Can you recommend a good lawyer? I must have a lawyer.' Well, if you give them the address of a lawyer at once, they will probably ring off, when what they really want to do is talk: the asking for a lawyer is just a way of beginning to talk, it's a way in.

It's ironic that, in the winter of '78, when I'd been doing this sort of first-hand work for about a year, my sister-in-law, Birgitta, committed suicide. Birgitta was the typical rich man's daughter, unstable because she is spoilt, yet, at the same time, because she has all this money, riddled with guilt, and espousing every cause under the sun, but in a second-hand way.

I was talking to a doctor at the Quakers' the other day, and she said, 'Some people are in such a bad state, wouldn't you, if you thought they were going to take an overdose, wouldn't you just let them?' I said, 'There's no way, as a Samaritan, you can *prevent* anybody committing suicide. If they really want to commit suicide, you have to give them the dignity of making that decision – if it is a *real* decision, if they don't want to be saved.' She said, 'There are times when I would advise it.' There's the rub, you see. I think she believes in Exit, and I don't think that I could ever actually *advise* anybody to commit suicide or help them do it. Only if they were in great *physical* pain, might I feel tempted.

I'm not sure that I could have prevented Philippe's death by making him talk. But, by becoming a Samaritan, I do understand what was the matter with him, and how I should have treated him, and I think I may have been able to help other people like him. I do now understand this sort of black depression for which there seems to be no real explanation. Of course, you can't ever *really* understand what it feels like unless you've actually felt it yourself, but a client once said to me that it was like a great hole inside her, a great black hole; she felt completely empty. If I could have made Philippe talk, made him tell me that he had these suicidal feelings which I didn't suspect at all, then *perhaps* I could have saved him. But people aren't always saved by talking to Samaritans or anyone else. Just before the suicide, there's often a period of cheering up and snapping out of it. This is quite consistent with Philippe's behaviour – the way he cleared his room and disposed of his papers, and got himself shaved and washed. This is how the vast bulk of suicides behave. You think they're better, you think they're recovering, and it's not so: it's this sort of bright period before they take their own lives.

The people I feel you can do most for are ex-prisoners. Some of them, when they are discharged, have nowhere to go, and ring up in a state of desperation. You feel that you are probably the first ordinary person that they have spoken to for a long time, that it is a kind of return for them to human beings who aren't concerned with crime or with keeping them in prison. I experienced this myself when I first came to London, and was homeless, and had to live with Louis and Bob in Newington Lodge. Most people there took it for granted that you were a criminal; you weren't exactly in prison, but there must be something wrong with you if you were in this hostel – you were a prostitute or something disreputable. But there was that one person, the Warden, who took you at your face value and believed what you said and treated you like a human being. So, when ex-prisoners ring up, I always think 'I hope you feel about me what I felt about that Warden.'

In the summer of '81, I recited some of my poetry for the Samaritans at an anniversary celebration of the movement; we usually have some sort of an entertainment every year, and everybody's asked if they can do something. I arranged several poems into a kind of imaginary trip around London, looking at different places and the different people who inhabit them. I did this monologue, and it was very popular. Everybody came up to me afterwards and said how much they liked it and asked would I tell them where I got the poems from. I said, 'Yes. They're from magazines, and they're all by the same author, Patricia Doubell.' Of course, they didn't know me as Patricia Doubell at all: they knew me as Pat Kass. So this was very interesting. It was like eavesdropping, because I heard the poems being talked about.

One poem people seemed to like in particular was 'The Man From Delhi', which I wrote at Bowyer House about the little grocer's shop where I used to do my shopping. This shop, with its Indian owner and its Indian flavour, at a time when there weren't so many Indians in London, bore out a lot of the things Philippe had told me about India, and I wrote the poem in the later part of

231

his life, when he was spending most of the day lying on his bed, doing absolutely nothing. India, then, seemed to have crept up on him. He wanted everything Indian – Indian food, Indian weather, and Vernon, the Indian student upstairs. He wanted me to be an indolent Indian lady and, on the other hand, an efficient Indian peasant woman, a servant able to deal with any situation of poverty: he was annoyed because I wasn't a good servant, but annoyed also because I had to be a servant at all.

You can 'befriend', if you wish, after you've been a Samaritan for a couple of years. The directors and Leaders decide at a meeting which 'client' you would benefit, then they call you in and tell you what they know and think of them, though they say at the end, 'Don't necessarily take any notice of this. Make your own judgement.'

You can meet the client at the Centre or, which is usually considered better, in a café. I've always met my clients on Saturday mornings first in a café to have coffee. It's funny – I've got used to it now – but very often I see two people in these cheap cafés, and I know that somebody is being befriended, though not necessarily by a Samaritan; you can somehow tell it at once. A man has to befriend a man, and a woman has to befriend a woman, and every now and then you report back. If you say the client is being very objectionable and abusive or is dangerous, they don't let you see them any more.

The last client I had was getting over a nervous breakdown, and your object is to get such people over their bad patch. She was very particular about what café we went to. We started off at 'Ye Olde Bunne Shoppe' in Croydon, which suited her very well, but then it was absolutely forbidden as it was taken over by Italians, and she hated foreigners. We then went to the Fairfield Hall, but she said the coffee there was very bad. We were rather stymied, but we then found a church which had a coffee morning every Saturday, so we went there, after meeting at the Fairfield Hall, and, later, we went shopping.

Good heavens, befriending has nothing to do with becoming a friend! Don't ever get that idea! I used to get very annoyed at group meetings, I said, 'We approach these people as friends, but what we're offering them is Gold Blend instead of real coffee!' It isn't a friendship because the befriender is always a nice, sympathetic person who never tells the client off, except for their own good; there are never any quarrels or fights as there would be with a real friendship; all the Samaritans offer is 'dutiful love'.

17

I'm leaving here to live in Scotland from August the 29th. Yes, to leave here must seem like a hasty and extraordinary decision, but it won't seem so *extraordinary* when I tell you why I made it. This spring, Louis told me that the cottage, Middle Cottage, next to his at Easter Rhynd, had fallen vacant. He said, 'What about it? Would you like to move up here? The rent is only £10 a week.' My first reaction was, 'No. I've got too many things going on down in London – Paray House School, the Quakers, the Samaritans, the unofficial Dulwich Group Poetry Readings . . .' Then I began to think about it. I thought, 'It *is* an opportunity to concentrate more on my writing. I've been neglecting it by doing so many other things in a sort of cage of responsibilities. Perhaps this is a pointer. Perhaps it's now or never.'

I was also coming up for sixty, which is the retiring age, though I'd had no intention whatever of retiring from the school because of this fact or the fact that the school was changing in character. When I went there it was a ballet school. We'd always taken one or two children who were slow learners or who had physical handicaps but, when Miss Williams retired as headmistress and Mrs Whitehead took over, we accepted perhaps five or six children, knowing that there was something a little wrong with them. They slotted in and, because we were small, we managed to do quite a lot for them, not by any trained methods, but simply by dealing with them as individual human beings and giving them a little single teaching. Their parents were very pleased and very grateful; one or two parents, in fact, voluntarily offered to pay higher fees. Gradually we got more and more applications for these sort of children; mothers talk, and we were getting a name for being able to bring on children with difficulties. I was able to work them into my plays somehow, though the new ballet mistress was very upset because anything she tried to do was always spoilt by these children galumphing about like elephants and never knowing where they should be. Anyway, the Co-operative held a meeting, and we decided to go over to being a Special School this coming autumn. Mrs Job, who was retiring at the end of the summer term, would be replaced by a trained ESN teacher, and Mrs Whitehead would stand down as headmistress in favour of her daughter, Mrs Sarah Jackson, who has recently qualified in the same way. I realised there'd be no call for French and that the plays would have to be completely different and that I would have to do *remedial* dancing, but I was resolved to carry on . . .

And then this cottage came up, and the rent of the cottage was low, and, oh yes, there was another factor . . . You see, everything happened at the same time, as though it was meant . . . Suddenly, the man who owned the shooting and fishing rights of the water meadows at Charlton Marshall died, and Felicity and Tim and I were able to make a good sale without him as tenant, and we each received about £10,000.

I decided, 'I'll take the cottage. Why not?' There's a Quakers' Meeting House in Perth, and, as there's a big prison there too, I may be able to help ex-prisoners, either through the Samaritans or somehow else. But I mustn't get bogged down again. Writing must take priority. Time is what I need to get my work into some sort of order. So, at the start of this term, I tendered my resignation to Paray House. Regarding my £10,000, my first impulse was to spend it – to go to see Felicity in Australia or to go to Mexico or to Spain. But I have a feeling that I may need the income, so I've put most of it into a Building Society to provide a supplement to the Retirement Pension which I now draw, losing the Widow's Pension I've had since Philippe's death. I also have a small pension from Austin Reed, which started on my sixtieth birthday – it's only £1 a week, but even £1 a week in the country will be quite useful. Easter Rhynd is a good seven miles from Perth, so I'll have to buy a car. Meanwhile, as Louis drives into Perth every morning to get his working orders, he can take me.

Middle Cottage is not at all a picturesque cottage, the roses-round-the-door type, though there *is* a nice little rose garden at the front: it's a very plain little grey Scottish cottage with a slate roof, joined to another two – Louis and Wilma's on one side and a retired postman and his wife on the other. In front, over the lane which leads to the cottages, is a field, and then the River Earn with swans going by and rushes; then beyond the river are hills which, even in summer, usually have white caps to them. At the back, there's part of a field, roped off to make a lawn for East and Middle Cottage, and, beyond that, there's a meadow with cows on it, and, beyond that again, a very high, wooded hill.

Both Louis and Bobby are borrowing a lorry which they'll drive down themselves to collect the furniture and Lulu and me. I find it hard to know what to take. I'm trying to get rid of my three-piece suite from the Ideal Homes Furniture Company; it's getting very uncomfortable and dilapidated – I shall manage, to begin with, on cushions, and a few chairs borrowed from next door. I'm taking the four-poster bed which I got to save myself from being smothered at Rosendale Road; also the desk which my husband made out of a piano. I'm also taking the large oak Regency bookcase which was one of my extravagances when I heard about the money from the water meadows. All the books will come with me – unfortunately, most of the children's went mildewy at Bowyer House due to a wet, crumbling wall, though I managed to retrieve one, a collection of animal stories by Kipling, which I hope to read to my grandchildren.

I'll take two old French chairs inherited from my mother, and the pictures of famous writers which Philippe framed. Other pictures I want to take are by Bobby and Louis. Bobby's is of seals in a circus; he did it when he was eight after going to the circus. Louis did his picture when he was twelve; it's of a dalmatian, which he was very taken with, and a car, which he always desperately wanted – but I think the car wheels were also inspired by a pair of roller-skates. Then there's a water colour of my great-grand-mother, on my mother's side, sitting on the verandah of her house in St John's Wood, painted by her son. She was a sewing woman to Queen Victoria. I've some mementoes of hers – a pair of baby shoes which belonged to Edward VII, and some fans which belonged to the princesses – but they're of no value as antiques, because they're without documentation. I'm also keeping a print of Grimaldi, inherited from Auntie Nora – my grandfather on my mother's side is said to be related somehow to Grimaldi.

Another thing I'm taking, along with the photos of my sons' weddings, is a bowl which Louis' first wife, Lynn, made at pottery class and gave to me one Christmas. I hope Louis has forgotten it. I shan't tell Wilma how it came into my possession . . . Oh, dear! I'm already getting cold feet about this move. Why did I *do* it?! I know this doesn't go at all with the idea of catching up with the writing, but I want as many people to come and stay with me as can. Louis is working *now* on installing a phone . . .

Perhaps I should mention the pots I'm taking – two cast-iron pots, a big one for cooking stews, and a small one I use for boiling milk and water for coffee and tea. They're usually rather expensive, but I got these at Quaker jumble sales in support of Oxfam and/or Christian Aid – the Quakers are very much concerned with these charities; I did flag days for them when it was Oxfam Day, and, during Oxfam week, I did house-to-house collections. I must say I enjoyed house-to-house collection, although it was time-consuming. There was a kind of fascination in knocking on doors and seeing what came out. One woman asked me to come in and write a note to her husband, in her handwriting, saying that she'd gone to see her sister. She was too drunk to write the letter herself. She'd promised her husband not to drink, and she had to go away somewhere to sober up so her husband wouldn't come home and find she'd broken her promise . . .

But the cast-iron pots. I've always had various little arthritic pains – all dancers have them in the ankles, the legs, the groin, the wrists, all sorts of places, which hurt now and again. Then a short while ago, I had a very painful back, and before that – I'm a blood donor – suddenly they refused to take my blood because they said I was anaemic (I started giving blood during the war and, apart from when I was up in Wales, I've given it at six-monthly intervals ever since). Well, my doctor prescribed a course of iron tablets, and these gave me a boost. Then I remembered that, although Welsh women in the Depression were pretty nearly starving and suffering from malnutrition, the one thing they never suffered from was anaemia because of the trace element of iron in the cooking pots they used. So, when I saw the first of these iron pots at a jumble sale, I thought, 'I'll use it.' And – it's absolutely amazing – not only has the anaemia gone, apparently, but all my aches and pains.

For my last production at Paray House at the end of this term, I decided to do *A Midsummer Night's Dream* – when I was a child, Miss Sayer, the headmistress of St Christopher's, took us to see *A*

236

Midsummer Night's Dream performed in a garden. All the words in my production were Shakespeare's, but I knew I could do only the fairy part, I couldn't bring in the sub-plots about Theseus and Hippolyte, Lysander and Hermia, and Demetrius and Helena, so I arranged all the fairy scenes into one little half-hour play that would stand on its own, including the Mechanics; you got simply the quarrel between Oberon and Titania, and the fairies doing a little bit of talk, and Bottom and the other Mechanics rehearsing their play, and the conspiracy against Titania, with her falling in love with Bottom, and the reconciliation and the ending when the fairies dance through the house after the wedding.

Ahmed Kassim, a bright young Egyptian, played Bottom to the life. His father asked us to do a special performance later so that he could make a video film of the play. Susheel Bellora, from India, was completely natural as Snug. Flute was played by a new boy called Michael. He was slightly spastic, but managed very well. To their clowning, Sean Condon was a beautifully solemn Peter Quince. James, a boy with something very, very wrong with him, had nothing to say, but he gave a star performance – every time the Mechanics came on, he came on with them. I always let him do exactly what he liked – and he always *saw* the Fairies, and would go up to them and stare.

In the scene where Bottom is being led off by the Fairies and Titania, the Fairy Queen, says, 'Come, wait upon him; lead him to my bower./The moon, methinks, looks with a watery eye;/. . . Tie up my love's tongue, bring him silently,' I made the Fairies fire off Party Poppers – they're tiny, brightly coloured cones, and you pull a string and they make a pop like a champagne cork and out pour liquid streams of colour which solidify and attached themselves to things. Well, I made the Fairies fire these at Bottom, so it looked as if he was all tied up with these strings, and then they pulled him off. James was so wonderful in this that we did special close-ups of him on the video, examining closely all these strings going out and playing with them and actually staying on after the others had gone, then running after them.

Sean Condon's sister, Annabella, a pale, slight little girl with long, straight hair, was Titania. She was wooden at first, but improved with rehearsal. She looked exactly right in a pale pink nightie and a crown of bent silver foil and white silk convolvulus. Catherine Bell was her Head Fairy, and I gave her quite a lot of Titania's lines to say, as Annabella was not very good at learning

237

words and Catherine was completely reliable. Theresa Vaughan was a wonderful Oberon. She's eleven, and she left this term, meaning to go to boarding school. She's a very nervous child, very tense, and she usually gabbles everything. I was in two minds whether to let her do that lovely speech 'I know a bank whereon the wild thyme blows . . .', but her mother made her a very pretty blue costume, and I think this must have helped her confidence because in the end, she did the speech so beautifully that I can still hear her. She achieved a lovely sleepy feeling, yet managed also to do what is so very difficult, maintain this with words of revenge, such as '. . . I'll streak her eyes,/And make her full of hateful fantasies.' Michelle Aylett was Puck. I gave her *carte blanche* for her two speeches at the end – 'Now the hungry lion roars' and 'If we shadows have offended' – and they were magic: she did them in the way that best suited her.

It was good to have a vague number of Fairies because, though half of them were ESN, they could all be dressed attractively in leotards with one chiffon scarf draped across the front and another at the back for wings, with matching silk flowers looping up the chiffon and in their hair. Apart from a dance at the end to Bach's 'Badinage', which *was* a bit of a struggle, though they managed it very nicely in the end, the ESN's didn't have to make much effort to be appealing, except for wafting their wings, and *all* the Fairies sang 'You spotted snakes', most beautifully, to an unaccompanied traditional tune I taught them. Eve Stylianides, a minute Greek who had just entered the kindergarten, knew the whole play by heart and acted everyone off the stage. In fact, 'The Midsummer Night's Dream' became the favourite game for the kindergarten at playtimes, and it was usually organised by Eve. I gave her two lines to say: 'Hence, away! now all is well./One aloof stand sentinel.' Her friend, Tamsie, four years old and slightly spastic, was too shy to appear until the dress rehearsal, but when she saw Eve dressed up in violet chiffon, she decided to come onto the stage in a hastily constructed costume composed of only blue chiffon scarves. The main incidental music was by Mendelssohn, and many of the parents brought fresh flowers to make the Fairy Bower.

After the play, which concluded the Open Day entertainment, Mrs Whitehead made a speech, saying that Mrs Job and I were leaving, and we were presented with bouquets – mine was white daisies with yellow carnations and jonquils. Many parents then brought us presents before the end of term. On the last day, before they were let go at twelve, I kissed all the children as I always did at the end of term anyway. With the little ones, I tried to make it as much like an ordinary end of term as possible – I hate saying goodbye (I'll hate saying goodbye to the Quakers in Streatham and to the Samaritans in Croydon). I knew if they cried I would, and vice versa. We packed everything away as usual, I gave up my key, and that was that. *Except* for a farewell lunch the same day, in Mrs Job's and my honour. Almost everyone connected with the teaching side met at our usual Italian restaurant in the King's Road, where I remember choosing trout, then raspberries and cream. Mr and Mrs Whitehead came, and Sarah Jackson, the future headmistress, and her husband, also Miss Williams, and the singing teacher and Lady Perowne, and John Smith, the vicar who was our landlord, and the accountant and his wife, and Gloria Odle, the swimming instructor at Chelsea Baths.

The extra ballet teacher had been invited, but she couldn't come, so that made thirteen of us at table. I'm very superstitious about this, so I put an extra chair at the end of the table and draped my shawl over it. I said, 'There can't be thirteen of us. *That* is the fourteenth guest! I'll give the price of my lunch to Oxfam, because I like the people who are sitting round this table, I consider them friends, I don't want any of them dead before the year is out.'

I must admit the lovely gesture of that lunch was something I hadn't bargained for. When it was time to say goodbye to Mrs Whitehead and Mrs Job, I cried. They *all* were, and are, my friends, but especially Mrs Whitehead and Mrs Job – we three had worked together, and there'd never been any altercation.

I'm not so certain of Miron Grindea's friendship: I now consider him even more of an enigma than ever. After not contacting me for four or five years, he rang me up at the beginning of this month [July] and said I must go to Canterbury Cathedral on the 15th, because the Archbishop was receiving him into the Anglican Church. Now, Grindea is Jewish; he is a Jew through and through; everything he does has a Jewish flavour. He has never been Orthodox – he prides himself on being part of the humanist movement – but the dream of his life was to do an *Adam* 'Jerusalem' number, which he eventually did, and on which I helped him. It was on the tip of my tongue to say, 'It simply *cannot* be true!' But he was very insistent. Not only was he being received by the Archbishop of Canterbury, but Mrs Runcie, who is rather a liberated lady, a new thing in Archbishops' wives, had converted him, and henceforth he would be a Christian.

So, very intrigued and not convinced, I decided to go to this ceremony. I half thought it was one of his phantasies and that, when I got to Canterbury, I should find that there was nothing happening and that it was all a tale. But on the train to Canterbury, the fast train, the eleven o'clock from Victoria, I found that it certainly wasn't a tale, because Grindea was on the train, not only with his wife and daughter and grandchild but also with a lot of *Adam* contributors I knew. I thought, 'That's it! It's true!' I still couldn't really believe it – all his life had pointed the other way. There weren't any seats near where he was sitting, but I did get a word with him. I said, 'You must have been thinking about this for a long, long time.' He said, 'Ah yes, I have. I did think a very great deal about it. It was a very hard decision to take.'

When we got to Canterbury, we all split up, because the ceremony in the cathedral wasn't till three o'clock and we all wanted to explore Canterbury. Well, after doing a bit of exploring and having lunch, I got to the cathedral early, just after two. I asked an usher, who was ushering a large queue into the cathedral, where would a service be held by the Archbishop for someone who was being received into the Church of England. He said, 'I don't know of *any* service going on today. In fact, there *can't* be any, because the cathedral's been completely taken over today for the presentation of degrees to the students of Kent University.' I said, 'Well, I've been *told* by somebody who is being received into the Church of England today that it is at Canterbury Cathedral, and it must be true because I've met the person himself, coming down on the train!' So he looked very puzzled. He said, 'The only part of the cathedral that's open to the public today is the crypt, where there are three little chapels. If you go along to the crypt, there *may* be something which the Archbishop has arranged himself.'

I toiled along to the crypt. Oh, *such* a hot day it was! At least the crypt was cool. I went down there, and I happened to meet somebody who introduced himself as the verger. I gave him details. 'Well, nobody can possibly be received by the Archbishop today, because his house is being repaired and he can't *stay* in Canterbury at the moment.' So I said, 'I don't know, but I understand that Mr Grindea has a great connection with *Mrs* Runcie, the Archbishop's wife. It was she who converted him.' Then this man began to look very doubtful. He went to another man, and *he* came up and said, 'We think it *may* be something to do with Mrs Runcie.' – I got the impression that Mrs Runcie was rather unpredictable. So they said, 'We will fetch the Dean.' I waited there about twenty minutes, and then the Dean arrived, and the Dean looked very worried. He said, 'It's very strange. The Archbishop is not here at the moment, but he hasn't said *anything* to me about this. It may be something that somebody's forgotten. Or else it might be that the Archbishop is trying to keep it very quiet.' He took me back to his house, and he rang several churches in Canterbury to ask if there was any ceremony to receive somebody into the Church. Of course, they all said No. I thought, 'This is a practical joke. But how does it come to be a practical joke when Grindea was on the train?!'

So I went back to where people were still filing into the cathedral, and I just happened to pick up a programme, and there, in large letters on the front, it said that Miron Grindea, the editor of *Adam International Review*, was to receive today the honorary degree of Doctor of Letters! Then, of course, I tried to get into the cathedral, but you could only get in by ticket. This is the usual practice with Grindea – he will invite you to some function where you can only get in by ticket and, of course, you haven't got a ticket. A woman at the door in a mortar board – a choir mistress? a don, perhaps? – said, 'A great many friends of Mr Grindea have arrived without tickets. Things don't usually happen like this. Fortunately there are places available.'

I went in, and really this was a very nice, interesting ceremony. I rather got my revenge on Grindea, because he looked very silly in a gown and velvet hat. It must have been dreadful for him and the rest of the people who were receiving their degrees, because they were all in these heavy gowns. I was frantically hot and fanning myself, and *I* was in a summer dress. All the names were read out, and the students went up and received their degrees, and it was somehow a very happy atmosphere, because you felt that they'd all worked so hard for these things and now they were let out of school. Then came Grindea and someone else who I've never heard of but who apparently has written a great deal of journalistic criticism. There wasn't much said by the Orator about the critic, but he made a long speech about Grindea. Of course, he said how much Grindea's magazine,

Adam, had done for literature, and how it had been started in Bucharest and brought in 1939 to London by Grindea, flying before the Nazis, and how remarkable it was that he'd actually been able to carry it on. And, oh, he mentioned the bit about how, when war was declared, the Grindeas were with Myra Hess and she immediately shut her piano and said that she wouldn't play again until peace came, and the Grindeas persuaded her not to pursue this resolve, with the result that she did, during the war, give a lot of concerts, especially the lunchtime concerts instituted at the National Gallery.

There was a reception afterwards at the County Hotel. I didn't take any notice of Grindea. I didn't speak to him at all, after a handshake when I came out of the cathedral. I knew Grindea of old; I knew that, at any reception, he has the habit of simply cutting you dead: he will walk right past you and will not see you, because he wants to talk only to famous people with a view to getting them to contribute to his magazine. He had Christopher Fry in tow, so I knew he would cut *me*. But, at tea-time, Grindea came over to where I was sitting, and said, 'Come over and talk to Christopher Fry!' and he introduced me, as usual, as 'a great poet'. I didn't really make any headway with Christopher Fry. He is a very old man, and I didn't think he would want to remember anything I said. He was rather distant and very tired, but it was very nice to meet him, because he's done some nice things. I *did* manage to get a word in with Grindea after this, and I said, 'I'm so glad that you decided not to take that serious step in the end.' He looked rather sheepish, and said, 'You didn't *believe* it, did you?!' And, of course, I hadn't believed it, but so many things seemed to point to its being true!

The remnants of what I still like to call the Dulwich Group are coming here for our last reading tonight [28 July, 1983] at eight o'clock. For various reasons, Pat Bradley, John Greatrex, Joe Winter, Molly Moorehead and Alan Gillot dropped away when I moved here to St Faith's Road. But Peter Meares, Michael Gerrard, Katherine Stenger and Stella Stocker continued, and Brian Dann, who's really Poetry in Croydon, came too, as did Valerie Elliott and John Power. Valerie Elliott was introduced to me by my former lodger, Mike Shirn. He took me to see a play of hers called *Sadie*, performed by the South London Theatre Club Workshop in her own home in Clive Road, Dulwich. She showed me some of her poems afterwards and, though they were not as remarkable as her play, I invited her to come to readings.

John Power, who is our youngest poet, came to us through seeing an old poster for a Crown and Greyhound reading which hadn't been taken down. He'd just come down from Hull, where he'd passed the examination for the Civil Service but couldn't get a job; he thought things would be easier in London, but they weren't, and his money ran out and he started squatting in Brixton. He's always, since he was a very young man – and he's still under thirty – written poetry, and he found in this rather miserable situation – he hasn't yet found work – that he was churning out a terrific lot of poetry and going around the place reading it and singing it. Poetry can be a kind of built-in safety valve for a certain temperament which might otherwise go over the edge. *So* many of the illusions and aberrations of people on the borders of nervous breakdowns are really poetic ideas. For instance, somebody came into the Samaritan Centre one day, and she said, 'There's a piece of glass on the floor!' She went panicky and shook. She said, 'I'm always afraid that it will get into my heart!' Now, she may at some time have read Hans Andersen's story, 'The Snow Queen', which *is* about splinters of ice getting into people's hearts. But it seemed to me that this was a poetic image which, in the hands of a poet, would simply turn into a poem on the page but, in the hands of a person on the edge of a nervous breakdown, becomes a panic or an obsession.

Stella Stocker, I'm sorry to say, has now left us. Michael Gerrard is something of a woman-hater, and he and some others criticised her poems one evening on the grounds that they were very feminine and a bit whimsy, which was not an unjust criticism. She was furious and she cried. She said, 'This is the only way I *can* write!' After that, she brought some more poems, which were inclined to deal with sex. They were, I suppose, in a way stronger but they were still written very much from a woman's point of view – after all, she *is* a woman so she writes like a woman. But she is very temperamental, and she couldn't bear further criticism. I didn't silence anybody, because this is not a group where people should be careful of what they say – that's the last thing I want. But I feel sometimes that they're doing something of the same to John Power. His poems *are* immature; he hasn't yet really found what he's looking for. He reads a lot, he's a terrific scholar in his way, and probably this is serving him badly at the moment, because his poems *are* coming out of books, there's no doubt about it. But then, this has happened to a lot of writers – they've begun by writing poems where the characters and everything are taken entirely from books; they go on later to realise that they must take from life and mix live characters, as composite characters, with what they've read. John *has* taken a lot of stick, and I've had to tell him not to be inhibited by this.

I read part of my latest and longest poem to the Group a few meetings ago. They didn't like it at all. It's about Ancient Mexico and it's called 'Reed Music for White Eagle Descending'. They criticised it very strongly not so much as poetry but because I've used a lot of exotic names.

> Chimalma, born of Ililinan
> In the city of Teotihuacan,
> Born in the Temple of the Sun,
> Schooled to the Fall at the Season of Flower and Beauty,
> Has grown old.
>
> Awaiting the promised return of my lord and love,
> I am old with the age of mountains,
> Older than any that I have ever known,
> Old with an age that priests have accounted divine –
> Toltec is death-in-greenness. . . .

The Group said it will turn people away because it's 'I know something that you don't' and it's wrong to write about a completely dead culture when there's so much to write about the present. But, whether I've succeeded or not, what I've *tried* to do is put universal human nature and universal emotions behind an ancient story. I've discovered, during Quaker sessions of Bible Study, that the only really interesting thing about ancient history is its relationship to what is happening now. Whatever changes may have happened to their life-styles, *people* haven't changed . . .

EDITOR'S NOTE: *The final meeting of the Dulwich Group [see p. 242] was attended, on 28 July 1983, at Flat 1, 19, St Faith's Road, Tulse Hill, London SE21 8JD, by Patricia Doubell, Brian Dann, Michael Gerrard, John Power, Peter Meares and myself.*